madam

madam

Antonia Murphy

SIMON &
SCHUSTER

New York · Amsterdam/Antwerp · London · Toronto · Sydney/Melbourne · New Delhi

MADAM
First published in Australia in 2024 by
Simon & Schuster (Australia) Pty Limited
Level 4, 32 York St, Sydney NSW 2000
This edition published in 2025

10 9 8 7 6 5 4 3 2 1

New York Amsterdam/Antwerp London Toronto Sydney/Melbourne New Delhi
Visit our website at www.simonandschuster.com.au

A catalogue record for this book is available from the National Library of Australia

ISBN: 9781761638152

Cover artwork © 2024 Tavake Limited, All Rights Reserved
Cover design by Christa Moffitt / Christabella Designs
Typeset by Midland Typesetters, Australia
Printed and bound in Australia by Griffin Press

The paper this book is printed on is certified against the Forest Stewardship Council® Standards. Griffin Press holds chain of custody certification SCS-COC-001185. FSC® promotes environmentally responsible, socially beneficial and economically viable management of the world's forests.

For the sex workers, madams and strippers . . .
and badly behaved women everywhere.

A Note on the Facts

This book is a personal account based on real events. Pseudonyms have been used throughout this book and certain details altered where necessary to protect the identity and privacy of all people referred to.

I do not pretend to speak for all madams or sex workers, who come from all countries and all walks of life, are of all genders, races, and sexual orientations, and who do this work for all kinds of reasons. I have written from my own memories, notes, and text messages from the three years when I founded and ran a legal, ethical escort agency in New Zealand. As with all memoirs, other people's recollections may vary.

Not all women who worked at The Bach are represented; it would be impractical to include the dozens of escorts who worked for me over the years – let alone the thousands of clients who visited. Some characters are composites of two or more actual people. A large proportion of the dialogue is quoted from memory, whereas almost all of the client texts are real.

If you live in a big city in North America, Australia, or Europe, then the price we eventually charged at The Bach for a 'Girlfriend Experience' – NZD $240 an hour, of which the lady received half – may seem surprisingly low. Whangārei, to put it mildly, is not New York City. It is a largely agricultural district of about 80,000 people. Most jobs don't pay very well, and most clients don't have much cash to spend. Between 2017 and 2019, the years in which we operated, the minimum wage in New Zealand was between $15.25 and $16.50 an hour. After tax, single mothers still had to pay for their childcare. By contrast, $120 per hour, with a flexible schedule and a child-minder on site, was a very attractive option.

The Bach offered free childcare for the first year we were in business, at which point I realized that most of our ladies were making more money than me. By then, they could afford their own babysitters, and they preferred to keep their children at home.

Prologue

Hey

u avail

??

Wats the cheapest deal you can do for me please?

My first day of running The Bach, I'm too scared to pick up the phone. *I'm not a madam; I'm a mom with a blended family of six kids.* Last night, I cooked spaghetti and read bedtime stories, and this morning I poured cereal and packed lunchboxes. There's a three-month-old baby boy in a rocker at my feet. But all day long, I get texts like these:

Hey do you have toys or suck without a condom

thanxx

Is that how they talk? I wonder, *when they don't have to pretend?* I feel like I have Google Translate for the way men actually think.

Show me pussy, face, tits and ass

Hey

u avail

DTF

I put down my phone and press my hands to my eyes. This is not what I thought I'd be doing with my life. I'm a city person, from San Francisco and New York. I thought I'd live at the center of where things were happening, have deep conversations about world events.

I am a 41-year-old American woman and I am running a feminist escort agency at the top of the North Island of New Zealand, in a small town called Whangārei. It's pronounced 'FAH-nga-rey', because in the Māori language, 'wh' is pronounced with an 'F'. That's the thing about New Zealand, which every foreign visitor learns sooner or later: at first you think it's the same as the little towns you grew up with, because there's KFC, and traffic lights, and everyone here speaks English. And then somebody hands you a raw sea urchin, or a plate of canned spaghetti on toast. Or a man passes you on the street with no shoes and a full facial tattoo, which is actually called a tā moko. Or you go for a dip and a penguin swims past. And you realize that you're at the bottom of the South Pacific, closer to Antarctica than you are to home.

Me? I opted out of big city life and sailed across the ocean with my husband, settling in a tiny farming community just outside of Whangārei. When you're young and dumb, you make choices on a whim because you think everything is reversible. And then one day, you realize it's not.

Purua is pastoral and green, all rolling hills and sheep, but it feels very far from the world. Once, I'd floated the idea of bringing in college kids from abroad, science majors who could enrich our kids' learning.

'That's not who we are,' my neighbor replied. 'We lead simple lives. We do our jobs, tend our veggie patches, and coach our kids' sports. Don't try to make this place something it's not.'

My phone buzzed, jerking me back to the present.

Hey

make me booking to fuck

??

Down here in New Zealand, so much is different. But some things are depressingly familiar.

Chapter 1

'Monogamy's not that important to me,' one of us said at the start of our courtship. I can't remember now if it was Peter or me, but does it matter? He was from Brooklyn and I was from San Francisco. We were drinking red wine on my sailboat. When one of us said it, the other one quickly agreed.

'My mom left my dad when he had an affair,' we both confided, sharing our parallel lives. The divorces had been painful and damaging, sending each of us bouncing between two parents' houses. Maybe that was why we'd soured on *normal*: a career track, a mortgage, a marriage with kids. We were ready to throw the whole thing in the trash and start over.

'Why do you have to break up a family?' Peter wondered. 'Why can't you sleep with who you want and stay married?' It turned out his parents had done that for years, swinging their way through the sixties and seventies. 'It was when he formed a relationship with a woman,' Peter told me. 'That's where she drew the line. It was when he fell in love.'

'But it doesn't even have to be like that,' I insisted. 'My parents' friend Claudine had a lover for *years;* she was married the whole time and her husband knew everything. We stayed at her lover's cottage in Normandy on vacation, that's how open it was!'

'Well.' Peter cocked his head. 'They're French.'

'Yeah, and they're *so much less* hung up on monogamy than Americans are,' I told him. 'I remember Claudine came to stay with us when the whole Clinton and Lewinsky thing was happening, and she thought it was hilarious. She laughed out loud. She couldn't *believe* there was a national scandal about a blowjob.'

Then we ducked down below and went into my cabin, which is where we spent most of our time early on. One day Peter was late for his job at the boatyard, and at twenty past nine, his phone started ringing. He dismissed the call, and it just rang again.

'Get your head out from between that girl's thighs and get over here!' I heard his boss shout down the line. I stuffed my face in the pillow so he wouldn't hear me laugh.

Three months after we first met, I was pregnant. By then Peter was living on my boat, and we were already talking about marriage. 'If it's a boy,' he said, his head nestled on my belly, 'we'll name him after my father – that is, if it's okay with you. We'll call him Joseph.'

'Joe? My first kid's going to be called *Joe*?'

'It's a good name!' He swatted my knee. 'Good enough for Jesus's dad, right?'

'Hmf,' I grumbled, 'maybe. He can always go by his middle name.'

Two weeks later though, Peter changed his mind. 'I want to go sailing!' he said. 'I want to have adventures. I *think* I want to be with you, but it's too soon to know for sure.'

'So, what?' I asked, incredulous. 'You want me to have an abortion? Abort this kid we just named after your dad?'

Peter wasn't looking at me. He was absorbed in the collection of books on my shelf. 'If you have it,' he said, 'I'll send money. But I won't be a part of its life.'

Get an education, my mother had said, *so if some man leaves you with kids to support, you can always find a way to get by. And make sure you get married before you have kids. That way, the law's on your side.* She'd told me stories about her life before, when she was raising my brothers alone. The gold lamé miniskirt she'd had to wear at her cocktail waitressing job, slinging drinks to red-faced, ass-grabbing men, while she chipped away at her master's degree part-time. The emotional scars my brothers still bore, since their father had left them so young. I didn't want that life. I wanted to be married with my husband committed, to sink a foundation before building a family.

So when Peter changed his mind, I didn't make a fuss. I took the pills and I had the abortion. He asked me to pay half the bill.

After that, we made plans to get married. Peter thought it was silly, just some words on a page, but I wanted the security the law could provide. Then we tossed out convention like confetti, starting our union by going to sea. We cruised through Mexico and Central America, then stopped in New Zealand when I learned I was pregnant again. This time, Peter accepted fatherhood: we'd been married for just over two years. Our plan was to stay temporarily, have a couple of kids and keep going. We'd cross to Australia, then through the Torres Strait to Jakarta – we had the sailing routes all worked out.

But first, we launched ourselves into parenthood. Silas was a beautiful, plump baby boy, and he nursed and he babbled on time.

He was my first child, so I didn't think twice when he only made one kind of sound. *'Da! Da! Da!'* he chortled, and I brushed it aside.

'Maybe he speaks Russian,' I bantered to Peter. 'And he's just this super positive guy.'

That our child should have a serious medical condition seemed inconceivable at the time. So far, we'd both been so lucky. Seeing no reason to pause our life of adventure, we decided we'd sail around New Zealand. If we couldn't take off for the wild blue ocean, there was plenty to explore near the coast. I'd been penning travel articles for sailing magazines, and I thought this could be a subject for my first full-length book. We'd travel the country and I'd sample its customs. We'd have zany adventures with our one-year-old baby, and I'd write a lightweight, funny travelogue à la Bill Bryson.

Three things came out of that trip, and none of them involved a publishing contract. The first was a surprise: we learned that I was pregnant again, this time with a baby girl. The second was a lesson which we swallowed the hard way: there's a reason New Zealand makes world-famous sailors. We nearly killed ourselves crossing Cook Strait, and after that we finished our trip in a van.

The third was a discovery – more my thing than Peter's, and I stumbled on it while reading the newspaper one day. 'No *way*,' I murmured out loud, and Peter glanced up from his laptop.

'What?'

'Prostitution is totally legal here. It's the *only* country in the world where that's true.'

Peter was only just mildly interested, but I inhaled the article, riveted. I learned that since the Prostitution Reform Act 2003, sex work wasn't just legal in New Zealand, it was decriminalized – which is even more liberal than that. In countries where prostitution is legal, it's often heavily regulated, and sex workers have to apply for a license. Not here. You just need to be an adult New Zealand resident, and remember to put on a condom. Legally speaking, selling sex in this country isn't much more regulated than selling a pizza. And running a brothel – being an 'owner operator' as they call it – isn't a whole lot harder.

Why, you might ask, did I bother to care? Didn't I have diapers to change and bottles to wash, booties to launder and storybooks to read? Well, remember, I was writing a book on this trip. So I did a little research, then I called up a brothel in Auckland, and got permission to come in and talk.

At the time, I thought I was a liberated woman, someone who could say 'anal play' in a sentence without stumbling over my words. But when I walked into my very first brothel, I came up against a lifetime of good-girl conditioning. This wasn't what private school and pony camp had prepared me for. Instead of playing it cool, I was self-conscious and nervous.

The bartender was unimpressed. He took one look at me and jerked his head. 'Oi,' he grunted, tapping the polished wood bar. 'This here's the lady I was tellin' yous about. The writer.'

Two young women glanced up from their drinks, then turned away. Heart thumping, I took a step closer and introduced myself. Would they be hardened? Angry and hostile? Up until that point, I'd thought of sex workers as 'other', denizens of an underworld that I'd never seen.

But you know what? Those girls were just . . . girls. Rein was tall and voluptuous, with a pretty, freckled face and sharp green eyes. Her skirt was short, and her boots had high heels, so she was dressed like my friends and me in college when we went out on a Friday. Veronica looked more Māori, with dark, wavy hair and big gold hoop earrings. Neither one was wearing much makeup.

'Hi!' I chirped. 'I was wondering what you guys thought about prostitution being legal in New Zealand?'

I figured they'd open right up about sex work, and how the Prostitution Reform Act protected their rights. But they didn't. Rein's green eyes narrowed. Veronica didn't look up from her Jack and Coke. 'Reckon it's what you think,' she muttered.

There was a pause. I stood there, a nervous smile twitching at my lips.

'It's gonna happen anyway,' Rein pointed out, giving me a sideways glance. 'You might as well make it safe.' She stirred her drink, then sucked on her straw.

To my right, Veronica shifted in her seat. 'People think we don't deserve the money. One of my mates, like, she said to me, "I work so hard at my job and you just lie around all day. At least I have a *brain*." They think we're stupid, and we're not. At *all*. You have to be smart to do this.'

We chatted for an hour, and by the time I left, it seemed obvious that sex work was . . . well, work. Sometimes they loved it, and sometimes they didn't, and sometimes they didn't feel like getting dressed to come into the office. You know, like a *job*. I added that experience to my book about New Zealand. And I filed it away in my memory banks.

Whangārei had been our first port of call in the country – and it was sunny and friendly, more affordable than Auckland or Wellington. We decided to settle there after touring around, and by then Silas's delays were too pronounced to ignore. At nearly two years, he'd just started walking, and he still had no words – only sounds. So the doctors ordered a blood test to analyze his DNA.

'Chromosomal microdeletion,' the geneticist said. 'On his twelfth chromosome. It's so tiny that just a few years ago, we never would have known what was wrong.'

'How tiny?' I asked.

'If the human genome is a thick Russian novel,' he explained, 'like your whole DNA is *War and Peace,* then Silas isn't even missing a sentence. Or a word. He's missing a letter, in the whole novel. And that's what throws everything off.'

Of course it threw everything off. When we learned about Silas's microdeletion, I knew we would stay in New Zealand. His medical needs alone would make living in America impossible – how could we begin to afford healthcare?

Our daughter was born, and we named her Miranda. Right away, I spotted the differences. Where Silas had been stocky and slow to get moving, Miranda smashed all of her milestones. She rolled, she reached, she babbled and crawled, and with every new skill I saw how different Silas was, how behind. All the cute little quirks that we'd fallen in love with turned out to be symptoms of his straitened fate: the middle finger he pointed with, the tongue that poked out, even the whorl of fine hair on his back that I kissed.

'He's moderately hirsute,' the doctors wrote down, 'and with a tendency to synophrys.' I saw them exchange looks, and I tried not to notice.

'Ball,' I told Silas, holding up a small ball. Just starting to walk, he staggered over and smiled.

'Ah-bah,' he babbled, his face lighting up.

'Ball,' I said again, emphasizing the 'l'. But he couldn't, or wouldn't, repeat it.

So I threw myself into helping him. I found speech therapy and music therapy; I wrote to researchers at the top of their fields. And Peter did the work that he had to do: he took a practical job in computers to support us.

We stopped talking about sailing away.

But I had another dream. If I couldn't get back on the sailboat, there was something else I could do: I could write. No one had published my book about New Zealand, but it was good enough to earn me an agent.

When Silas turned five we moved to Purua, a tiny farming community half an hour outside of Whangārei. Among the gentle hills and wildflowers, the plump cows and sheep, I found a charming one-room schoolhouse where we thought he might thrive. The kids there kept bees to make honey, and in America it would have been exclusive and Waldorfy, only for the children of technocrats, but in New Zealand it was just country living.

At first, we housesat for a neighborhood family who had traveled to Germany for the year: we cared for their chickens, a cow and a goat. After big city life, the farm was a shock. I dealt with misshapen eggs when the chickens were sick, and maggoty compost as the weather got warm. When the goat felt unwell, the vet asked for a stool sample, and I found myself driving to town with goat shit in my purse. But I wasn't put off – I found the whole thing hilarious, and soon I was writing a new book. My literary agent got three publishers interested, and when it sold, they titled it *DIRTY CHICK: Adventures of an Unlikely Farmer.* Despite Silas's disabilities, and the goat shit in my purse, it felt like we were all on our way.

Our landlords came home, and it was time to move on. By that time, I'd bottle-fed calves and lambs, and I'd tended to two baby goats. I'd nursed a chicken when she had a sore wing, and raised up a turkey for food. We'd even bought three alpacas, a choice our neighbors disdained.

'If ya can't eat it or milk it, an' it don't lay eggs, then what the hell's the point of keepin' it?' one asked.

'I mean . . . fiber, I guess?' I said unconvincingly. But that was a lie. Mostly I just thought they were fluffy and cute.

Leaning into our lives as dilettante farmers, we purchased a house on twelve acres. I planted vegetables, and we raised livestock and chickens. I brewed fruit wine. I milked the goat and made my own chèvre. We found friends in our rural community, sharing raw milk and hosting dinner parties where we all grilled fresh mussels, or stuck a sheep on a spit. Our property was what the Kiwis call a 'lifestyle block', a lifestyle that my American friends envied.

'Are you *kidding me?!*' they squealed over Skype. 'You have *alpacas.* You have *bees.* You *literally won life.*'

Okay, maybe.

But *fuck*, I was bored.

I will only tell you a little bit about being the mother of a disabled child, because I know that it makes you uncomfortable. When you get up in the morning, you go to his room and you clean the shit off his body and you dress him. Then you take him by the hand, you walk him downstairs and you feed him with a spoon. You put his liquid epilepsy medicine in a syringe, and crush the pills in another spoon with some honey. While you are waiting for the school bus, he might pee on himself and the couch, so you peel off his wet clothes and change him.

He does not talk. He does not kiss, because he can't pucker his lips. You're not sure if the distant, dreamy look in his eyes is from the intellectual disability, or the epilepsy, or the medication you are giving him for the seizures.

You feel profoundly ripped off by the universe.

Once the children are on the bus, you do the dishes, you make the beds, you feed the chickens and milk the goat. The only voices you hear are on podcasts. If you have an article to write about farming or cheesemaking, then you work at your laptop. You think about what you'll cook for dinner. The children come home and you cook the dinner. The husband comes home and he's tired and bored. *You're* tired and bored.

The days are so repetitive that you feel like a robot: *UP make a meal send the children to school – OUT tend the chickens, and the goat and the garden – IN do the housework, greet the kids when they're home – then cook the dinner and put everyone DOWN.* The routine takes the shape of a four-sided box, your sense of self so compressed that it's about to explode.

It's always hard to parent small children, but having a disabled child is lonely. Nobody wants to hang out with him unless you're paying them money. People get uncomfortable when your kid is incontinent, and yelling out sounds instead of saying real words.

I was tired of feeling so exhausted and isolated. I didn't want to be just a farmer and housekeeper, a caregiver and a cook. I wanted to feel like a woman again. I was desperate to break out of the box.

When Miranda was four and Silas was six, I flew to New York to record the audiobook for *Dirty Chick.* Stuck at home, Peter went to his job and took care of the kids. We had backpackers staying with us who helped out, but he had to do some cooking and cleaning. He had to change Silas's diapers, and coax little Miranda into her bath.

One day when we spoke on the phone, he asked how I'd feel about getting another dog. 'John's got a litter of puppies, and he said we can have one for free. It's a sheep dog, so it's got a ton of energy, but they're so smart and so easy to train.'

'No,' I told him. 'No way. We have twenty-six animals on that farm and counting. I don't want to train another dog. I'm way too busy with the kids and the book, and you're off at work during the day.'

'Okay,' he said. 'No problem. I'll tell him we can't take it.'

One week later, I was back in New Zealand. And Peter had adopted the dog.

—

What happens to a marriage when the power dynamic flips? It's worse than cheating and falling in love. *Why are YOU suddenly in charge when I used to be? I didn't agree to this! You never asked!*

'I want to quit,' Peter said one night, as we were sipping peach wine on the deck. 'That computer job's sucking my soul. It's killing me.'

'Okay,' I hesitated. *That's dramatic.* 'And what would you do instead? Did you want to retrain, or . . .'

'Captain a tall ship,' he announced. A tall ship is a huge, old-timey sailing vessel. Think Russell Crowe, in *Master and Commander.* They still get around on the water today, but most of them are modern replicas. I knew Peter had worked as a deckhand on a tall ship twenty years ago, when he was a young man with no real commitments. He'd loved it, and of course he did – why wouldn't he? Shimmying up and down masts like a lost boy from *Peter Pan,* learning complicated knots and testing himself out at sea. But we still had two young children to raise, and one them needed full-time care.

'But that's like . . . a job from the eighteenth century,' I said. 'Are there any twenty-*first* century careers you might like? Or . . . twentieth, even?'

Peter was adamant. 'I don't think so. I really want to captain a tall ship.'

How much do you get paid to captain a tall ship? I wondered. *Do they pay you in cash, or in silver doubloons? And how am I supposed to take care of Silas alone, while you play Renaissance fair out at sea?*

'Is there even a tall ship, here in New Zealand? Would they hire you?'

'Yeah,' Peter nodded. 'It's called the H.M.S. *Capricorn.* They wouldn't give me a job right away, but I could start with an unpaid internship. And I could work my way up from there.'

'Huh.'

I loved Peter, I really did. We laughed and we traveled the world together. And I wanted to honor his dreams. But inside my head, a small voice was saying: *I care for the kids. I coordinate Silas's needs. I clean the house. I cook all the meals. I manage the farm animals and the vegetable garden. I take care of the household accounts.*

You: do a job to earn money. That's what you bring to the table.

So here's my question: If you stop going to work, what are you contributing to this family? Seriously, I'm asking, Peter. What are you even doing here?

At that point, I knew I had to take charge. When the father of your children says he wants to run away to play pirates at sea, it's time to start looking at options. I started thinking about starting a business then, and I had an idea of what I wanted it to be. A clean, supportive place, where women could work. I remembered that girl Rein, five years ago, working at a brothel in Auckland.

It's gonna happen anyway, I remember she'd said. *You might as well make it safe.*

Chapter 2

Five months after Peter said he wanted to quit, in a little house in California, a blood vessel burst inside my mother's brain. A friend came to collect her for a museum trip the next day, and found her collapsed on the living room floor. My brothers and I all rushed to her bedside, and for the next two months, she was reasonably conscious, though the stroke had killed off half of her brain. She sat up in hospice and greeted her children and grandchildren; she turned up her nose at the inferior food. She drank white wine on the terrace at sunset, and I *think* she was aware of my book launch. She stayed alive long enough to say goodbye to us all, and then after two months, she was gone.

I didn't have the guts to start a brothel until my mother died, so maybe I should tell you a little bit about her. She was a dedicated, life-long feminist, and throughout my childhood she seemed frightened of nothing – except the possibility that I might one day have sex. When I was twelve years old, she made me wear a camisole under my T-shirt so my barely-there nipples wouldn't 'give the boys erections', which she worried might be embarrassing for them. Years before I was born, she'd put herself through a master's degree by cocktail waitressing while raising two sons on her own, and she drilled into me the critical importance of education – not so much to liberate my mind as to defend against the time when some man would dump me with two kids to support.

Well, she wasn't wrong there.

A few weeks after my mother died, I started to blow up my marriage. Peter and I went to a dinner party at Patrice's house, a nearby neighbor who was separating from his wife. I don't remember what we ate that night, but I do remember slipping my right foot out of my sandal and stroking Patrice's calf, just to see what he would do. He froze. Peter was telling a funny story about something, and the guest on his left burst out laughing. Then Patrice pressed his foot against mine, and I knew he was trying it out with me; he wanted to see if I meant it. So I told a lighthearted anecdote that complemented the story that Peter had shared, and under the table I stroked Patrice's leg and he pressed against mine, and eventually I could tell that he *did* have a hard-on, and I wasn't the least bit sorry about it. Actually, I was thrilled.

By the time the night of that barbecue rolled around, Silas was seven and could say just ten words. They were half-formed syllables like MIH for 'milk', and PEES for 'please'. Sometimes, he repeated nonsense sounds, like 'BUSS-ah-buss-ah-buss-ah-buss', and 'WHORES!! WHORES!! WHORES!!' I had no idea where those syllables came from. But they were weirdly prescient, now that I think about it.

'I want to sleep with Patrice,' I announced to Peter soon after the barbecue, and he thought the idea was hot. The past few years of speech therapy and diapers, doctor's appointments and household chores had ground us both down, and we were ready for the next big adventure. We felt strong and secure in the bond that we shared. It wasn't something a little casual sex could break down.

So Patrice and I started sleeping together, and then Peter started seeing Selma, a local woman he met on Tinder. And it all just felt exhilarating, two parents sharing the childcare while the other two had sex like sixteen-year-olds: all night, no babies to look after, no dinners to cook, no consequences.

Sex with two people, sex with three people. Once Selma and Patrice started sleeping with us, nothing was too crazy for us not to try. It was such fun to have a wicked secret, in our quiet, uptight little town.

But then something deeper happened: Patrice and I rediscovered a world. He thought he'd given up France, when he married a New Zealand woman. His Kiwi family only spoke English. Like many French expats, he'd resigned himself to a life of mediocre cheese and supermarket wines. He'd learned to bake his own crusty bread.

But I *did* speak French. My family had lived on the French Riviera when I was little, not because we were rich and glamorous, but because they wanted me to learn a new language. Villefranche-Sur-Mer in the eighties was a cobblestoned village, a simple, quiet place where you did your laundry in a bathtub and your grocery shopping on foot, with a basket slung over one arm. It formed the core of my early memories.

That time was long in the past, and sometimes, when I spoke French in bed, Patrice couldn't help but laugh. 'You talk like you're still five years old!' he teased. 'Your language – it's so *enfantin!*'

'But I *was* a little kid the last time I spoke French!' I protested. 'So, teach me some grownup phrases. Teach me how to say something filthy, like . . . I don't know, how do I say *you have a beautiful dick* in French?'

Patrice blushed. We were only just getting to know each other. '*Vous avez une belle bite*,' he said, lifting the sheet from my body. '*Et vous madame, vous avez un cul d'enfer*.' *You've got a smoking hot ass.*

'*Merci*,' I responded politely. 'You see? They never taught me that when I was a little kid in French school.'

'*J'espère bien!*' He laughed. *I should hope not!* Then he went quiet. Slowly, he traced his finger down my side, along my ribcage and the dip of my waist. '*Effleurer*,' he murmured. '*Je vous effleure, Madame*.'

I swallowed. 'What does that mean?'

'It means to touch so softly, it's like touching with the petals of a flower.'

—

As the months went by and nothing bad happened, the four of us brought up outlandish ideas, like forming a family, and raising five children together. It made so much sense when we talked about it, late at night as we sat by the fire: we could pool our resources, our money and love, and our kids would have more parents in their lives.

Six months after my mother died, my inheritance came through, and I paid off the house. Everything seemed possible, all of a sudden: maybe we could pay off both houses, or all live in one. Maybe we could build a second house in the paddock. Maybe we could build a creamery, and export our own cheese!

Then one day, Selma changed her mind. She'd been seeing another man all along, and now she thought she might be in love with him. Abruptly, she broke up with Peter.

And that's when everything soured.

'You have to break up with Patrice,' Peter told me. 'If I don't have someone, then you can't have anyone either.'

That didn't make sense to me. 'Why? We're not talking about two bowls of ice cream. I have a relationship with Patrice. He's a friend.'

Peter dropped it that time, but I could tell he still felt resentful. And for the first time since I'd met him, I just didn't care. *I bought the house. I have a writing career. He doesn't even want to* work *for a living! Why should I do what he says?*

Out loud, I said, 'No. I don't want to go back in the box.'

It was right about then that Patrice and I stopped using condoms. We didn't talk about it explicitly, which was odd because we're both reasonable adults. But there were some things I couldn't explain. Like when your child has a genetic mutation, and you wonder if your marriage was a biological mistake. *Is the damage in me?* you wonder. *Is it in him? Is it the mixture of the two of us together, that shouldn't be making more babies?*

And how do you tell your lover that when you close your eyes during sex, you're conjuring the image of a little blonde boy, running through the grass on your farm? A little boy with no disabilities, a boy who can laugh and talk? How do you tell him that when you get the image just right, you come in a white hot instant, so fiercely do you wish for that child?

When Selma left, Peter spent a full day in bed, and I wasn't sure what was wrong. What happened to ideas of super-sized families? Of making our own cheese? Of adventure? Outside the box, my life felt expansive – but there was Peter in bed, curled up in a ball. His devastation felt like more than the loss of a girlfriend. I think he already knew I was gone.

A brothel. A brothel? Could I open a brothel? I never could have done it when my parents were alive. Sex workers are whores, and brothel owners are pimps. As everyone who's ever been a woman will tell you, our sexuality is the whole world's business.

When it came to my parents, both my father and mother, protecting twelve-year-old boys from their tiny erections was really only just the beginning.

'Don't be a cocktease,' my father advised me at thirteen. I wish he'd explained how the stock market worked, but this was the wisdom he wanted to share. 'Whatever you do, don't be a cocktease.'

'But do you *enjoy* the sex?!' my mother wailed, when I told her I was sleeping with my high school boyfriend. Then she flew across the country, determined to yank me out of boarding school. (And what? Lock me up in a nunnery? It was never entirely clear.)

'He has abused his position of authority,' declared the Columbia athletics department, when they found out I was sleeping with my former crew coach. Poor Jon got fired, though he wasn't even my coach anymore, and I was the one who had seduced *him!* Yet someone convened a panel to discuss our consensual, adult relationship.

Be more sexy. Be less sexy. Be sexy, but only with this man, not that one. Don't be too sexy, or you might get knocked up. Then he might leave you, if you're too sexy. Or not sexy enough.

Prostitute. Floozy. Jezebel. Tramp. Wasn't this what my parents had warned me about? In French all these people even have their own name: the *demi-monde,* the half-world for people on the fringe – the criminals, the addicted, the whores.

Did I have the courage to open a brothel? I didn't know. I wasn't sure if I *wanted* to. But I was pretty confident it could make some good money. With Peter spiraling and aimless, I knew I'd soon need a job. And I wanted to learn more about it.

So the next morning, I started Googling brothels in Auckland. *Allure . . . Firecats . . . Femme Fatale.* **I'd like to start a brothel in Whangārei,** I wrote to six different places, cutting and pasting the email. **I'm in Northland so I won't compete with you. Would you be open to meeting with me, so I can ask you some questions?** Most of them ignored me, but not all: a woman called Luvely Lacey, who ran a business for erotic massage, replied. **I'll talk to you,** she said. **Come down Friday at 2. I'll meet you at the cafe on the corner.**

When I got to the coffee shop she had suggested, the place was practically empty. One customer sat in the corner, a young guy in a blue T-shirt and khakis, his profile framed by his tousled brown hair as he looked down at his phone. I ordered a coffee and took a seat at a table, unsure how long I should wait.

I looked around. The young man seemed like he was studying me. *Is he . . . hitting on me? No, that's not the vibe.* He jabbed at the screen on his phone.

Two minutes later, a beautiful young Chinese-Kiwi woman walked in, rocking skin-tight jeans and clear platform heels. She strode to the guy in the corner and he stood, kissing her lips before he walked out the door.

Then she approached me. 'Antonia? Sorry 'bout that,' she said, 'that's my partner. I wanted him to make sure you're all sweet. Just a minute, let me order a coffee.'

Six minutes later, Lacey sat across from me, sipping at her steaming flat white. She fixed me with a skeptical eye. 'A brothel, eh?' She put down her cup. 'And how d'you think I can help you with that?'

'Well, uh . . . basically, I don't know what I'm doing,' I admitted. 'Do you have any advice for me, starting out?'

'First off, have three different ways to check your accounting,' she said. 'Everyone steals. Everyone lies.'

'Really?' *That seems paranoid.* 'Why do they lie?'

'Think about it.' She licked the foam from the edge of her spoon. 'The whole business is built on lies. Illusions and lies. Your clients are probably lying to their partners about coming to you. Your girls are lying about their identities so no one will find out what they do. And everyone's paying in cash. You'll spend ninety percent of your time babysitting, and that's the truth.'

'But if you're operating in a way that supports women, if you pay them fairly and they feel happy about coming to work—'

'Look,' Lacey said, putting down her spoon. 'I don't do full service – my business is massage. If you want to run a business like *that*,' she said, 'then you'll need to do your own research.'

'Research? But that's why I'm talking to you! The full service places I contacted – none of them even wrote me back! They all ghosted me, every single one. So who do I talk to?'

Lacey raised an eyebrow. 'Stop trying to call people if they don't want to talk.' She pantomimed her hands on a keyboard. 'There's plenty of other ways to find them out there.'

'So what, I go . . . online?'

'There are forums.' She inspected her perfectly manicured nails. 'Reddit's a good one. But don't search for *sex,* or *sex work.* And *definitely* don't search for *prostitution.* Too many of the posters are off in America, or other places where it's against the law.' She reached into her sparkly handbag and pulled out a pen, then jotted a note on a napkin, pushing it across the table to me.

r/seggswork

'Try that,' she suggested, capping her pen. 'There's loads of good information out there. You just have to be a bit clever to find it.'

Back in Whangārei that evening, I told Peter my idea while I gave Silas his bath. 'Remember on our trip around New Zealand, when I interviewed those sex workers for the book? I'm thinking of starting a business like that.'

'You want to open a *whorehouse?'* he asked.

'A brothel, more like.' I soaped up a washcloth and ran it along Silas's back, while he flicked the water's surface with his fingers.

Peter ran his hand through his hair. 'You don't want to do something *normal?* Like writing and editing? Or law school?'

'This is *interesting,'* I said. 'What if sex work doesn't have to be awful? What if it can be done in a way that puts *women* in charge of their sexuality?'

'Whores are in charge of their sexuality?'

'They prefer to be called sex workers.'

'Okay, sex workers. And how are you going to pay for this . . . brothel?'

I stood up, drying my hands on my jeans. 'There's fifty grand left after paying the mortgage. I'll put it in a separate account, for the business.'

Peter was still processing the news. 'And then can I quit my job?' he asked. 'Because I can't keep doing computers, Antonia. I can't keep this yoke on my neck.'

'I guess,' I said. 'It sounds like you're going to anyway. And then you'll—'

'Captain a tall ship,' he finished, and I felt about a million years old.

'But that's not a *job*,' I burst out. 'It's a *hobby*. It's for someone with no responsibilities. You're a father now; you have a family. What are you going to *do*?'

'I don't know,' he replied, sounding lost.

He left the bathroom then, and I heard him go down the stairs. Down in the living room, he sat on the couch. I knew he was searching online with his tablet – I'd seen him do it dozens of times. *Passive income streams . . . captain a tall ship . . . buy a junk rigged sailboat to charter in Fiji . . .* dreams, dreams, dreams and escape hatches. Dreams without plans that would never come to anything.

I pulled the plug from the bath. I held up the towel, and dried Silas's head, then wrapped him and lifted him up in my arms. I put him in pajamas; I brushed his teeth. I found Miranda, made sure her teeth were brushed. I got into bed with them; I read them two stories; I sang three songs and we cuddled.

And the whole time, I was thinking about the brothel I could start. It wasn't a dream that could never come true. I'd met Lacey that day, and she'd done it. Sure, she only did erotic massage, but her business was sex work – and she wasn't some monster, or some sleazy pimp. She was just a smart-as-hell woman who ran her own business.

And I thought *maybe* it was possible – if I found the courage – that I could run one just like her.

Chapter 3

The next day, once the kids were packed off to school, after I milked the goat, hung out the laundry, did all the dishes and weeded the garden, I sat down at my laptop with a ham sandwich and coffee. I typed in Lacey's magic word:

r/seggswork

The screen loaded with a page full of Reddit threads. I flicked through the headings, then clicked on the first one.

wh0re_galore
The world's first hooker was a force to behold. She was just like back up there Ramses III, this pussy ain't free

territor!al: Yeah that's what they're scared of
wh0re_galore: Who's scared?
territor!al: Clint and his gummy worm

manogator8: Girl I used to clean up cum at a Travelodge for $7/hr. Now I still clean up cum but I'm making some bank. THAT's what they're scared of.
territor!al: Pull out that gummy worm Clint you will PAY. GTFO with that wee-wee stick till you bring me my BAG.

Clint and his gummy worm? This was . . . unexpected. I clicked on the next one.

prettybaaaby
Stupid Client of the Day! Wrong answers only:

saturninmercury11: so he sez do you have any restrictions? uuuh no you may chop off my knee caps and harvest my organs please be my guest sir
normie4neva: when it comes to being a seggs worker you gotta stroke more ego than dick tbh
bimbobaggins: Keep getting requests for COT and COF lolol. Today I ducked my head or he woulda shot me in the eye!!

COT? COF? Opening a new tab, I googled 'COT and COF sex work,' which brought me to a list of abbreviations I couldn't unsee. *Come On Tits and Come On Face . . . okay, good to know.* Then I kept reading, and instantly regretted it. *I'll never think of snowballs the same way again.* Wincing, I clicked back to the chat.

normie4neva: Puts it in my butt and says 'I slipped' 🤦 um no Chad that has literally never happened in the history of the world

trixR4kids: Makes a booking then asks what special extras I offer I WILL LITERALLY HAVE SEX WITH YOU what more do you want??

hair0nfyre: I think he forgot to ask for your soul

badbabybiatch: Had one ask me if the extras cost extra. YES JIMOTHY THAT'S WHY THEY'RE CALLED EXTRAS

I caught myself snorting at a couple of the comments, and I set down my coffee so I wouldn't inhale it. I scrolled down, past more snark and dark wit until one of them made me stop short.

phryne: I don't know, sure some clients are dumb but then some are just shy. Some have terrible anxiety. One of my clients has a brain injury and this is the only way he'll ever experience intimacy. If they didn't have us, where else could they go? Those who think it's wrong to give people joy should consider what it is they're afraid of.

'Huh,' I said out loud. I squinted at her avatar, the head of an ancient statue, her stone eyes blank and unseeing. 'Phryne . . . who are you *really,* though?' I hovered over her username and her profile appeared.

Dominatrix – FSSW – Seductress – Kink & Fetish Specialist – AU/NZ

I hit Chat. Then I stopped. What did I want to ask her, exactly? *Hello, random stranger, can you tell me how to open a brothel, please?* Was she even a *she*? And would she get offended?

I flexed my fingers, feeling surprisingly nervous. Putting my actual questions in writing made this whole thing seem real, somehow. Then I just started typing.

MadamAntonia: Hi! I'm new to all this, and I was wondering if you could tell me a little bit about being a seggs worker?

She had to accept my message request before I'd get an answer, so I flicked back to the main forum while I waited.

cruelladechill
What people don't get about being a seggs worker GO

payORgoaway: no one believes me when i say s3ggs is only 5% of our jobs. like really you think i'm out here getting railed for six hours?? DEBBIE I AM NOT A TRAIN SET
queenvagine: when people say sw is not a 'real job' like please tell me deryl what does a 'financial analyst' do??
trixR4kids: how bout when the lady rings your groceries up at checkout and its $130 but inside ur like 'that will be 1.3 bl0wj0bs pls'

These girls don't sound downtrodden, that's for sure. They sounded like a bunch of smartass, funny women bitching about their crap day at work. I scrolled down further, landing on a picture of a giant, juicy burger sitting next to a pile of onion rings. The caption read: *This is the special treat I just earned for farting inside of a man's mouth.*

My laptop dinged. There was an alert in the top-right corner of the page. I clicked.

phryne: Why do you want to know? Are you some trick with a fantasy?

There was a pause, then she added:

My time is valuable. Are you going to pay? If not, don't waste my time.

Okay, that's fair. She probably gets this shit all the time. I took a minute to collect my thoughts, then I jumped in.

MadamAntonia: I want to open an ethical brothel. I'm in New Zealand, so it's legal. I want to start a place that's fair to the women, where they feel good about going to work. Problem is, I'm a newbie. I don't know anything. 😅 Would you be open to answering some questions?

I hesitated, then I added: *yes I can pay.*

I heard Miranda's school van pull into the driveway, and I checked the time. *Crap. Three already??* Downstairs, the front door slammed. 'Mama??' she called out.

'Up here!' I yelled. 'In my study!' I turned back to the screen. Several more lines of text had appeared.

phryne: You don't want a brothel then you want an AGENCY. An escort agency. I'll answer more questions but you pay in advance. $100 per question so you should choose wisely. I usually charge $500/hr in Melbourne & I assure you I'm worth it.

I could hear Miranda clumping up the stairs. 'Mama? Is there some snacks?' Quickly, I tapped out a reply.

MadamAntonia: OK done! I'll message you this evening. You're in Melbourne, right? 9pm?

The door swung open behind me, and I quickly closed the chat.

Miranda skipped over, peering curiously at my laptop. 'Oooh! Is that a burger?? Could I have a burger? 'Cause today we had swimming and I'm so, so, so starving!'

I closed out of the Reddit window so she couldn't see the caption. 'We don't have burgers, but how about a cold chicken drumstick?'

I took her down to the kitchen and got her set up with a snack, then loaded the Reddit app on my phone while she ate. Silas's school van pulled up, and I went out to get him. When I slid open the door, his face lit up with a smile. 'MIH! PEEES!!' he demanded, and I walked him inside, then helped him out of his gumboots and got him some milk. He slurped at his sippy cup while I slathered peanut butter and honey on bread.

'Mama?' Miranda pushed a crumpled worksheet across the kitchen counter. 'I'm supposed to learn these heart words for spelling and also I have to read an owl book and it's SO DUMB 'cause—'

My phone dinged with a Reddit alert.

phryne: Here's my email for Paypal. AUD $500 buys you 5 questions.

I blinked. *Okay,* I thought, *I guess I'm doing this.* I went upstairs and drew a warm bath for Silas, then got him stripped off and sat him down in the water, giving him an empty yoghurt container to play with in the suds. Then I sat on the toilet while I listened to Miranda stumble her way through the world's longest bird book. 'Kuku the ruru could not learn to fly,' she read. 'He tried and he tried, and he didn't know why!'

Kuku the ruru can fuck off and die, I thought irritably. *I need to get to my into my Paypal account!* I pulled out my phone, checking the time difference in Melbourne.

'Kuku the ruru liked insects and mice,' Miranda went on. Then: 'MOM! You're not supposed to look at your *phone!* I'm READING!'

'Okay, okay, *sorry.*' I stuffed it back in my pocket. *It's two hours earlier. So I have until eleven here – that's 9pm in Melbourne.* Seated in his bath, Silas was absorbed with his plastic container, filling it up and then pouring out the water. 'BUS!' he babbled happily. 'Bus-ah-bus-ah-bus.'

After two more renditions of Kuku the ruru, Miranda went off to have her screen time and I got Silas up and out of the tub. *'Whores,'* he growled, when I pulled out the plug and he saw the water draining out of his bath. *'Whoooores.'*

'I'm *trying,*' I assured him, lifting him up in his towel. 'I just gotta figure out how it all works.' I guided him to his bedroom, laid him out on his bed and fastened his nappy, then eased him into a pair of fresh, clean pajamas. 'How about a little *West Side Story*?' I suggested, and Silas bounced happily on the bed.

'Bus!' he declared, so I put on the music, then arranged his plastic zoo animals all around him. Finally, I made my way down the stairs, carrying his dirty clothes to the laundry. Peter was sitting at the kitchen counter, though I hadn't heard him come in. He had out the plastic container of cold chicken, and he was gnawing on a drumstick as he scrolled on his phone.

'Hey,' he greeted me, his mouth full of chicken. 'I'm *starving*. What were you thinking of doing for dinner?'

That night, I waited until I heard Peter snoring before getting up and slipping on my bathrobe. The summer night air was gentle and warm, so I didn't even bother with slippers. I grabbed my phone and I glanced at the time. *10.54pm. Perfect.*

I crossed the hall and stepped into my study, shutting the door softly behind me. As quietly as I could, I slipped the lock in its catch. The room was dark, but the curtains were open, and the windows let in a faint glow of moonlight. I sat down at my desk and opened my laptop, then clicked on the chat box for Phryne. I didn't know who this woman was, but I'd just sent her five hundred real Australian dollars. And I already knew my first question.

> **MadamAntonia:** Hi again. Okay, so here goes. Why did you say I want an escort agency, but not a brothel? I thought they were two terms for the same thing?

Whoever she was, this person was prompt. Once I hit Send, she started typing right away.

> **phryne:** They are NOT the same thing. There are good brothels and bad brothels, that's not the point. It's more about working conditions. At a brothel, the ladies have to all work on shift.

It could be 8-12 hours, and they might not even get a client. Plus they have to hustle, like go out and do lineups for the men. Escort agencies are by appointment only. The girls don't even have to be on site – they can go to school or be home with their kids, or just be out there, living their lives. The clients call you, then you reach out to her if she gets a booking.

That was your first question. Four more.

I read through the message, then I read it again. I could see how an agency might be better, especially for students or stay-at-home moms.

MadamAntonia: But it's the same work in the end, right? The madam tells them when they have a booking and they go have sex with some guy?

phryne: Well. There's sex and there's sex. What do you plan to offer?

I don't know.

MadamAntonia: I don't know? Sex is just sex, right?

And did that count as one of my hundred-dollar questions? Because if it did, that's a rip-off.

phryne: Don't worry, baby madam. We're still on the same question.

What, is she psychic? Outside, a native owl called out from the bottlebrush tree. This was the ruru I'd heard all about. Since Miranda had read me the book three times through, I knew she'd be sitting in her nest with two babies, waiting for her mate to find food. *You and me both, Kuku,* I thought to myself. *Just here in our nest, making sure we provide.*

Meanwhile, Phryne was still typing:

phryne: Different kinds of 'sex' could be (but are not limited to):

Full service: vaginal and oral sex on him, only – this is the basic, for guys who just want to get off.

Girlfriend Experience, or GFE: that's the full fantasy. All of the above, plus oral on her and kissing. GFE's more psychological . . . she acts like his adoring girlfriend.

Porn Star Experience, or PSE: another kind of fantasy. All of the above, plus lots of dirty talk and different positions. She'll probably have her legs pinned up around her ears. Can involve Greek, maybe a striptease. More of a performance – she's doing the whole 'filthy slut' routine.

Okay. I read on. *What's Greek?* But Phryne wasn't finished:

Then there's BDSM, kink and fetish work . . . but you shouldn't go there until you know what you're doing.

Three more.

Frowning, I typed back.

MadamAntonia: So why is 'Greek' a part of the Porn Star Experience? Is that like a role-playing thing? Like with togas and stuff?

phryne:

Umm . . . did I say something dumb?

phryne: No togas. Greek is anal sex. Usually costs extra, and not everyone offers it.
Two more.

TWO more??

MadamAntonia: But that last one was more of a clarification, don't you think??

phryne: My time is valuable. Two more.

Jesus, this lady's a hardass. But what did I expect? She's a dominatrix. I considered my next question.

MadamAntonia: So let's go back to the whole escort agency business model. A client calls up, makes a booking, and then I call the lady? And tell her to come in?

phryne: No.

Now that can't *be a whole-ass answer.* I prodded for more.

MadamAntonia: So how do I get in touch with her then?

phryne: You can call her if you want, or message her, or however you choose to get in touch – the issue is CONSENT. If you want to run a 'fair business', as you say, then you don't *tell* the women to do anything – you ask them. The women must consent at all times, and they can withdraw their consent anytime.

I typed quick to get in my follow-up, before she could slide in a 'Next question.'

MadamAntonia: So just asking her instead of telling her – that's what makes it more fair?

phryne: No.

This time, the pause was so long, I thought she might have given up on me. I listened to the ruru calling from her tree, wishing that stupid book wasn't stuck in my head. *Kuku the ruru eats insects and mice. Kuku the ruru thinks spiders are nice . . .* Then Phryne replied:

phryne: Consent is much more complex than that. For example, women can never be in debt to you or your agency. If they're in debt, they might feel like they *have* to take a booking, even if they feel unsafe. That's how a lot of the bad places force women to see clients, even when they don't want to. They charge her room fees, or they fine her for being late. Once she's in debt, she can't say no.

Drugs are another issue. Some places turn a blind eye, because they know an addict will always feel pushed to make more money, and that's good for business. But if she's working to feed her addiction, she can't consent of her own free will. Plus with drugs on site, you'll get a lot of problem clients. Avoid.

Blackmail's another. There are parlours out there that will threaten to 'out' a woman online if she doesn't do what they say. Protect the privacy of your workers, always. Even when it's legal, the stigma can ruin lives.

That was your fourth question. You have one more.

I took my time to think about it. I didn't want to waste my last hundred-dollar question. This invisible Phryne was my genie in a bottle, and she had just granted five wishes. When I was a kid, I thought I had the perfect hack for those stories: *Ask for unlimited wishes!* I'd tell all my friends. *Do that just once and you'll have more wishes than you could ever use up in your whole entire life!*

But that wasn't an option. My hands hovered over the keyboard. Finally, I typed:

MadamAntonia: What do you think is the most important thing for me to know about being a madam? If you could give me one piece of advice, what would it be?

phryne: Hold your power.

I waited, but that's all she wrote.

MadamAntonia: That's it?? Hold my power? What does that even mean?

phryne: Sex is a power negotiation. The clients will push, but you don't give an inch. It always starts small . . . they'll whine about taking a shower, or they'll come early, or stay late so they can use up more time for free. The next thing you know, they'll take off the condom. Or try to hurt her, or hold her down during sex. DO NOT MAKE EXCUSES. DO NOT APOLOGISE. DO NOT BACK DOWN.

That was your last question. Good luck.

I leaned back in my chair, trying to think. Who were these men, who paid women for sex, who I'd have to force into line? Obviously, Phryne had real-life experience. Could I come across just as tough in my texts? Could I make men play by *my* rules?

Off in the bottlebrush tree, the ruru fell silent. *Hope you got something to eat tonight, Kuku. Make sure you take care of those babies.* I shut down my laptop and headed to bed. But first, I downloaded my chat history.

—

The next morning, I made omelets for Silas and Miranda, I packed up their lunchboxes, and I milked the goat. But I didn't even glance at the laundry or the dishes. Instead, I started calling up rental agents.

'I want to start an ethical brothel,' I said to each one, trying to be up-front and honest. *Big mistake.*

The agents did not sound impressed. '*Ethical brothel?*' one of them asked. 'What's that when it's at home?'

'I want to protect women's rights!' I clarified.

'You want to sell girls for sex,' he corrected.

'So is that a no?'

The agent made a snorting sound. 'The problem,' he explained, as though I was stupid, 'is that the business is viewed in a negative light.'

'But how does that matter? It's legal, isn't it?'

He sighed. 'Legal, yes . . . but not *acceptable or desirable.* Landlords still view it as a dirty business. Fair or not, they see it as tangled up with drugs and crime. Gang violence, that sort of thing. So from a landlord's point of view, it's all a lot more trouble than it's worth.'

'Oh,' I said, my new sense of purpose deflating. 'I get that. I guess.'

Be more sexy. Be less sexy. Be sexy, but only with this man, not that one. What I was discovering was one more rule telling women how we should fuck. *Whatever you do, don't sell sex for money. Once it's transactional, you've really crossed the line.*

I still didn't want to do the goddamned laundry. I decided to get back on Reddit. This time, I wouldn't just listen and lurk. It was time to start asking some questions.

badbabybiatch

WHY does he have to tell me he's white in his first contact?? Just pay my deposit Brayden IDGAF what color your skin is SMH

normie4neva: Honestly that's a big 🚩🚩🚩 for me. Usually it comes with 'I'm young and handsome not like your usual old guys' like dude I ♥ my old guys. They're polite and they don't go for hours lol

bimbobaggins: People are just racist idk it's gross

queenvagine: Where I worked b4 at a br*thel the skinny white girls always got picked first and there were some banging latina chicks but 🤷‍♀️🤷‍♀️🤷‍♀️ some guys are stupid and blind

payORgoaway: SO skinny like size 4-6 no tits no ass WHY ARE MEN

I read through the rest of the posts, frowning. *Skinny white girls, huh?* It was harsh, but these women were speaking from experience. I pictured a line-up of girls at a brothel, different sizes, ages, body shapes, and skin tones. It was easy to see how that could just be degrading, especially if you didn't look like a magazine cover. Getting judged like a product for sale on a shelf.

But then again . . . what if we were talking about modeling, or acting? When they pick out women for their looks it's just normal. *We need an Asian size four for the Spring/Summer line. The director's looking for a slender white actress with fair skin, a size six or an eight.* There are so many jobs where we're judged on our size and appearance, and whether we're able-bodied or not. Models and actors, athletes and soldiers, hostesses in high-end, busy restaurants. It might not be fair, it might not be right, but it's silly to pretend it's not real.

And if there was one thing I saw with these sex workers online, they didn't give a shit about 'PC' or 'woke'. They said what they thought, and they kept it real.

I took a breath, then posted a question:

MadamAntonia: Are you saying white girls make more money?

payORgoaway: depends on where you're at . . . sometimes white guys want a black girl, a thicc girl, or an asian. Why, MADAM, r u doing market research?? 😂😂😂

MadamAntonia: kind of. I want to start a high-end agency.

queenvagine: 'high end' = white and skinny. Sry not sorry that's just how it is.

afrodite4hire: Hey **u/MadamAntonia**, your profile says you're in NZ . . . have you talked to the NZPC? Because they have a lot of resources if you're getting started.

The NZPC?? Never heard of it. I opened a new tab and searched. The first link took me to the New Zealand Prostitutes Collective. *Run by sex workers for sex workers. We advocate for the rights, safety, health, and well-being of all sex workers.* The banner on the homepage had a crowd of smiling people in red, holding up matching umbrellas. They were mostly women, but not all of them – there were some men and some trans folks. I scrolled down to the bottom of the page.

Locations: Wellington – Christchurch – Auckland

Well well well, I thought to myself, clasping my hands like a cartoon villain. *Auckland NZPC, you're my next stop.*

'I need to go down to Auckland,' I told Peter over dinner that night. The children had both cleaned their plates, and Silas was listening to *Fiddler on the Roof* in his room while Miranda put on her PJs. 'I need to do some research, for starting my agency.'

He pushed away his plate, still oily with salad dressing, and poured himself a glass of homemade honey mead. 'Okay . . . for how long?'

'Just one night. I want to check out the New Zealand Prostitutes Collective, see what they're all about. I think they've got tons of resources, health and safety information, a bunch of stuff about the law, and—'

'Who's gonna take care of the kids? And get them to school? I can't be back here when they get home at three. You know I'm out of here by seven-thirty, and then there's dinner at night. I mean, I can make pasta—'

I put down my fork. 'Okay, but they *are* your own kids, you know? And don't worry, I found a French girl online. She can be here next week. I'll show her the routine, I'll teach her how to milk the goat – it'll be fine!'

Peter pressed his lips together. 'What about your boyfriend? Why doesn't *he* do it?'

'I guess he could, if you'd let him stay over . . .' I stopped. This felt like uneasy ground. 'Let's just get the French girl to help. It's only one night.'

In the end, the trip was easy to organize. Violette came on Monday, and by Wednesday she was milking the goat by herself. Plus it didn't hurt that she was gorgeous, and liked jumping on the trampoline with Silas and Miranda, flashing her legs when her sundress flipped up.

'Go ahead,' Peter said Wednesday night. 'Have fun in Auckland. We'll be just fine.'

—

The next day, I woke up before dawn, getting on the motorway to Auckland before it clogged up with rush-hour traffic. I got off at the exit for Karangahape Road, which everyone just calls 'K Road'. It reminded me of Times Square before they kicked out the peep shows: an exciting, dirty street full of thrift stores and sex shops. I steered my hatchback into a tight little parking spot, then walked to an unmarked building with frosted white windows. I buzzed and the door swung open. 'Oh hello,' a tall, friendly Māori woman greeted me, her streaked blonde hair tied back in a ponytail. She stuck out her hand. 'I'm Diana. Come on in. Welcome to the NZPC.'

Waving me inside, Diana led me to a pair of armchairs at the back of a cluttered office space. There was one other woman in the office, an Asian lady absorbed in her computer screen. 'That's Anya, by the way.' The lady looked up and waved. 'She speaks Japanese, Korean, and Chinese. She writes up the info packs, for the ladies who don't speak English. Sorry, did you want a coffee?'

'No thanks, I had some on the road.' I sat in the chair she was pointing at, and took in the scene all around me. 'I can't get over that this is all legal, and . . . *fine*,' I said. 'You mean nobody gives you a hard time?'

'I wouldn't say *that*.' Diana made a face. 'There's always the stigma. That's a lot harder to get over than the legal side of things. But prostitution was always legal in New Zealand. It was just the *acts surrounding it* that were criminalized, like living off the earnings, or soliciting. Which I guess is what you want to do.'

I nodded. 'But I want to do it right, and I want to make it safe. So what do you guys, I mean – what do you *do* here?'

She smiled. 'Funny you should ask. Not many people know, outside the industry. They hear "Prostitutes Collective", and they think we're *collecting prostitutes*. It's not like that at all. We've been supporting their rights for thirty years now. The girls who work in the sex industry *these* days,' she shook her head, 'they wouldn't have the faintest clue what it was like to work pre-law reform.'

'What *was* it like?' I asked. 'I mean, if prostitution was always legal, how bad could it be?'

Her smile went flat. 'Anyone who worked in a brothel had to go on a police register, with your real name, and your real details. Then the cops would come in about a week later, and they'd be undercover. They'd pay to have sex with you, then they'd arrest you.'

'Wait a minute,' I had to interrupt. 'You mean the cops would get *laid?* And *then* they'd arrest you?'

'*Yes.*' She nodded her head emphatically. 'It wasn't the johns who were prosecuted; they were free to go. Only the sex workers. And then you'd get done for soliciting. You were a criminal. It was a double standard law, written by men for men. And yeah, *the cops got laid*.'

'So how did you get the law passed? Did people make a fuss?'

She gave me a hard look. 'We almost didn't make it. People thought there was going to be an explosion of prostitution. They thought it was gonna be a toxic waste for this nation. We had a lot of hatred toward us. But that's not what happened.' She leaned back in her chair. 'Sex work isn't a toxic waste, that's obvious. But it isn't some feminist fantasy either. It's just a job. It's a real job. It's my life, you know? My body, my choice.'

I pulled out my notebook, where I'd listed some questions. 'Could we talk about sexual health for a second? Because I know condoms are required, for working in the industry—'

Diana pointed at the far end of the room, where stacks of boxes were piled in neat rows. 'They *are* required, and we'll supply you for free.'

'For *free?'* I repeated. 'Sorry, I'm American. Not much is free where I come from.'

She shrugged. 'Just makes sense, really. If you want workers to use them, you have to provide them. Otherwise, the most vulnerable providers, the ones who might not be able to afford them, might not use them. And that puts everyone at risk. Especially since the men will always try to get out of it. They'll ask you for "natural", or "premium services".' Her fingers made air quotes around the words.

'And that's—'

'Industry lingo for sex without a condom. Don't put your workers in the way of it.'

'Okay, got it.' I glanced at my notes. 'So . . . what about STIs, infections and stuff? Should I require the ladies get regular testing, or—'

Diana held up her hand and I stopped. 'Let me ask you something. If you go in to have a heart operation, do you ask your surgeon if he's been tested for STIs?'

'What?' That seemed kind of random. 'No, of course not.'

'Why not?'

'Well, I mean, he's a *doctor*, and—'

'Exactly. And you think he's more *clean* than a sex worker, because he's spent a few years in medical school. He's literally *inside your chest cavity,* and you're not going to ask if he's been tested?'

'But, I mean . . .' I tried to recover. 'I just figured—'

'Well, don't figure. It's illegal for you to force your ladies to get tested, and it's illegal for you to tell clients you guarantee that they're disease free.'

'It is?' I put my notebook down.

'It's their *private business.* Besides, they could have been tested last week and contracted something two days before. So who knows?' Her voice softened. 'That's why we use condoms, every time. And the truth is, most sex workers are scrupulous about their health. They're not stupid, and this is their livelihood. But anyway,' she rose to her feet. 'You're parked just out front, right? If you want, I can get you stocked up with four sizes of condoms straight away. There's lube, too, and starter packs. Here, let's get you all sorted.'

—

Peter wasn't expecting me until the next morning, so I found a bench by the harbour and relaxed near the sailboats, listening to the halyards clanking against the metal masts. I pulled out my phone and opened the Reddit app, hoping for more comments from sassy sex workers online.

manogator8
Top secret trixx of the trade – GO!

Oh, this should be good. I pulled out my notebook and a pen.

wh0re_galore: Get him into the shower and get him worked up in the suds. That way he'll go right away. Two minutes of seggs then ppbbbbt BYYYYE!!
territor!al: Pineapple juice before golden showers. YOU CANNOT DRINK TOO MUCH PINEAPPLE JUICE 🍍 💀🍍 💀 🍍 💀
afrodite4hire: Best way to get chili oil off a dick? Dish soap.

Say what? I decided to ask.

MadamAntonia: Why would you put chili oil on a dick lolol?

afrodite4hire: BECAUSE MEN

saturninmercury11: Look him in the eye when ur giving head.

bimbobaggins: Shove a bit of lube up in there right b4 a booking. Then you can go oooh you make me so WET!

saturninmercury11: Good tip lol like babe IDC how hot you are, I'm dryer than the Sahara rn

saturninmercury11: Actually scratch that DON'T TOUCH ME JUST GIVE ME YOUR MONEY

I kept reading and scribbling. *Parsley for garlic breath? Latex gloves for anal play? VAMPIRE GLOVES??* I was absorbed in the conversation, furiously scribbling notes, when my phone buzzed with a notification. It was a message:

afrodite4hire: Speaking of chili oil. Do you want to learn how to torture a dick?

Um. I don't know, do I?

MadamAntonia: Yes!

Of course I do.

afrodite4hire: Can you make it to the CBD tonight 9pm

I sat up straight.

MadamAntonia: Yes! Auckland, right? But . . . how did you know I'm here?

afrodite4hire: I'm mates with Diana at the NZPC. Go to 87C Ambassador street at 9 tonite. That's the dungeon where I work. Do not come early and do not come late. Ring at the frosted glass door and I'll buzz you inside.

Someone let out a short, sharp laugh and I jumped. A couple of corporate-looking office types were walking right past me, wearing slender dress pants, leather messenger bags slung on their shoulders.

Startled, I put down my phone. The sun was still bright in a radiant sky, the white yachts and dinghies rocking gently in their slips. *And here I am, making a date with a stranger, to torture a dick in a dungeon tonight.* I flicked my phone off and stuffed it back in my pocket, feeling like I had something to hide.

Ambassador Street was just off K Road, and by nine all the bars were crowded with partiers. I wasn't sure how to dress for this mystery date, and I didn't have much to change into. I'd found some high-heeled leather boots in a shop on K Road, and I kept on my black jeans and T-shirt.

Number 87 was a narrow, dark building with eight buzzers out front on a panel, each one labelled with a neat, typeset name. The one for Unit C said **Ms F. Ryn.** *Wait . . . F. Ryn? Like Phryne? Where's Afrodite?* Lacey was right: this business was illusion. I buzzed, and the front door clicked open.

At the end of the dim hall a door opened, revealing a slender shape in the gloom. She wore a plain white mask, a thin plastic toy from a dollar store, and a high-necked, white lab coat over trim charcoal slacks. When I got there, I saw she was reedy and tall, with long, sculptured fingers and fine, sharp wrist bones. She held out her hand, her fingernails clipped exceptionally short.

'Hello, Antonia. Or should I call you Madam?' She gestured inside, and clicked the door shut. I couldn't see her face behind the white plastic, but I could make out her shining dark eyes. We stood in a small, simple sitting room, the walls painted black, a grey couch and side chair stiff against the back wall. A small lamp with a flexible neck gave off a red glow. A spare kitchenette was off to one side, a full teacup steaming on the counter. Beside it was a paperback, open face-down. I couldn't read the cover but I saw the word *Fantasy,* with a picture of a black leather whip.

'Are you . . . Phryne?' I asked, thrown off by the name change. 'I thought you were in Melbourne.'

'Don't believe what people say, if you want to madam.' Phryne perched on the couch. 'Everyone lies.'

She lowered the red lamp so it lit just her hands, folded demurely on her lap. Outside the red glow, her body stayed dark and vague. I moved to the chair.

'You can stand.' Phryne sat immobile. 'It's good that you're doing your research. You came down to Auckland; you spoke to Diana. You stocked up on condoms and lube.' She lowered her voice to a whisper. '*But that's not what this job is about.*'

'It's not?' I shifted in my new boots. There was a blister coming up on my right heel, and it hurt.

'No. It's about *holding your power.* I told you before.' She sounded impatient. 'Would you like to try?'

'Try what?'

'A domination session.' She took a phone from her pocket. 'I'll charge you one thousand, and he can be here in five. Henry Ball Bondage. Or that's what I call him. Most of them give us fake names, of course.'

'And he wants to be . . . dominated? Like, right now?'

'Are you interested?'

'Yeah,' I said, 'I mean I think so. I'll give it a shot, anyway.'

'You have my Paypal.' She glanced at her phone. 'Perfect. He's just outside.' She stood and walked past me, pressing a button that was fixed to the wall.

'Henry!' she called, when he came to the door. 'This is Mistress Antonia. She'll be in charge of your session tonight.'

A red-haired man stepped inside, and she shut the door behind him. He was fair and freckled, his pale green eyes rimmed with fine, almost invisible lashes. He met my gaze and then quickly looked down.

'Yes, Mistress. Thank you, Mistress.'

'Come with me.' Phryne stepped to a door on the right side of the room. 'Henry *loves* to have his nipples pinched. Don't you, Henry? And his balls trussed nice and tight.'

She swung open the door to a well-lit dungeon, its crimson walls lined with leather and stainless steel tools. 'Your tools are there on the trolley. Pegs, fishing weights for his balls, some laces. There's nipple clamps, too.' She pushed a rolling steel cart to the center of the room. 'It won't hurt him when you put the pegs on – it's when you're taking them off and the blood rushes in. The restraints are there, on the wall.' She gestured at some leather straps, fixed to the floor and the ceiling. 'Check his feet and his hands, when they're cuffed. You need to make sure they're not cold. And as far as binding his balls go—' She tittered. 'Don't worry, he'll tell you *exactly* how he likes it.'

She moved to the door. 'Think I'll go have my tea now, and finish my book.'

'You're not staying?' I felt like I was on stage with no script.

One delicate hand on the doorknob, Phryne tilted her head. '*Are* you a madam, Antonia? Because this is the job.'

Which is how I ended up alone with Henry Ball Bondage, his bare ass covered in goosebumps as he bent down to pull off his socks. He folded his things in a neat little pile, then turned around, his pale pink penis waggling between his legs. *Run away!* the small voice in me screeched. *What are you doing in a dungeon with this strange freckled man, who wants you to torture his balls!*

'Right,' I said, steeling my courage. *I can do this.* 'Let's find some cuffs for you, shall we?'

'Yes, Mistress. They're right over there on the hook, Mistress.'

I started to thank him, then bit my tongue. *Mistresses don't say thank you.* Instead, I snapped the cuffs on his feet, then clipped them to stainless steel anchor points on the wall. 'How does that feel? Too tight? Or is that good?'

'Yes, Mistress. Feels right, Mistress.'

He raised his left hand to be cuffed. *Did I ask you to raise that hand? No, I did not. Put it down again, you eager little fool.*

Whoa. What voice was that, just now in my head? I didn't say it out loud, but I wanted to. 'Raise your other hand,' I said instead, attaching his wrist to the end of a hanging bar. 'You like your nipples tortured, don't you, Henry?'

'Yes, Mistress.'

'I'll usc these metal clamps then, they're pretty.'

They were also very sharp on one side. I traced the curve of Henry's spine with the edge of one clamp. He let out a deep, shuddering breath.

I think I'm starting to like this. I'm in charge, and he can't do a thing. I opened the clamp, closing it around his left nipple, twisting it as it bit down.

'Yes, Mistress. Thank you, Mistress.'

I pinched his right nipple the same way, then I stood there, inspecting his helpless, hard cock. Usually when I'm in the presence of an erect penis, there's a man there who wants to stick it in my body. He's the penetrator, and he's in control. Usually I like it that way. But not this time.

'You can't touch me, even if you want to.'

'No, Mistress.'

'Good. Too fucking bad.' And that time, I *did* say it out loud. *Who am I?*

'Guess we'd better truss up that cock, Henry. It's hanging out far too free.'

'Yes, Mistress.'

I picked up a long black bootlace with a loop secured in the middle of it. 'So, how do I do this, Henry? Show me.'

'Yes, Mistress. You place the loop at the center, just there under the balls. Then you wrap it forward. And back again. And up and over the shaft of the penis.'

It isn't fucking rocket science, I wanted to snap. *You're just wrapping your nuts in a shoe lace.* But I didn't say that, because I was still a little worried about hurting him. I'd thought balls were so fragile, so vulnerable to a swift kick or a knee. We're always taught to be gentle with them, and here I was, lashing his up nice and tight.

Then I remembered. 'Oh, weights! We haven't put any weights on you yet.'

'No, Mistress.'

I moved to the cart, which contained a collection of fishing weights, metal spheres weighing a pound or two each.

'We'll start with a smaller one.'

'Yes, Mistress.'

I knelt between his legs and clipped a weight to the loop beneath his ball sack. Henry groaned with pleasure, so I figured he must want some more. I clipped the other ones on, so he soon had what looked like a bunch of iron fruits suspended from his dick and balls. It must have been four or five pounds' worth.

'Do they just hang there like that?'

'Yes, Mistress. Or you can . . . swing them back and forth.'

'Oh! That sounds like fun.' I gave them a nudge a first, then I started knocking them into one another, like those steel toys people keep on their desks. 'You're my own little toy, aren't you, Henry?'

'Yes, Mistress. Thank you, Mistress.'

I wasn't afraid of this guy anymore. I literally had his balls in a sling.

'We'll be done soon, Henry, but first I have to smack your ass.'

'Yes, Mistress.'

'And I do like these paddles.' I took a large, flat wooden one from the wall, and smacked it against my left palm. *Shit, that smarts.* Henry was in for a treat.

I moved behind him, raised the paddle, and slapped his left cheek. He let out a grunt of pain. I slapped him a few more times, until his ass got nice and pink.

'I'm going to release you now, Henry,' I told him.

'Yes, Mistress.' I pulled off the weights and unbound his dick, feeling pride at each groan of pain.

Then I reached up and unbuckled the cuffs, touching his hands to make sure they were warm. His legs were still cuffed to the floor, but I paused.

'Pick up those pegs.' It felt absolutely wonderful not to say please.

'Yes, Mistress.'

He gathered the pegs up awkwardly, crouching to the floor with his ankles still restrained. When he straightened, he tried to hand them to me.

'Don't give me those. Put them on the table with the other tools you've soiled. We'll have to wash them now, Henry. They're filthy.'

'Yes, Mistress. May I get dressed now, Mistress?'

'Sure.' I unclipped him, and Henry tugged on his underwear, wincing when the elastic touched his backside. He finished getting dressed.

'You may go now, Henry.'

'Yes, Mistress. I'll be calling your name tonight, Mistress!'

'Really? Because I've already forgotten yours.' I turned, pretending to be bored.

But the truth is, I was exhilarated. That man did exactly what I told him. He loved every minute. And I've never felt so free in my life.

'You did well,' Phryne said, when I came out of the dungeon. She was standing at the far end of the room, in the dark. On the low metal table, in a pool of red light, sat a discarded white mask. She stepped toward me, into the light that spilled from the now-empty dungeon. She smiled in sympathy when she saw my face.

'It's tough for you,' she said, her voice deeper than before. The hollows in her cheeks matched her long, slender hands. Her Adam's apple bobbed at her throat. 'Because you're starting from scratch, and people don't know you.'

I tried to act casual. 'But sex always sells, right? I'm sure I'll figure it out.'

'Mmm.' She tilted her head. 'Don't think it's a license to print money, Antonia. It's hard work, especially now that it's decriminalized. The industry was *swimming* in cash when it was illegal, but not anymore. Plus, you're competing with Tinder now, and the sugar daddies, and . . . the "chicks with dicks", as we're known in the industry. Single most-downloaded porn, by the way.'

Phryne smiled. 'You can let yourself out. I'm sure I'll see you online.'

Chapter 4

The next two months were busy with Christmas, then New Year and the long summer holidays. Heirloom tomatoes and rock melons grew lush on their twisted vines; I brought home a pig we could raise for prosciutto. I found a length of black plastic to spread on the grassy slope by our orchard, then soaked it with water and dish soap so Miranda could slide. I spent the night with Patrice whenever Peter agreed, introducing fantasy, role-play, and games. Even apart, we found ways to touch. We wrote each other letters more swollen and erotic than anything I'd experienced in my adult life.

Then one day in February, my period was late. When the test came back positive, I checked with a calendar. Patrice was definitely the father.

But the three of us loved each other, right? Or we had. Maybe we could live in a throuple. Wasn't a throuple a thing now? We were open-minded people, not bound by the laws of monogamy. For Christ's sake, Patrice was *French*. If Selma didn't want to stay in our super-sized family, we could have a *menage à trois.*

As they say in New Zealand, *yeah nah.* When I told him the truth, Peter got in his truck, drove to Patrice's house, and punched him in the face. Then he moved out.

'*Tsk, tsk,*' people hissed. 'Of course he did.'

'She had an affair!' *We had an open marriage.*

'She fell in love with Patrice.' *I did not.*

'She's so selfish to get herself pregnant!' *I just wanted a healthy baby.*

'I don't love you,' Patrice said. 'I hardly know you. But sometimes in life, you hold hands and jump, and if you want to do this, I'm in.'

News traveled fast in our little community, and people stopped returning our calls. We thought we had friends, and if they were upset, I figured that they'd tell us why. But here was a side of Kiwi culture I'd never encountered: no one came round; no one yelled; no one said a damned word. They just cut us dead. I wrote an email to one friend to tell her what happened; I poured out my story and she never wrote back.

I know I should feel like a terrible person, for trying to get pregnant without my husband's consent. But I don't. At the most basic, biological level, it's the women who decide who we mate with. We choose our partners for all kinds of reasons: wealth, good looks, great sex. But underneath that is the animal drive to pick a partner with good DNA. And Patrice had three beautiful, healthy children.

There's an old story my family used to tell, from when I was five and my brother Brian was back home from college. We'd just had our lunch, and there was homemade chocolate cake for dessert. For some reason, he'd nearly finished his cake, but I'd only taken one bite.

'When I finish mine,' Brian growled in a monster voice, 'I'm going to start eating YOURS!'

'NOOOOO!' I hollered, grabbing my barely-touched slice, the whole thick wedge of it between my two pudgy palms, running into the bedroom next door, shoving it into my mouth, packing it in until I couldn't physically close my jaws and it ran down my chin in a sticky, brown stream.

'RAAAAAA!' Brian roared, bursting into the bedroom. I was laughing so hard I almost choked.

He lunged at me, my wild big beast of a brother. 'I'M GONNA TAKE YOUR CAKE!'

I wiggled away delightedly. On my hands and knees on the cold tile floor, between the bed and the wall, I managed to swallow. I choked down the wet, thick wads of chocolate. I won.

When we told the story later, it was always about how greedy I was, even at the young age of five. That I would rather humiliate myself, run away, practically choke, instead of sharing my cake.

But here's the thing. It was my cake. It was always my cake. I just wanted to keep what was mine.

In April 2016, Patrice managed to pack up and leave his old life, and he moved into my house with my kids. His children came to live with us week-on and week-off, so every other week, our lives were a whirlwind of laundry and Lego.

'You know I'm going ahead with the agency, right?' I told him before he moved in. 'I've been learning a lot online, in the forums. It's a risk, but I think I can do it.'

'The *maison close,*' Patrice clarified, his blue eyes twinkling. 'It's an excellent idea; I think it will work.'

'Why?' I pulled back. 'You just think it's sexy, right? You think it's hot.'

'No.' Patrice looked surprised. 'Because it's good business! It's like a restaurant, right? People need food, and people need sex. You'll always have clients. And what should I call you? You're no longer with Peter, but you're not *mademoiselle.*'

'No, you're right,' I told him. 'I'm still *Madame.*'

'Madame *Antonia.*' He kissed me. '*Ça, c'est chaud,*' he whispered in my ear. '*That's* hot.'

It had been three months since Peter punched Patrice, and it was clear that our marriage was finished – but he still called me now and then, trying to see what he could pick from the wreckage.

'I thought what we had was sacred,' he told me one day. 'Not the sex, but the having children part. Our family.'

Sacred, I thought, *huh. Like that baby you asked me to flush down a toilet, because you wanted to go for a sail?*

And since I'm a history major, I thought about how that word has been used through the centuries. Women who were too sacred to get an education, because it was our God-given duty to raise kids. We were too sacred and pure for the workforce, because our God-given place was in the home.

Too sacred to go to war.

To hold office.

To vote.

To wear *pants,* for Christ's sweet sake.

Too sacred to fuck who we want. And *definitely* too sacred to charge for it.

Why do men always tell you you're sacred when they're trying to keep you in line?

Chapter 5

After Peter punched out Patrice, I put the throuple idea on ice. Then I made an appointment to see a divorce lawyer.

'So why are you here?' the lawyer wanted to know. 'Are you worried your husband's going to run off with countless millions?'

'No,' I told him truthfully. 'There's no millions. But there's a house, and fifty thousand dollars I inherited from my mother. I'm afraid he's going to clean out the money and sail away.'

'Mmm,' the lawyer acknowledged. 'Sail away . . . that's what I'd like to do. Usually on a Thursday.' He cleared his throat and leaned back in his chair. 'But if the money's in a joint account, it's half his. What do you want the money for, anyway? Maybe you should just let him sail off and good riddance. Fifty grand would be getting off cheap, I should say.'

'I want to start a business.'

'And what are you now?' He glanced down at his notes. 'A *writer?*' He arched one eyebrow. 'What sort of a business do you want to start?'

'An ethical . . . escort agency.' I felt nervous saying the words, like I was doing something dirty.

But the lawyer let out a bark of a laugh. 'Oh, thank *Christ!* I was afraid you were going to tell me you wanted go into *publishing* or something. An *escort agency.* At least you'll make some money at that!'

I hope so, I thought. *I need it.* But now the real fighting began. Peter had moved into an apartment in town, and he was pressuring me to buy him out of the house. This involved a toxic series of texts:

You disgust me.

You have to buy me out.

I can't even look at you.

You owe me money.

You have benefitted financially from being with me.

But then I remembered Phryne's words. *Sex,* she'd said, *is a power negotiation.* I went back to the lawyer, to talk about how I could protect the money I'd put aside for my business. 'He said I have to pay him,' I told the lawyer. 'A lot more than what he's put into the house, I mean. Because I've benefitted financially from being with him.'

'Hmm,' the lawyer mused, jotting something down on his notepad. 'So, what were you doing *before* you married him?'

'I was . . . running a children's theatre.'

The lawyer bit the tip of his pen, and I had the uncomfortable feeling he was trying hard not to laugh. 'So, you weren't making much money then. And you didn't work while you were married, except the one book. So actually, he's right. You *didn't* contribute financially.'

Really? I thought about the two children I had birthed. The years of interventions and therapies for Silas. The constant care for both babies, Silas with his disabilities and healthy, vigorous Miranda. The elaborate gourmet dinners I cooked. The bills I took care of. The sewing of curtains and upholstery. All the sex we'd had, over more than a decade: in the mouth, in the vagina, in the ass. The homes I made. The farms I ran. The friends I made. The parties I threw. The life I made for the four of us.

'No,' I agreed. 'You're right. I wasn't contributing much at all.'

Help me to understand, was what I wanted to say. *If a man supports a woman while she's having sex with him, then he decides he doesn't want her anymore and asks for a refund, is that marriage? Is that sex work?*

What's the difference?

In a week, the lawyer found a precedent that meant the money I'd intended for the business was mine. 'If you've parked it in a separate account,' he explained, 'and you both understood it was intended for a specific expense, like starting a business, then you can keep it in the divorce. It's yours.' So I mortgaged the house to pay Peter, and he stopped sending threatening texts.

One day, I discovered a sex shop in town, where I met an intriguing new friend. Tall and strawberry blonde, Karli was bubbly and warm, always excited about the next shiny new thing. She was unpacking a box full of dildos and vibrators, and when I told her I wanted to open an escort agency, she practically squealed in delight. 'Are you *kidding me?*' she asked. 'There's *nothing like that* in town. You'll make *stacks* of cash! Well,' she corrected, wrinkling her nose, 'there *is* the Velvet Lounge. But *yuck,* no one goes there but crackheads and losers.' She flicked on a large purple vibrator, buzzing it back across her shoulders. 'Aw, these things are the *best,*' she sighed in delight. 'And the extra-long ones get the tough spots!'

She switched off the vibrator and put it on a shelf, then looked at me curiously. 'What are you going to call this place? Pleasure Therapy? Pleasure Palace? Pleasure . . . Paradise?'

'I don't know,' I admitted. 'I have the idea, but I don't have a name.'

'It's got to be something fresh, up here in Northland.' She ran her tongue over her lips, considering. 'Something that makes people feel . . .'

'Like they're leaving their worries behind!' I finished. 'Like a beach house, where you'd go in the summer!'

'Well, that's it then.' She twirled both her hands. *Ta-da.* 'But if it's a beach house, you'll call it a *bach.*' She rhymed it with *catch.* 'That's what we call beach houses here.'

'Really?' I tried out the word in my mouth. 'A . . . *bach?*'

'No, silly.' She giggled. '*The* Bach. Believe me, you'll be the only one in town!'

Karli had even more tricks up her sleeve. Born and raised in Whangārei, that girl knew everyone. When I complained that I couldn't find a place for my business, she tapped her long coral nails on her glass display case. 'Hmm. Let me make a few calls.' The next day, she texted:

I know a guy. His name is Gavin.
He's not too friendly but he's the most successful
commercial real estate agent in town. Call him.

I breathed a sigh of relief. It felt good to have a woman on my side again. Since I'd shown myself to be an adulterous slut, no one in Purua still spoke to us. And now that I was opening the new brothel in town, I had a feeling I was going to need a friend.

—

Gavin swept into our meeting in a long black overcoat, his slight, pointed overbite giving him a rattish expression. Sitting down, he got straight to the point.

'I own a motel,' he explained, 'as an investment. But I don't want to run it. If you manage it for me, then you can do your brothel there or whatever. Karli told me your idea. I don't care what you do. Just manage the place and keep things on the up and up. I'm happy to look the other way.'

By this time, we were well into the month of September, and I was enormously pregnant. Gavin rolled back the passenger seat in his truck, and cleared away some bottles so I could climb in. Then he drove me to the Marina Court Motel to inspect it, and right away, I knew it could work. Perched on the banks of the Hatea River, the property had eight rooms, each with its own ensuite bathroom. Spread across two cinderblock buildings, the units were basic and worn, with dusty venetian blinds and carpet that had seen better days. There was a third building on the property as well, with the reception and laundry for the motel, Gavin's own private apartment, and a small one-bedroom unit intended for a hotel manager. Gavin pulled a crumpled profit and loss statement out of his pocket which said that the place broke even, and how hard could it be to run a hotel with only eight rooms?

So I signed a three-year business lease. With the rent and insurance, it was eight grand a month.

—

Matisse was born at home on a crisp October night, a three-quarters moon hanging bright in the sky. 'This baby will come *fast*,' my midwife had warned Patrice. 'You'd better be ready to catch it.'

When the contractions got sharp and more frequent, I lowered myself into the hot tub. 'And then you screamed like one of those heavy metal guys,' Patrice told me later. 'I didn't know a person could make such terrible sounds!' He'd tried to comfort me, stroking my naked, wet back.

'Touche pas à mon dos,' I snarled. *Do not touch my back.*

In just forty minutes, I felt myself open. The head came out, this child that was half-fish and half-human, that could stay underwater without breath. 'Keep the baby under until he's all the way out,' the midwife had said. 'If his face touches air, he'll start breathing.' Then I pushed one last time, with a scream that tore open the world.

I reached down and brought the baby up to my chest. Patrice leaned over to kiss me, holding us awkwardly in the water. Our son made little mewling sounds, like a new baby kitten. Patrice went to get a hat and a blanket.

I was there in the starlight, alone with my baby. The weight of him warm on my chest. There were three rolls of fat on his neck, a head of dark, wet hair, and the feel of him breathing. The feel of him healthy. The feel of him strong.

Did I reach out of my marriage and take this baby from a man who hadn't quite finished his?

Maybe.

Sometimes, when you feel ripped off by the universe, you take what you think you deserve.

Chapter 6

My business lease started at the end of November, just six weeks after Matisse was born. We'd agreed that Patrice would stay home at first, but while I was nursing, the baby was with me. Running a motel and founding an escort agency – all with five kids and a breast-feeding infant – felt like an impossible feat. I was a brave woman, but I wasn't insane. I knew that I needed help.

'Do you think you might like to work with me?' I asked Karli. 'As my co-madam? It seems like this business is all about connections, and from where I stand, you're the unofficial mayor of Whangārei.'

Karli was intrigued. 'Oooh! I *think* I could do it, at least a *few* days a week.' She shrugged. 'I'm not selling many vibrators in this uptight little town, so why not?'

My next move was to hire a full-time caretaker to manage and clean the hotel. Wiry and strong, her grey hair clipped short, Debra was an old-school Kiwi woman, who'd raised three kids plus her grandkids. When she found out the job came with a free place to live, she said she couldn't care less about our little escort agency. As far as she was concerned, it made for less work at the motel.

'Just *look* at what you've dug up!' Karli flipped through my notebook. 'All this research you've done! GFE, PSE, *tie and tease* . . . and what's this?' She pulled out a folded sheet of paper, a list of prices and services that I'd found online. *'Five hundred dollars an hour?!* Could we *really* get that much money?'

'In Auckland and Wellington, sure.' I reached out a foot and pushed Matisse in his rocker. He gurgled contentedly, his blue eyes fixed on my face. 'But people in big cities have the money. Plus there's international businessmen, celebrities coming through—'

'Well, we won't get those prices in Northland.' Karli took out a pencil. 'No one's got *that* kind of cash.' She jotted a few lines on a blank page in my notebook. 'How 'bout this?' She held up the page. 'Three hundred an hour, that's one-fifty to us, one-fifty to the girl. That's the one-hour price for a girlfriend experience. Less for massage, we'll make that two hundred. More for fetish, or if they want Greek—'

'So how much can we earn then?' I interrupted. 'With one room, at first?'

Karli tapped her pencil against her bottom teeth. 'Well, I reckon . . . If we run from ten until nine . . . that's eleven hours . . . minus one for turning over the room . . .' She looked up and grinned. 'Between two and three thousand a day!'

Matisse screeched from his rocker, and I felt like joining him. *Two or three thousand a day sounds just fine.*

Next, we shut down two of the motel's eight units. Room 1 was a three-room family suite: we'd use that for the agency's office, and a dressing room and hang-out space for the girls. 'They need to relax and hang out between bookings,' Karli reasoned. 'And they can share all the goss that way! This one likes to have his nipples pinched; that one likes a finger in his bum.' Plus, we had a whole other plan for the lounge room: we wanted to offer free childcare. Why not? We were both experienced mothers – why couldn't we look after some lady's kids while she made $150 an hour?

The second unit we cordoned off was the nicest one in the motel – Room 6, the only one Gavin had renovated. This one was two rooms, a lounge space and a bedroom. The carpet was new and unblemished, and it had a brand-new bathroom and shower. Room 6 would be our very first service room. I'd asked the ladies online for advice:

MadamAntonia

So what do you DO in a 60-minute booking? You're not having seggs the whole time, are you??

trixR4kids: I mean sometimes but it's RARE. Every now and then you get Jimmy Jackrabbit pounding away for the whole dam hour but those are THE WORST

prettybaaaby: Rule #1 is PROTECT YOUR VAGINA I should tat that on my titties lololol

trixR4kids: No more than 10 minutes is what you should go for. Break it down like this:

10-15 minutes, offer him a drink, have a little chit chat . . .

15-30 minutes, get him in the shower. He'll tell you he's clean. HE IS NOT CLEAN.

hair0nfyre: Plus if you hop in there with him you can get him worked up in the suds

trixR4kids: 30-45 minutes, you might actually have to shag him 😭

Then the last 15 minutes, one more shower, put your clothes on and BYYYYE

MadamAntonia: I offer him a drink? Like for free?

prettybaaaby: 🙈 you can charge but if it's GFE then it's all about the FANTASY. So throw Jimbo a beer or a soda or something and he'll think it's a date

trixR4kids: Plus it's safer. Have a drink, get to know each other. Like you're an *actual human*, not a hole he's paid money to fuck

We kept all that in mind when we set up Room 6, stocking the mini fridge with sodas and beers. We decorated the lounge room like a classic Kiwi bach, hanging paintings of Northland beaches, with Nikau palms and ferns. We picked out cute little cushions and throw pillows, in teal and bright lemon yellow. We put strings of twinkling lights in glass vases, and set up the bathroom with fresh orchids and mouthwash. Next to the bed, we set out pump bottles of lube, coconut oil in a bottle warmer, and a selection of four different condom sizes, the ones the NZPC had supplied. 'You can't have just one,' Diana had said. 'You'll need four kinds of condom, at least. Your basic Durex, that's the most popular. These Glide ones, those are the XL. You can stick your head up in those. Then you've got the 49 Degrees – the small ones. Flavored ones are for blowjobs, and make sure you choose the pink ones. That way, if she's starting her period, he won't notice a thing.'

'So do you just let the client pick one?' I'd asked, packing the boxes into the trunk of my car.

'*Definitely* not.' Looking around to make sure no one was near, Diana leaned in to explain. 'Anytime you leave it with the client to choose, he'll go extra-large – guaranteed. I don't care if it's like *this*,' she said, holding her fingers three centimeters apart, 'he thinks his winky's a masterpiece.' She lowered her voice, as though she were confiding a secret. 'You won't believe this, but some of them will poke a hole in it if you let them. They get off on it – I think it's to do with control. So no, don't *ever* let the client choose his own condom. Right from the start, the provider's in charge, even though she's making him *think* he's in charge. *That's* the art of it.'

Once Room 6 was set up, Karli and I checked the feed from Gavin's security cameras. They were placed to give the widest possible view of the property, so we could see cars pulling up and clients going to the room. 'But that's not enough.' Karli looked worried. 'How can we see the guys' faces when they get here?'

'Does it matter?' I shrugged. 'We'll talk to them when we make the booking. We'll tell them the rules, and we'll find out as much as we can. After that – it's not like we're running a dating service. What, is she gonna turn him down if he doesn't look cute enough?'

Karli rolled her eyes. 'This is a *small town,* though. What if she knows the guy? What if it's her dad's fishing buddy? Or even – fuck my life – what if it's her *dad?* We *have* to let them cancel a booking, if they don't feel like they can go through with it – even if they don't like the vibe.'

I hadn't thought of it that way, but of course she was right. *The women must consent at all times,* Phryne had said, *and they can withdraw their consent any time.* Plus, Diana had talked about the Prostitution Reform Act. It was right there, in the letter of the law.

'So, what if she *does* cancel? Do we pay her anyway?' Between the free drinks and the pay-outs, *ethical* was sounding *expensive.*

Karli shrugged. 'I think so. *Definitely,* if she's taken her clothes off or shagged him. We don't want her to feel like she has to keep going if she doesn't feel safe, right?'

Room 6 had a large, plate glass window by the door, and I hired a glass company to tint it so the client couldn't see in. That way, the lady could lock herself inside before the booking, and only open the door when she was ready. Then Karli found out the glass company also put in custom mirrors. 'A MIRROR,' she squealed, rubbing her hands in delight. 'A GIANT MIRROR! Floor to ceiling, right by the bed. Antonia, we *have* to!'

It was impossible to say no when Karli got so excited, and I had to admit, running her sex shop had given her some great instincts. By the time we finished, Room 6 had exactly the look we were going for: it was clean and comfortable, with a breezy, beachy feeling, a mini fridge stocked with cold drinks, an expansive bed with crisp white sheets, a selection of lubricants and oils, four different kinds of condoms, and a floor-to-ceiling mirror that could have come right out of Vegas.

We were ready to open The Bach.

Or . . . almost ready, since we hadn't yet found any women. Like so many things in this business, hiring sex workers wasn't straightforward. In New Zealand, most people look for jobs on a website called TradeMe, and that was the first place we tried to advertise:

The Bach is Hiring . . . Ready When You Are.

Opening in January 2017, The Bach is set to become Northland's premiere high-end escort agency. We are woman owned and operated, and we make it our mission to protect your health, safety and right to consent. Earn $150 per full-service session, while we take care of all your photos, pay for your advertising, and provide beautiful dresses and shoes in a fun, supportive atmosphere. Free childcare available. Send an email with a current, un-edited photo.

I thought it was pretty good copy, but our ad never made it online. We were instantly flagged for 'inappropriate content', and TradeMe refunded our fee. 'But it's legal!' I complained to the company. 'How can you censor us when we're not doing anything wrong?'

'TradeMe is a family-friendly website,' came the corporate, canned reply. 'We don't accept ads for sex work or any sexual content.'

'Mmmm.' Karli tapped her nails on the desk, thinking. 'What about WINZ?' She was talking about Work and Income New Zealand, the government welfare office. 'This town is full of young solo mums on a benefit, and our job pays ten times the minimum wage. Let's see if they'll take our listing.'

But when I sent out an inquiry, WINZ made it clear that our ad was a total non-starter. 'The government deems such work unsuitable,' they explained. 'Moreover, the high wages that are paid in the industry could cause some women to feel coerced into prostitution, so we do not accept job listings of an adult nature.'

'Bloody hell,' Karli swore, when I showed her the email. 'These ladies are *adults,* not helpless babies! If they want to fuck and make $150 an hour, that's their business!'

'I know,' I told her, scrolling through the job listings that *were* being offered through WINZ. 'And just look at what the government *does* deem to be "suitable". Cleaner . . . cleaner . . . *bathroom* cleaner . . . cook at a rest home . . . and, oh look, McDonalds. None of them paying more than minimum wage.'

Karli leaned back in her chair, swinging her blue suede stilettos on her desk. She shut her eyes and pinched the bridge of her nose. 'Well . . . leave it with me,' she finally said. 'I might know someone.'

'Really?' I practically jumped out of my chair. 'Why didn't you *say* something?'

'Because she's not ideal, to be honest. She's my friend's old flatmate. She used to be in the industry, then she buggered off to Australia. I'll need to check if she's back in town.'

Three days later, I was sitting outside my Room 1 office when a young woman drove in and approached me. She looked pleasant enough, but I was a madam now. I tried to appraise her with the eyes of a pimp.

She was medium height, with dark blonde hair and a reasonably pretty face. Her pink and blue tie-dye dress billowed around her figure, so I couldn't quite tell how slender she was, but she had big boobs, and when she got closer I made out her best feature: her startling ice-blue eyes.

'I'm Amber,' she said, her voice high and girlish. 'Not my real name. Obvi.'

I shook her hand and we sat down together, but she didn't make eye contact, looking instead at a spot just behind me. 'I used to do this work, couple of years ago,' she said, 'before I moved over to Oz. I started off selling my virginity online.'

'*Pfff.*' I snorted out loud. 'And that *worked?*'

'Yep,' she smiled shyly. 'All seven times! Then the guys started recognizing me, so I moved away. But I got my kids taken off me, back in Perth.'

Aha. 'Why?' I asked. 'What happened?'

'I'll be straight up with you. It was drugs.' She pulled a cigarette from her handbag, then lit it and took a long drag. 'But I'm getting my life sorted now. I want to save up, get a place, get my kids back.'

'What sort of drugs was it?' I asked.

'P,' she said, and when I looked confused, she clarified. 'That's what we call meth in New Zealand. But I haven't done it in ages, I swear!'

She sounded sincere. *And she's getting her life back together,* I thought. *We can help her.*

Then I thought: *I need you.*

Then I thought: *you'll do.*

It wasn't my first choice to hire an addict. But Karli and I were desperate, and we were running out of ideas. 'Sounds good to me,' I told Amber. 'When do you think you might want to start?'

Chapter 7

With just Amber on board, we were hardly an agency – it was more like we were pimping out some girl Karli knew. Meanwhile The Bach had an even more serious problem: nobody knew we were there.

Although sex work in this country is decriminalized, it's up to individual town councils to decide how to zone and regulate brothels. In Whangārei, that meant we couldn't put a sign on the street. The local tourism board gave out a map for visitors, many of them yachties and sailors spending the storm season at the local marina, but we could barely get them on the phone. 'We're a family-friendly publication,' they told me. 'The visitors who use our map want to know about *boat chandleries* and *ice cream shops*, *not* prostitution and brothels.'

'Riiiiight,' I responded, my head in my hands. ''Cause if there's one thing that sailors *don't* want, after spending three weeks at sea, it's sex.'

But I couldn't change anyone's mind. When it comes to sex work, everyone has a rock-hard opinion, and most of the time, it's not good. Especially if they don't know what they're talking about.

One company that *did* want our money was an online directory called New Zealand Girls. They dominated the market for sex work ads, despite a clunky website that looked like a relic from 1995. And they weren't cheap, either.

'A hundred dollars a week, that's per girl,' the bored sales rep informed us. 'Course, once your agency really gets going, we can do larger packages with a daily roster of ladies, but individual ads are best if you've only just got a few.'

'Those guys are *creepy*,' I told Karli when I hung up the phone. 'They say they want a "verification photo", which is a full-length picture of the girl *showing her face,* holding up a piece of paper with her working name and the day's date.'

'Like a mug shot?' Karli frowned.

'Yeah. They say it's to make sure she's a real person, and not using someone else's pictures. But that's not the worst part. When you sign up with them, you have to tick a box, that says not only do you agree not to advertise on any other website—'

'Okay, *that's* super illegal,' Karli cut in.

'I *know.* But also that NZ Girls owns all the rights to your pictures, forever.'

Karli bit at her thumbnail. 'So essentially, they could hold onto the photos and years later, they could use them for blackmail.'

'Basically.'

'Like if the woman wanted to go on to become prime minister or whatever, NZ Girls could just pop up like a bad rash and publish her verification shots.'

'Yup. Far as I can tell, they're the biggest pimps in New Zealand.'

But we couldn't avoid them. New Zealand Girls was the single biggest online sex work advertiser, and without them we'd never get business. So we placed an ad, and we opened The Bach. And I spent all day in a dusty motel room, too chicken to pick up the phone.

Hey babe can I get any fucks for 50?? I'm sexy btw

I can't believe what an idiot I am. Why did I think I could do this?

Now that men were calling and my phone was ringing, this business was starting to feel dangerous. Wasn't I doing what women are *never* supposed to do? What both of my parents had warned me about?

Don't wear such a short skirt. Do up your top button. Watch your drink when you go to a bar. Don't jiggle; don't move your hips like that. Don't smile if you're leading him on. Don't be a cocktease, my father had said.

Hey bb

u working?

u do sex in the annal

??

When I was a kid, my friend's little brother used to feed live goldfish to his pet garter snake. We'd watch, enthralled, as he pinched the fish's tail between his thumb and index finger, then lowered it, thrashing and jackknifing, into the tank. The snake's head would snap up at the motion, then it would slowly uncoil, slithering over to see what was for dinner. The boy would drop the goldfish in a small dish of water, where it would flail for a second or two until the snake struck, snapping up its meal in one swallow.

Sitting in that beige motel room, holding my phone in one sweaty hand, I was starting to feel like the fish. But wait . . . no, that wasn't right. *Amber* was the goldfish. And I was the one lowering her into the tank.

I'd been sitting there all day without making a booking – which wasn't surprising, since I hadn't once answered the phone. Dinner-time was approaching, and I figured I'd close early. *I'll be braver tomorrow. I just need to get used to these horrible texts.* I was heading out to my car, Matisse strapped to my chest, when the jaunty glockenspiel of my iPhone rang out.

Okay. I have to do this.

They can't all be awful.

If I want to run this place, I'm gonna have to pick up the phone.

I tapped at the screen. 'Hello, welcome to The Bach, how can I help?'

'Oh hello, good evening,' an older man's voice replied. 'Is this The Bach? The, ah, the escort agency?'

'Yes.'

He sounded almost as terrified as I was. 'I wondered . . . I wondered if I could ask you a bit of an odd question?' *He doesn't sound Kiwi, I don't think. English maybe? In his seventies or eighties?*

'Sure, how can I help?'

'I was wondering . . .' He trailed off as he gathered his courage. 'I was wondering if any of the ladies *don't* shave? You know, their private bits.'

'Uh, I don't know,' I told him. *Am I supposed to be keeping track of bikini lines?* 'I can *ask*.'

'Ah, yes, that would be so kind of you.' He cleared his throat. 'I'm a child of the seventies, you see. And I *do* like a nice bush.'

We chatted for a while longer and then I hung up, promising to ask the ladies about their intimate grooming habits. *There,* I told myself. *That wasn't so bad, was it? Just a friendly old man who likes a nice bush.*

Then my phone buzzed again.

I only want quick 20 mins massage hand job 70 bucks

I shifted Matisse on my chest and replied.

The lovely Amber is available for sensual massage.
30 minutes is $140.
When would you like to see her?

There was a pause, and three little dots:

Thats to much baby
any cheap girl available today

That cheeky fucker! I thought to myself.

Hold your power, Phryne had said. *The clients will push, but you don't give an inch.*

Right, I thought. *Here we go.*

We don't have cheap girls at The Bach, just cheap customers. Amber gives excellent service. Would you like to make a booking with her for $140?

Another pause. Then he texted:

yes please. sorry to offend.

any chance I could see her at 7pm?

Good boy, I thought, and once I checked in with Amber, I sent him the confirmation text we'd prepared.

30 minute sensual massage at 7pm with Amber, confirmed. $140. Come to the Marina Court Motel, 56 Riverside Drive, at the correct time for your booking. Do not come early and do not come late. Park in space number 6. Go upstairs to Room 6 and knock. She will open the door when she is ready.

Holy shit, I thought. *I just did it*. Then I texted Amber, and she was annoyed that he didn't want sex. 'Just sensual *massage?*' she asked on the phone. 'What a cheapo. Ah well, I'll see if I can get some extras out of him.'

One hour later, at 6.45, she was up in Room 6 for her date. Her client, who would come to be known as Bobby BJ, showed up on time and parked where I told him. The door opened, he went in, and it closed. I set my timer for thirty minutes.

'Sold him a gobby,' Amber announced, when she came back to the office. 'Plus kissing, so that's a hundred in extras.'

'How was he?' I asked. 'Was he nice?'

'Supa nice. He came in about thirty seconds. Said it had been years and years. You know what? I just think he was lonely.'

And really, that's all there was to it.

—

'There's another one, too,' Karli mentioned the next week. 'I wasn't sure if she'd do it at first, 'cause she's got a nice little business on her own. But then I told her about The Bach, and how cute the room is, and she reckoned it might be nice to not have punters showing up at her house.'

'And she does *sex work?*' I asked, practically drooling. Matisse was nursing on my lap, and he snuffled and fussed. I turned him and gave him my other breast. 'Like, full service and everything?'

'Mmmm . . . no,' Karli winced. 'That's the other thing. Haley only does sensual massage. But she's really bloody good at it, and she doesn't do drugs, so . . . yay!'

I'll take it. Karli gave me her number, and I called up Haley.

That evening when she came by the office, she flashed me a bright white smile. Haley was petite, perky, and trim, and her handshake was brisk and professional. 'Pleasure to meet you,' she said. 'Karli's told me all about you. I think what you're doing is *amazing,* by the way. This town needs a safe place to work.'

'So . . . how long have you been in the industry?' I asked, showing her inside.

'A few years now.' She put her bag down and took a seat on the couch. 'I used to be a cam girl, if you can believe it.' She snorted. 'I used to think I was balling, making money just by sitting at my computer, showing my little titties all day. But guys would ask for weirder and weirder stuff. One guy asked me to open a can of baked beans and pour it on my head. I think I made thirty dollars that day, and I was sitting there all sticky, tits out, with baked beans all down my front and in my hair. And I just thought: *pfff.* It's not worth it, ay?'

'I guess not,' I agreed, hoping it wasn't obvious how much I was checking out her figure. *You're gorgeous,* my pimp voice wanted to say. *You're intelligent, well-spoken and charming. Why oh why don't you offer full service?*

'Plus, it's lonely. You spend the whole day by yourself, in front of the computer, dealing with these men. And some of them can be *quite* gross.'

'Well, yeah,' I conceded. 'I've been getting a taste of that already.'

Haley nodded, and for a moment her smile flickered out. 'You'll probably hate men by the end of this.'

'I will? Why?'

'Just trust me.' She shrugged. 'You'll see.'

'The great thing about making the boys book ahead,' Karli enthused the next day, 'is that it adds that element of fantasy. They can ring up and book on a Monday, then spend the whole week looking forward to their date. It's so much *sexier* than just rocking up to a brothel, and having a quick shag with the first girl they see.'

But that was before we knew about the Dick Emergency. One of the first things we learned on the job is that while *some* men plan ahead and enjoy it, they are not the majority. They were not even half of our male clientele. The plan-aheads were a tiny percentage, while most men were more like the customer we nicknamed Fuckwit Wants It Right Now.

Fuckwit, as we called him for short, made contact shortly after Haley joined us, when we had only two girls on our website.

where is the bach

Welcome to The Bach. I see you haven't yet made a booking. Have you had a look at Amber and Haley online? Do you know who you'd like to visit?

you give me address
i come now

No you do not come now. We are by appointment only. Who would you like to see, at what time?

no
you tell me address
now
now right now

Which is how we came up with our first 'client code' at The Bach, a way to organize hundreds, and eventually thousands, of men. Fuckwit was clearly a 'Now Right Now' client, which we coded as NRN. Most men, we learned, thought about hiring a sex worker only when they were already horny – or, as Karli put it, 'when he's got his dick in one hand and his phone in the other' – which is why they were in such a hot rush. At first we were baffled by this, then exasperated. But eventually we flipped it around. Whenever a lady needed to earn as much cash as she could, we suggested she come in and hang out – so she could pick up the NRN bookings.

Is it $140 for a 30min massage? No chance of any discount?

No, our prices are fixed and we're worth every penny 💋

Hey can I get a blow job for 100 pls

No. You know this. We keep telling you this.

hi all ur ladies are drop dead gorgus

Thank you so much! That's so sweet 💋

do i get a discount then?

No.

Three weeks in, I noticed a trend in our messages. 'I have to admit, it's impressive,' I said to Karli as I scanned through the phone. 'How they just assume we give discounts!'

'I *know!*' she burst out. 'I got one just yesterday, who wanted to pay us in crayfish!'

'Like *lobster?* He wanted to pay us for sex with some *seafood?*'

'Yes. *And* he wanted the lady to squirt! I put him in the contacts as "Solo Dad Obsessed with Squirting Wants To Trade Seafood for Sex". In case you want to have a chat to him, you can find him again.'

'It's incredible,' I said, 'the entitlement. Listen to this one:

I can get 200 GFE for an hour with an extra
thrown in.
Can you match or beat that?'

'What did you tell him?'

'I said he could get a one hour GFE with his right hand, for free! Tell you what, that shut him right up.'

Karli scoffed. 'You wouldn't ask for discounts with your *therapist.* You don't go to Pak'nSave and buy your groceries on tick. But they think because we're women, we're timid and weak.'

'And sex workers,' I added. 'Don't forget. We're a bunch of dumb sluts who don't know how to add.'

With Amber and Haley as a part of our team, we started to take on a few clients. When I look at my logs from the very beginning, we did three or four bookings a week. But that wasn't anywhere near what we'd hoped to bring in. I was beginning to see that 'three thousand a day' wasn't just looking on the bright side of things. Karli and I were probably deluded.

Now it was February. We'd been open a month, and I was rapidly burning through my cash. Two hundred a week went to New Zealand Girls, and a thousand a week to pay Karli. We'd put a couple of thousand into decorating Room 6, including that fabulous mirror – and now at the end of the month, I owed Gavin another eight grand.

'So here's what we do,' Karli proposed. 'We say yes to *everything*, try *anything*.' We threw ourselves into recruiting more girls, using

Facebook ads to reach local women between eighteen and forty-five, but we kept getting thrown off the site. Surprisingly, the problem wasn't that our job was in prostitution – but that the hourly rate we were promising flagged us as an online scam.

Then I got an email from a woman named 'Ruby'. A qualified radiologist in her late twenties, Ruby had a few too many drinks one night and got hit with a DUI – so the government yanked her medical license, and she'd been working a terrible job at a call center. *I'm a European BBW,* she said in her email, *and very sexually confident. If you'd take a chance with a larger woman, I know I'd be a fantastic fit.*

'What's a BBW?' I asked Karli, because she knew all the internet slang.

'Big Beautiful Woman,' Karli replied. 'Check out her photos. She's got them there in the attachment.'

I clicked on the first one. Ruby was *definitely* plus size. But she was pretty, with a mane of corkscrew curls that she'd dyed a bright, cherry red and a fun, flirty look on her face. 'I don't know,' I hedged. 'Online, they say high-end escorts are skinny. Like, sixes and eights. No higher. And Amber's already a sixteen . . .'

'I know, but what kind of body fascism is that?' Karli scoffed. 'Aren't we past all that nonsense by now? Here's a big, beautiful woman – and don't you think some men have fantasies about that? Besides,' she lowered her voice, 'it's not like the world's beating a path to our door. Say *yes,* Antonia. To everything. Or we won't be around much longer.'

I couldn't argue with that. I was down to my last twenty grand. So I shot off an email to Ruby and asked her when she could come in.

In the next few weeks, Karli and I said yes to everything, sometimes stretching the limits of 'ethical'. We set up sock puppet accounts on Tinder, pretending to be straight men looking for women. If a lady swiped right, we told her what was really going on, telling her we were all about consent, and hoping she'd hear us out before she blocked us. We scraped the internet looking for men for our profiles, and it was working – until one of Karli's high school friends sent her an angry text.

'You know that picture of "Mike" we flicked up on Tinder, the one of him holding a fish?'

'Yeah,' I said. 'It's a good one. Had a couple of swipes already.'

Karli looked pained. 'We have to take it down. I guess, ah . . . it's my friend's ex-boyfriend? And actually he's married? So . . .'

'Oh, *shit.*' I grabbed at my phone, before I blew up the poor guy's life.

Amber, Haley, now Ruby. We were headed in the right direction, but I knew it was far too slow. The first week in February we had just one booking: Amber did a thirty-minute GFE that brought in all of $100. With this burn rate, I'd soon be unemployed and bankrupt – and still on the hook for a quarter-of-a-million-dollar business lease. *I could lose my house,* I thought with a chill. Gavin didn't seem like the cruisy kind of guy who would just let me out of the lease.

Ruby got a couple of bookings, but I noticed her clients kept pushing her limits. I got the feeling that because she was fat, they thought they could get away with it. As though an overweight woman was lower value, or too desperate to turn down their cash.

One day a client put through a shot of his abs, and I had to admit, he looked good. *Probably in his twenties, and he does lots of sit ups. Good for you, buddy.* I replied right away:

Welcome to The Bach!

Don't you look sexy . . . I'm sure our ladies would just love to meet you! 💋

But Six Pack Abs wasn't mucking around:

How much for a quick blowey?

Which girl gives the best head?

Isn't that charming, I thought to myself. *At least he gets straight to the point.* But I was getting used to that kind of talk. I sent through a photo of Ruby.

Ruby is our gorgeous European BBW . . .

How about a 30 minute GFE for $200?

I'm told she gives the best head in town! 💋

Three little dots, then he started his sales pitch.

Sounds good. My name's Rick.

I'm 28 years old, with an 8' cock and I last for hours.

You should probably be paying ME haha 😉

Haha, I answered, not laughing.

So how bout a discount?

My eyes rolled so hard, I think I tickled my brain. Hadn't I heard about this guy online? *Didn't they say it was a major red flag?*

But then, I wasn't swimming in clients. I tried to be tactful.

We don't bargain, but our ladies are the best! Would you like to book with Ruby for $200?

He agreed, and then made a booking for the next afternoon. And sure enough, in spite of his gym bod, Ruby was less than impressed. 'That guy wants a Porn Star Experience, *not* a GFE!' she said with a grimace. 'Dirty talk, come on my tits, nine hundred different positions . . . plus he was *so rough.*'

I didn't like the sound of that. 'Did you charge him extra? For PSE and COT?' It was easy to get lost in the alphabet soup, but 'Porn Star Experience' and 'Come on Tits' were some of our more common requests.

'Yeah, I did, but probably not enough, if I'm honest.' Ruby smoothed out her rumpled skirt, then fiddled with her bra strap. 'I'm really *sore* after that, actually. He definitely needs to start paying more.'

I pulled up Rick's contact, which I'd saved as Rick Six Pack, and this time I gave him a new name: Ricky Come on Titty. *Huge ego,* I wrote in his client notes. *Good looking, but he thinks he's God's gift. Too rough with Ruby in a PSE – warn him to behave.*

The next time he booked, Rick had more questions.

If I see Ruby at 3, will I be her first?

I think so! But why do you ask?

Because I want her clean. Not some cumster whos seen 8 dudes already.

Nice! Ricky's keeping it classy. I tapped out the lie.

Of course you'll be her first booking!

Confirmed, 60-minute PSE at 3pm. $400.

Pay an extra TWO hundred and she'll grow back her hymen, I thought to myself. *Shit, it worked great for Amber.*

At 2.47, I spotted Rick in the parking lot, a tall, lanky white guy in jeans. I texted him that he was early – but he ignored me. So I went out there and got in his way.

'You're ten minutes early,' I told him, in a friendly-don't-fuck-with-me tone. 'You'll need to walk around the block so Ruby can get up to the room.'

He had very blue eyes, with thick, dark lashes. He turned down his lips in a pout. 'How 'bout I wait?' he asked me flirtatiously. To my surprise, he sounded American. 'I'll just hang out here. It's fine.'

I had a feeling this guy was used to getting his way, especially when he turned on the charm. 'How 'bout *not*?' I told him. 'She doesn't want to parade past you.' I pointed at the sidewalk. 'Go take a walk. I'll text you when she's ready.'

Don't give an inch, Phryne had warned me. *It always starts small . . . the next thing you know, they'll take off the condom. Or try to hurt her, or hold her down during sex.* And sure enough, Rick didn't stop there. 'I asked him to back off when he was behind me,' Ruby said. ''Cause he *is* pretty big, and it was starting to hurt. So then he tried to take back his money! Cheeky! Can you believe it?' She opened her bag, taking out the cash from the booking.

'Luckily I was on to him, and I'd hidden the money whilst he was in the shower. So then he *accuses* me of stealing his mobile. Are you *kidding me?* Like I want his rubbish Nokia when my mum got me an iPhone last year. *Pfff,'* she scoffed. 'To be honest, I was about to call you to come kick him out, but then he went to put his pants on and *ta da!* His mobile fell out of his pocket. Awful booking, though.' I counted the cash and gave half to her, and she took it and initialed her pay stub. 'Won't see him again, I'll tell you that.'

My cell phone buzzed with a message from Rick.

That slut gives terrible service. Plus she's too fat.

Sorry to hear that, Rick. Maybe you'd like to book with another lady next time?

Nope, I've got someone else in mind.
No uppity bitch that thinks her pussy's made of gold either. Have a good day and please don't solicit my number anymore.

'You know what?' I told Ruby. 'Rick won't be seeing *anyone* again. 'Cause he just got himself banned from The Bach.'

I made a quick note on my phone. And I thought that would be the last we'd see of him.

—

By Valentine's Day I was starting to panic, not sure how we'd ever connect with our clients. 'How are you supposed to *promote a business*,' I asked Karli, 'when you can't even *talk* about it in polite conversation? It's not like I can give out free samples in the street!'

Karli was lying on her side in Room 1, wearing just a G-string and bra. She was taking sexy selfies for her husband while we worked, and Matisse was doing tummy time nearby. 'I know,' she agreed. 'It's awful. Same problem I had with my sex shop, in the end. Men lie to their wives to go there, people are ashamed, feel like they have to sneak around. Not a good way to make money.' Karli had shuttered her shop two weeks earlier, since she hadn't been turning a profit. Now she needed The Bach just like I did.

'D'you know anyone in media?' she asked, rolling toward me. 'Like, someone who can help get the word out?'

'Hang on,' I said, thinking. '*Yes.* I think I do.'

Rachel had been a Kiwi exchange student at my high school, and now she was running a production company in Auckland. She'd even messaged me on Facebook when I'd opened The Bach, asking if she could make a TV show about my pivot from farm life to sex work. 'It's not farm-to-table,' she'd laughed on the phone. 'Not you! It's . . . what? Farm to full service? Bullocks to blowjobs? Oh God, it's *such* a New Zealand story!'

'Yeah, well this story's about to fade out,' I told her, 'if I don't get some media exposure for the business. Nobody even knows who we are out there! And it's *impossible* to advertise. No one will even touch our money.'

'Ah.' Rachel stopped joking around. *'You,* my friend, need the kind of publicity you don't have to pay for. Let's get the *Herald* to run a story on you.'

'The *New Zealand Herald?'* I was skeptical. 'That's the biggest newspaper in the country. Why would they do a piece about me?'

'Because, darling,' Rachel reminded me, 'sex *sells*. Let me make some calls, and I'll see how I go.'

Which is how, two weeks later, I found myself sitting in Room 6 with a journalist and film crew from the *Herald*. 'There's no reason why sex work shouldn't be ethical,' I spoke into the camera. 'This is a job where a young woman can set her own hours and be entirely flexible, earn a hundred and fifty dollars an hour plus tips, *and* have free childcare on site. And that's the kind of working environment that I think it takes *women* to provide for women.'

'The Ethical Brothel: Bringing Sex Work Out of the Shadows' was published in print and online with a video, and the comments section quickly blew up.

'What are they saying?' Karli asked, covering her face with her hands. 'I can't look; I'm too nervous!'

'It's not the prostitution that's pissing them off,' I reported, scrolling down the screen. 'It's the *free childcare,* if you can believe it.'

'Why's *that?'* Karli peeked out from between her hands. 'What's wrong with giving the kids tea while their mum has a shag?'

'I *think,'* I said, reading more, 'that they think we're going to *involve the children* somehow.'

Karli leapt up, reading the comments over my shoulder. 'Those *sick muppets.* What kind of *monsters* do they think we are?'

'Here,' I said, pointing at the screen. 'Look at that.'

That's DISGUSTING! someone had written. *Any mum who would have her kids cared for in such a place should be investigated by the police!*

Revolting! screeched another.

She should take her disgusting ideas and go back to America!

'Hey, but what about this?' Karli brushed her finger over my touchpad. *Oh get over yourself,* someone had said. *It's a legal business in New Zealand.*

'And this—' *Would you be so upset about it if the women were making less money? Maybe you're jealous?*

And right beneath that was the one that really hit home, the comment I wouldn't forget:

I wish there were more jobs that paid $150 an hour with free childcare.

Chapter 8

Patrice heaved a copper pot from the oven, two roast chickens sizzling and spitting in their fat. He spiked them onto a carving board and began slicing them up with expert efficiency.

'I'LL NEVER LET YOU HAVE HIM!' my six-year-old daughter Miranda shrieked, barreling into the living room with her beloved stuffed turtle held high over her head. She scrambled to the kitchen and grabbed a steak knife from the cutlery drawer, then brandished it over the turtle's fur belly. Patrice's son Titou, who was only a few weeks older, dashed down the stairs and froze when he took in the hostage crisis.

'I'LL KILL HIM,' Miranda threatened. 'I'LL CUT OUT HIS GUTS BEFORE YOU CAN HAVE HIM. I'LL NEVER LET HIM GO.'

'NOOOOO!' Titou wailed in horror. 'DON'T DO IT!'

'Miranda!' I jumped to my feet. 'Put that knife down *right away*.'

Realizing she'd gone too far, Miranda reluctantly put down the knife. Which is when Titou, seizing his chance, pounced and yanked the turtle out of her hands, then made a dash at the open sliding door and exploded into the garden at top speed. Miranda shrieked and tore out after him.

'Close the bloody door, *bordel!*' Patrice shouted, tipping a tray of hot roasted potatoes out into a serving bowl. After sixteen years in New Zealand, Patrice spoke fluent English, but he still swore in his native French.

Silas had his portable blue music player to his ear, exuding delight as he bounced to the Broadway soundtrack for *Avenue Q*. Happy Muppets were belting out tunes about racism, and he didn't get the irony, but he thrilled to the music.

'HONEY!' Silas suddenly yelled. 'HONEY! PEEEES!'

'Okay,' I told him soothingly, placing a gentle hand on his knee. 'Dinner's almost ready.' Patrice slid a Pyrex cup onto the counter, then spooned in a few pieces of chicken and potato, along with a hefty slug of warm cream. I plugged in the immersion blender and turned it on, pulverizing Silas's food so he'd eat it.

A chicken wandered in through the open glass door. '*Casse-toi, la poule!*' Patrice growled, snapping at the bird with his dishcloth. 'They don't see the doors in this house? Do they have shit in their eyes? They can't close the door?!' The chicken fluttered past and took shelter under the dining table, where it promptly pooped on the floor. 'KIDS! *A table!!*' Patrice called into the garden. 'AND PUT THIS THING BACK IN ITS COOP CHICKEN!'

'Chicken coop,' I corrected automatically, helping Silas to sit at the table. 'And we don't really say kids have shit in their eyes. It hits a little harder in English.'

'Do they have shit in their ears, too? I just called them to eat. *A table!*' he shouted again, deglazing the copper pot with wine and whisking in a big hunk of butter. Tossing the dishcloth over his shoulder, he brought steaming platters of food to the table, the smells of rosemary and roast chicken permeating the room. 'HONEY!!!' Silas roared, when my spoonful of food wasn't fast enough. 'WHORES!!!'

Miranda and Titou charged back through the sliding door, Miranda now clutching her stuffed turtle like a child she'd just saved from a kidnapping. 'I'll get the chicken, Papa!' Titou sang cheerfully, crawling under the table to nab it.

'Miranda?' I pointed at the green and white puddle on the floor. 'Would you wipe that up, please?'

My daughter was incensed. 'Why do *I* have to clean up the chicken poop? Titou *started it* when he took my turtle, and anyway *last night—*'

'Miranda.' I shot her a look. 'Do as you're told, please.'

Silas finished his purée and howled. 'WHORES! WHORES! WHORES!'

'I only have three,' I told him, catching Patrice's eye with a grin. 'And they're not working right now. You want something else?'

'MIH,' he announced, bouncing up and down. 'PEEES.'

'Sure, I'll get you some milk.'

'Nova! Maris!' Patrice called over his shoulder, pouring himself a beer and placing a glass of red wine by my plate. *'A table!'*

Titou came back from the chicken coop and launched himself at his chair, grabbing at a drumstick with one grubby hand. *'Titouan,'* his father glared at him. 'Wash your hands for dinner, please.'

'But I'm *not dirty*,' Titou whined, reluctantly dropping the bone.

'Si tu n'aimes pas les règles, tu peux changer de crémerie,' Patrice told him, which means 'If you don't like the rules, you can just go

to a different cheese shop', and it probably makes sense in French. Titou got the message and got up to go wash his hands.

'This family is SO LOUD,' Maris announced, breezing into the dining room. 'How can five people make so much noise? I can hear you all the way at the other side of the house!' A bright and bold fourteen-year-old, Maris mostly spent her time drawing, listening to Imagine Dragons on repeat, and testing the limits of her father's patience.

'HIIIIII!' Silas yelled when he saw her. He liked to draw out the word in an exaggerated sing-song, the way his teachers did at his special needs school. They'd recently taught him that this was a better way to greet people than pinching them, and now he tried to use his new word all the time.

'Hi, Silas,' Maris said, taking her seat at the table.

'It's *dinner?'* Nova floated down the steps, pulling her headphones off her long, golden curls. 'Why didn't anyone *tell* me?'

'HIIIIIII!' Silas yelled, and she waved at him.

'Do you want a white or a thigh?' Patrice asked, serving his oldest daughter the chicken. A talented artist who could spend hours grazing fruits and vegetables from the garden, Nova could seem part-pixie, not entirely concerned with the world.

'Hey, Papa,' Maris gave her father a wicked grin. 'How do you say the worm goes toward the green glass, in French?'

'That's stupid,' Patrice said. 'Why don't you say it?'

'Because I don't speak French, silly! *Baguette, baguette!* Honh honh honh!' The last sounds she made with an exaggerated French accent, which she knew would piss off her father.

'That's racist,' Patrice told her.

'It's not racist if you're both white,' Nova corrected.

'Just *say* it!' Maris insisted, spearing a roasted potato with her fork. 'The worm goes toward the green glass!'

'Le ver va vers le verre vert.' Patrice sighed, and Maris burst into helpless laughter then choked, coughing bits of potato into her napkin.

'TITOU! You're hogging ALL the roasties!' Miranda yelled, gazing in anguish at Titou's plate, where a towering pile of potatoes threatened to spill out onto the table.

'Don't be a *piglet,* Titou,' Nova scolded her brother. 'There's other people here, you know.'

'WHORES!!!' Silas shouted, since no one was saying hi to him. 'WHORES!!!'

From down in the nursery, Matisse started fussing. I went down the stairs and lifted him from his cot, nestling him on my lap for a feed. He pushed hungrily at my breast and latched easily to the nipple, gulping milk so fast it trickled out the side of his mouth. *'Shhh, shhh,'* I hushed. 'It's okay, there's no rush. You've got all the time in the world.' He kept nursing frantically, grinding his head when the milk wasn't fast enough. *'One two, buckle my shoe,'* I sang softly, hoping to lull him to sleep. *'Three four, shut the door . . . Five, six . . .'*

He seemed to calm, slowing down until his eyelids began to droop. Soon, his pink lips parted in sleep, releasing my nipple as his mouth went slack. I settled back in the armchair, holding him close.

Only now, I was thinking about numbers. *ONE escort agency, with TWO or THREE ladies working, earning less than FIVE hundred dollars a week, makes . . . not nearly enough money to take care of SIX kids.* I wasn't being negative; that was just math. I had to come up with a better idea. And unlike Matisse, I didn't have much time.

Chapter 9

No thanks don't want to work with yous. Heard about yr brothel down there and not interested.

'*Christ,* I can't even get an *electrician* down here to fix the wiring!' I grumbled, jabbing out a reply on my phone.

Sorry to hear paying women $150 an hour offends you. Maybe we should all shut our mouths, keep our legs crossed, and stay on the benefit!

I showed Karli the screen. 'Oooh, good one,' she cooed. 'Well he can get stuffed if he won't take our money. There's other sparkies in town.'

Yeah, but can I pay them? I'd called the first guy because he was cheap. My own checking account was down to two digits, and I'd taken cash from The Bach so Patrice could buy groceries. But no matter how thin I spread out the money, I knew there just wasn't enough.

It had been two days since the *Herald* article, but the publicity wasn't turning things around. Gavin's girlfriend had called me in a rage over the weekend because he'd neglected to tell her about our real business. 'I just don't know if I can *live* in a *brothel,'* she'd spat, as if the word was a turd in her mouth. I couldn't blame her for being angry at Gavin, but their private lives weren't my problem. *My* problem was finding new girls to hire, before I went totally broke.

I pulled up Tinder and started flicking on prospects. The drone of a bulldozer came from next door, then somebody started a jackhammer.

'What are they building over there, anyway?' I asked. 'Have you had your ear to the ground?'

Karli, who was organizing lingerie, piped up with a cheerful smile. 'Yeah, I think it's a Māori kindy – you know, like an early childhood center? My aunt knows someone on the board.'

Oh God. Brothel next door to a day care. 'Wait till the press gets a hold of that one. It sounds like a reality TV show.'

'No such thing as bad publicity!' Karli knelt to start sorting the shoes. She'd recently scoured the thrift shops in town, and we had a rainbow collection of heels, in sizes from seven to ten. Now we just needed some feet for them.

I turned back to Tinder and saw a woman had matched with me. *Blonde, curvy, nice Roman nose. Full lips.* She'd blurred out the lower half of her face, but it *looked* like she might be Italian.

'What about this one?' I handed Karli my phone.

'Definitely,' she nodded. 'I'd fuck her.'

'Oh God,' I took back my phone and sighed. 'Is this how we talk about women now? Would I fuck her or not? Can we convince her to work at The Bach?'

'Please.' Karli rolled her eyes. 'That's how men have been looking at women forever. We're just putting our little pimp hats on!' She pulled out a lime green thong and stretched it out over her head. 'How d'you like mine?'

I flicked to my Notes app and grabbed the canned text we'd written for Tinder contacts, explaining that I wasn't actually the man this woman had swiped on, but the madam of an ethical escort agency. 'Here goes nothing,' I said under my breath. 'Either she bites or she blocks us.'

My laptop chimed with an email from Booking.com.

Your January commission payment is now overdue. Attached is the invoice for February. Total amount due on receipt: $3258.

'Three thousand—' I put my head in my hands. 'Gavin said this motel *made* money. I didn't think it was going to suck me dry!'

Karli gestured at the room she was standing in. 'Well, we *did* take two rooms off the market. And this one's a three-room family suite, so that's like more than a quarter of the motel?'

'But The Bach was supposed to make up for it!' I scrolled through my inbox, which seemed to be nothing but bills. 'Look at this! Power, internet, water, *trash collection* . . . Christ, I even have to buy those stupid little bottles of shampoo and conditioner for the rooms!'

'You could stop giving free samples, I guess,' Karli suggested. 'Only those mini hotel toiletries are so much fun. One time, I was staying in Raro, and got these frangipani-scented wet wipes, and I was *in love*, because—'

Her phone jingled in the pocket of her miniskirt, and she wiggled it out and swiped. 'Welcome to The Bach,' she cooed. 'This is Madam

Karli . . . how can I help?' She listened. 'Yes? . . . Yes! *Absolutely,* that would be wonderful! We'll be here! Okay byyyyyyye!' She tapped off the call and beamed at me. 'YES!' she shouted. 'I knew it!'

I pulled down the screen of my laptop. '*Please* tell me it was a woman who wants to work here.'

'Nope.' Karli grinned. 'It was *two women* who want to work here. They're mates and they're coming here now!'

'Then I guess you better take those undies off your head,' I told her. 'We need to start looking professional.'

Piper and Sabra, as they would come to be known, tentatively knocked just a few minutes later. And I didn't need my pimp hat to judge them. Anyone with eyes could see they were gorgeous.

Sabra was in her early twenties, her black hair cut in a stylish bob, dark bangs emphasizing her melting brown eyes. She had a perfectly round birthmark, just above her left upper lip – the kind of detail that makes men fall in love. Both hands were stuffed deep in her pockets, probably because she was nervous. Or worried about what kind of monsters we were.

Piper was barely five feet tall with her shoes on. With her big brown eyes and delicate rosebud lips, she looked like a life-size doll – but she stuck out her hand with a grin. 'I heard you in that Facebook video and I thought *hell, yes!'* she said, pumping my arm up and down. 'Why *shouldn't* I be able to fuck who I want and also make heaps of cash!'

'The free childcare's massive as well,' Sabra said, as I showed the two girls inside. 'Both of us have kids. And I just started nursing school, so it's . . . a lot.'

'*And* the jobs in this town are all shit.' Piper took a seat on the couch. 'Fifteen an hour, plus you have to pay childcare.

And WINZ does fuck-all to help. They just *lecture* at you to *budget* better, and I'm like, bitch, *you* add up the rent and the crèche fees! Plus groceries and power and petrol – sitting there with your gold jewelry and that judgy little look on your face? *Pfff.* Bunch of wrinkled-up cows.'

'The DPB is humiliating.' Sabra sat down beside her. She was talking about the Domestic Purposes Benefit, the small sum of money that single parents can get, to keep them out of the worst kind of poverty. 'And the student allowance isn't much better, except now I just need more childcare.'

'It's like a – what do you call it? A *vicious circle.'* Piper spun her finger in the air to demonstrate. 'So we thought, if we can make in *one hour* here what it takes *ten hours* to make at another job, *plus* have our childcare covered . . .' She threw up both hands. 'Even I can do *that* maths! And I never finished Year 12!'

'You *do* look very young,' I mentioned. 'Do you mind if I ask how old you are?'

'Nineteen,' she shrugged. 'I'll show you my rego. Had to leave school when I had my baby, and his father's a useless prick.'

'Mine too,' Sabra said. 'My baby daddy's long gone.'

'Why don't I get us some tea?' Karli chirped, getting up to turn on the jug.

Sabra shifted uneasily on the couch. 'So . . . what *is* ethical sex work? Like, apart from the childcare, I mean. How are you guys different from . . . all the other places?'

'Oh, honey.' Karli came back with two mugs. 'Have you *seen* the Velvet Lounge?'

'No.' Sabra shook her head. 'I don't really know much about the business, if I'm honest.'

'Is that the *grotty* old place down on Vine Street?' Piper stuck out her tongue in disgust. 'Didn't the owner get done for chasing some guy with a meat cleaver?'

'Yes!' Karli clapped her hands. 'I forgot about that! People used to call him The Butcher.'

My phone buzzed and I glanced at the screen.

100 dollar mean bj pls

I ignored it. 'Forget about the Velvet Lounge,' I said. 'What we're doing is totally different.'

It buzzed again. This time it was Gavin.

Water rates were due last week and are now overdue. By the terms of your lease, you have three days to pay.

Then the first guy started in again.

Half hour bj
Half hour bj

'Sorry,' I said, looking up. 'You were saying?'

'What makes it ethical?' Sabra asked again. 'I mean, the businesses are the same, right? We sleep with the guys and we take their money. Then we give you what – a third? On commission?'

The guy was not going away.

pls I want fat cock sucked.

I put my phone on Do Not Disturb. 'Half,' I corrected. 'The house actually takes half. But you get a *helluva* lot in return.'

'Like *what?'* Piper asked. 'We're the ones doing the sex, right?'

Karli crossed her long legs and leaned in. 'For starters, you don't have to work out of your home. Which is actually really dangerous? Like if the punters know where you live. We have a *beautiful* service room, we've done it with paintings and flowers – it's *so cute.* And the sheets are all changed between bookings.'

Please don't go, please don't go, please don't go. I ticked off more points on my fingers. 'We take all your pictures, and we protect your privacy. No faces, ever. We pay for your advertising on New Zealand Girls. We provide all your outfits and shoes, including some really nice lingerie. Here, want to see?'

I felt like I was talking too fast, like it was obvious how desperate I was. *Pull yourself together,* I told myself. *No one wants to get on a sinking ship.* We took the girls into the dressing room, and Piper went right to the lingerie, pulling out a lacy black teddy. 'Oooh!' She held it up in front of the mirror. 'I would look *fierce* in this one!'

'How are you even supposed to put this one *on?'* Sabra asked, dangling a tangle of elastic black straps from one hand. 'If I got myself into it, I'd come out looking like a rolled roast!'

'It's . . . doing a BDSM thing.' Karli took the straps and stuffed them in a bag. 'That's why we've got lots to choose from, though! We want you to feel *gorgeous* and *amazing;* that's the whole point.'

'And it's about your well-being,' I added. 'You don't have to buy your own clothes, and that helps. But also, it keeps your two worlds apart. The person you are at work is this goddess that all men desire . . .'

'And then you hang it up on the rack!' Karli finished. 'And go back to being a student and a mum.'

Piper glanced at her phone, and I felt like I had to keep talking. 'Do you . . . want to see the service room?' I asked. 'It's just across the parking lot, up there on the left.'

'Sure,' Piper shrugged. 'We still have an hour before pick-up.'

We took them both up to Room 6. 'Okaaay,' Sabra said, taking in the paintings and flowers. 'This *is* nice. Way better than I expected. But . . .'

'What is it, hon?' Karli asked

'What about safety?' she finally asked. 'What if a guy gets rough? Or he doesn't want to leave when it's time?'

I chose my words carefully. 'Nothing's a hundred percent,' I told her. 'But it's a lot more safe than a Tinder date.'

Piper looked doubtful. 'How do you reckon *that?*'

'Because people are watching,' I explained. 'There's cameras all over the property. Not in the bedrooms, but outside, in the car park. When they come here, we have them on film. We get their license plate numbers. And they know that a madam is watching.'

'If you were some kind of a sex maniac,' Karli reasoned, 'wouldn't you rather get a girl drunk at a bar, then take her back to your house where it's private?'

'And if you ever feel uncomfortable, you can stop the booking,' I added. 'It's always your choice. No exceptions.'

Piper frowned. 'So like . . . we don't have to work if we don't want to?'

'Never,' I said. 'You fuck who you want, when you want. It's always your right to consent. And if you want to stop the booking early, I'll pay you out – even if he hasn't paid. Also, there's no line-ups.'

'What's *that?'* Sabra wanted to know.

'At a regular brothel,' Karli said, 'like the Velvet Lounge or whatever, they make you come out and prance around, so the men can go "Oooh, I want that one". It's *super* gross. I mean, what are you, some kind of *cow*?'

'We're by appointment only,' I said. 'And you work as little or as much as you want. So if class gets out early on Thursdays, you can tell me you're available then. A guy sees your photos online, and he calls up to ask if he can book you.'

'Then you ring us and tell us he's coming?' Piper asked.

'No. Then I *ask* you if you *want* to see him. I talk to him first, or Karli will, and we find out as much as we can. We make sure he's polite and respectful. And after that, it's always your choice.'

'And is it just sex?' Sabra asked. 'Or . . .'

'What we offer is a "Girlfriend Experience",' I told them. 'It's sex, mutual oral, and kissing. But what it's *really* about is making him feel like you're his "adoring girlfriend".' I put that last part in air quotes.

'All men want to feel like a king.' Karli sighed. '*Especially* the boring ones you'd never date for free.'

I pulled a flyer from a drawer by the minibar, with a description of prices and services. Piper took it from me and scanned it. 'Sounds easy. I could bounce on a dick for one-fifty. Better than scrubbing out toilets, for *sure*. Why didn't I think of this years ago?'

'Because years ago, you were a *child* in *high school*,' Sabra reminded her.

'Yeah,' I said, 'about that. I would like to see some ID, if you don't mind. And also – kind of an awkward question, but . . .'

Both girls looked at me expectantly.

'Is there any chance one of you *doesn't* shave? We have this client who really likes a nice bush.'

Sabra and Piper promised they'd think about it, and when they left Karli cheered and high-fived me. '*Two more,* you hot sexy madam! If we get those two, I *know* we'll take off. That makes five girls, with Amber, Ruby and Haley!'

'I know.' For the first time in weeks, I could breathe. *We have six kids to take care of at home.* And since I got knocked up by the neighbor, it felt like all eyes were on me. *What's more fun to gossip about than the slut who blew up her marriage? I know! The one who also started a brothel, then failed spectacularly – that's who!* There was no way I was letting that happen.

Karli went back down to the office to put the finishing touches on the dressing room, and I sat on the couch in Room 6, checking the messages I'd missed in our meeting.

Eny pussy pic

Sorry mate, no pussy without a paid booking!

Hy can i see bubs and vagine

No.

Hi, is Haley available at 6:30?

I think so! I'll check

How much to root for a hour?

We don't sell 'roots' here, but a 60 minute GFE is $300, including sex, mutual oral and kissing 💋

Then I clicked out of the texting app, and I saw I had a message on Tinder. *Please be the cute blonde girl, please be the cute blonde girl . . .*

shit im out here banging these mongrels for free might as well give it a go

Thank fucking God.

Awesome! Could we meet up for a coffee sometime? I can tell you all about how it works

Then I sent a message to Karli.

Babe I think we might just have SIX girls. That blonde chick got back on Tinder 🤞🤞🤞

When I first glimpsed the woman who called herself Bee, I knew right away she would kill it. Sitting alone in the crowded coffeeshop, she was jabbing at her phone with one long, silver nail, her platinum hair slicked back in a ponytail. Her figure was compact and tight, in white denim jeans that were straining to hold in her curves. 'Bee?' I asked, tapping the table to get her attention. 'Are you here to meet Antonia?'

She sucked her teeth when she saw me, jerking her chin out to show I should sit. 'Look atchu, fancy white lady! Pimpin' all round Whangārei!'

That's when I noticed her chin tattoo: a swirling black design that extended from her lower lip all the way down to her jawline.

So not Italian, then. Māori. 'I guess I have the right person,' I smiled and held out my hand. 'I hope you weren't offended when I texted you.'

Bee flicked her fingers dismissively. 'Bitch, please. This girl a pirate and a whore already. Ain't nothin you can do to corrupt *me*.'

'So you've . . . done this work before?'

She held up one hand to stop me. 'Nah, don't *even*. I said I'm a whore, not a whore like *that*. Least I wasn't, 'cept that cunt fucked off and now I got my babies to care for. Nāna te hē mō tana hara, know what I'm saying?'

'I don't know,' I admitted. 'I don't understand te reo.'

'Means he's just a idiot cunt with big ideas an' a small cock. Basically.'

'So you'd like to try working at The Bach?'

Bee picked up her phone and read something, then jabbed out a message and slammed it back down on the table. 'BLOCKED. He wants to see me again, he can pay me. Idiot pounds away like a jackrabbit, with a ure like Tāne Mahuta. His dick was from *here* to *here*,' she said, tapping her arm at the elbow and wrist. 'So either I got some real short arms, or he's got a *huge as* cock.'

'So . . . a not-so-great Tinder date?'

'They *all* not-so-great, boss lady! They all hooked on porn, and *none* of 'em knows how to bang! I gave that idiot your number. Said if he wants to pound, he can pay.'

'Glad to hear it,' I said. 'I'll look out for him.'

'Pfff,' she shook her head in disgust. 'You can't play a playa. *Ride* with me or *collide* with me, know what I'm saying?'

'Yep,' I nodded. 'I *definitely* know what you're saying.'

After her first booking, Karli and I crowned her Queen Bee.

'Can you see Paul Yum Yum at noon?' I asked her that day on the phone. '60 minute GFE. He's white, mid-fifties. Amber just saw him last week, and Haley's seen him for sensual. She thinks he's a sales rep, like for farm equipment or something.'

'Uuuuuuungh,' Bee groaned. 'What *time* is it, boss lady? I was out with my besties all *night*.'

'It's just ten,' I said. 'You have plenty of time to get ready.'

'Aw, *shit!* No, I didn't!'

'What's wrong?'

'Lady, I just pulled up my bank balance and there's *nothing*. Think I shouted the whole bar!'

'So do you want it?' I asked. 'It's a hundred and fifty for the hour.'

'Yeah, I'll take it.' Bee yawned. 'One question, though. Why's he called Paul . . . Yo Yo?'

'Yum Yum,' I corrected. 'Because that's what he says when he comes.'

One hour and forty-eight minutes later, Bee was dressed and made-up for her booking. She'd layered a tight black lace dress over her red satin underwear, topping it off with six-inch red leather heels. I let out a whistle when I saw her.

'Don't hate me 'cause you ain't me!' she sang out. 'Paul Yum Yum don't even deserve this ass.'

'He'll *love* you,' I told her. 'You're gorgeous.'

Paul's silver Toyota pulled in right at noon, and I watched him go up to Room 6, then set my timer for an hour. Fifty-six minutes later he was back in his car, and Bee was in the office, tossing three hundred dollars on my desk.

'How was it?' I asked. 'Did he say it?'

She shrugged. '*Psssh.* I don't know. Didn't even bang him.'

'You didn't have *sex*? Was he upset about that?'

'Boss lady, *please.* I put on Nicki Minaj, did a striptease. He *loved it.* That boy just paid me to twerk.'

And that's when we crowned her Queen.

—

'It's sort of like building a fire,' I told Karli. 'You start with some kindling, then you add bigger sticks, and finally you start feeling the heat.' Now that we had a few women on board, we were getting more calls from new clients.

'I think the boys just like variety,' Karli mused, loading a hamper with clean towels and sheets. 'Maybe it's a power thing? Like they want to be the ones who can choose?'

I scrolled through the texts from that morning.

Hi are there two girls slim under 30 available at lunchtime

Weres the Bach and how many girls on

I really want a bj babe bt only have 100

Do any of the ladies wear langara?

'What the fuck is *langara?'* I asked Karli, showing her the phone.

'Oooh, what do you bet he means *lingerie?'* she said. 'Silly boys in this town. They can't spell!'

Later that week, Sabra had her first booking with a guy we called Mark Jungle Fever. **Dyou have any maori girls,** he'd texted. **Got a bit of the jungle fever.**

'That was *so easy!'* she beamed, handing me a small stack of bills. 'I *cannot believe* how *easy* that was!'

'So he behaved himself?' I asked, filling out her pay stub.

She flopped on the couch and kicked off her heels. '*Yeah.* He kept touching my face, telling me I'm the most beautiful woman he's ever seen.' She shook her head. 'It's just weird, because I don't actually think of myself that way? But he said I was the most beautiful girl *ever.*'

It wasn't just Sabra – I saw it with all the girls. Once they took a few bookings, their self-confidence soared. Clients told them they were gorgeous, incredible, desirable – and most of them started to believe it.

'I got myself a special perfume,' Sabra said, 'that I only ever wear here at work. It makes me feel dangerous and sexy. Not the boring mummy everyone thinks I am. Anyway,' she said, getting comfortable. 'How did Piper's first booking go?'

'That girl is a *hustler,'* I said. 'I can't believe it.'

Sabra nodded. 'Thought she'd be good at this. She's had to fight for pretty much everything she's got. So what happened?'

'There's this guy we call Fuckwit Wants It Right Now – 'cause whenever he calls, it's a Dick Emergency. Anyway, he booked her for a one hour massage, and when his time was up, I texted. But she didn't answer. I knew she was safe, because Fuckwit's a regular, but after six minutes I got kind of pissed, so I called her.

'And she goes, "Whoops! My bad! I didn't want to kick him out because he's so nice!"'

'Nice don't pay the bills,' I told her. 'Don't give him your time for free.'

'Ha! I know, right? Never again,' Sabra laughed. 'I'm not giving *anything* away for free. No more!'

'Right?! So when he finally left, I go up to clean up the room. And Piper's *literally* throwing fistfuls of money in the air. And she goes, "Nice don't pay the bills, huh?" And I'm like, "Where did that come from?" because Fuckwit is notoriously cheap.'

'So how did she get it?' Sabra asked. 'Did she overcharge him? Or—'

'It was tips. She took off her clothes and she *danced* over him, but she wouldn't let him touch her unless he paid.'

'That's brilliant,' Sabra said. 'I don't know if I'd have the balls for that, to be honest.'

'That girl earned $230 for a sensual massage, and she didn't even have to touch the guy's dick.' I laughed. 'She's gonna make a boatload of money.'

One person who *wasn't* making much money was Ruby, and I was starting to feel pretty guilty about it. 'It's because she's too big,' I told Karli. 'We never should have gotten her hopes up. We need more size sixes and eights.'

'I hate it *so much,'* Karli said. 'Did you know I used to be a fat kid? I've got stretch marks from when I was little. And I've spent my whole adulthood dieting.'

'It's not just size, either. A lot of men are asking for white girls.'

'Ew!' Karli winced. *'Why?'*

'Racism, I guess.' I pulled out my phone to show her. 'They think white is more valuable, and when they're paying that much, they want what they think is the best. Look at these messages.'

Hi have you got any slim size 6 white girls available today?

I am seeking a slim DD

Have you got a natural blonde white girl?

Is that the best you have something skinnier?

Who's the smallest European girl working tonight?

I don't like any fat

'Pretty, skinny white girls.' I flicked at the screen. 'How enlightened. We might as well come up with a shorthand. Let's call them PSWG.'

'Who's a pretty skinny white girl?' asked Queen Bee, who was coming back from finishing a booking. '*You* a pretty, skinny white girl, Boss Lady. Why don't *you* suck some dick for some cash?'

'I did,' I said, 'for ten years. Then my husband left. How was Danny Rock My Jocks? He said he wanted to go the whole hour – did he do it?' Danny had earned his name in his first booking, when he'd pointed at Amber and said *get over here and rock my jocks.* He probably thought this was sexy. We unanimously agreed it was not.

Queen Bee held up her hand. 'Bitch, *please.* He think he gonna last the whole *hour* with me? I told him, do your seventeen seconds of *unh-unh-unh,* 'cause that's all you got. Ha. It touched the rim of the flap and it cummed.'

'What's that in English?' I asked.

'Nah, I forgot you don't speak hood. His *penis* touched my *vagina* and *ejaculated.* Like, right away. Said it was the best thing that's happened to him in fourteen years.'

'Impressive,' I told her. 'I have to admit, you got skills.'

'That's *right* I do. Feel my *wairua,* bitches! Those boys who want pretty skinny white girls? They best come *correct* with Queen Bee.'

My phone jingled, and I was still laughing when I swiped on it. 'Welcome to The Bach, how can I help?'

'Antonia?' It was Debra, the woman we'd hired to run the motel reception. 'There's somebody here from the Council? They say we don't have a resource consent for a brothel here. We have a month before they shut us down.'

Chapter 10

'A *resource consent?*' I spluttered. 'Why would I need a *resource consent?* We're already *zoned commercial* here. This place is a working motel!'

'Sorry, yes I'll give it to her.' Debra was speaking to someone else in the background. 'All right, thank you! I'll tell her. He's gone now,' she said.

'Thank *Christ.*'

'And he's left quite a big envelope here for you. Shall I bring it round?'

'You boss ladies take care of *your* business.' Queen Bee shrugged and pocketed her cash. 'Then get this Bee some more bookings. I want Bach bitches to pump!'

Bee swung open the office door, nearly colliding with Debra, who was standing right there with the envelope. I took it and thanked her, pulling out a long legal document on official Whangārei Council letterhead. 'What the actual,' I muttered as I read. 'Traffic impact assessment? District plan compliance? Lighting? *Signage?!*'

'What're they on about?' Karli was reading over my shoulder.

'They want me to apply for a resource consent. But this is going to cost *thousands.* Effects on the *environment? Flood susceptibility?* How am I going to *pay* for all that?'

'I don't think you're meant to,' Karli said. 'I think they just want you to shut down. But how did we get up their noses? We're not bothering anyone here.'

'And we *already* run a hotel,' I moaned. 'Where people *pay* to come for a night and have sex. What's the *difference?*'

'Let me see that.' She took the document, running her glittery pink nail over the paragraphs of legalese. 'BOOM. There it is.' She handed it back to me. 'Effects on the character of the surrounding land, including the *already consented childcare.*'

'Fuck,' I swore. 'The kindy next door. I'll bet they're the ones who complained.'

—

'What do they think we're going to do, anyway?' Amber grumbled. 'Toss our used condoms over the fence?' She was just back from seeing a new client named Scott, and we'd filled her in on the kindy's complaint.

'Maybe they think it's contagious?' Karli asked. 'Like the kids will all grow up slutty if their sandpit's too close to a brothel?'

'It's not even a *brothel,'* I cut in. 'It's an *escort agency.* Why does no one get that distinction?' I paused for a second, making a mental note to read up on the law. 'Anyway,' I turned back to Amber. 'What should we call this new Scott guy?'

'Scott Wanks Back To Front,' she said right away.

'Excuse me?'

'He does! He holds it like this, *overhand.'* She bent her hand in a claw shape, like someone had broken her wrist. 'So that's what we should call him. Other than that, not much to report. In his forties, I guess, and white. Likes to get himself off at the end, which is why I saw how he wanks it.'

'Why?' I asked. 'There's a pretty girl right there in front of him, and he wants to jerk off with his hand?'

'A lot of them do,' Karli said. 'They've got porn dick. They're so used to jerking it in this very specific way, so they can't get there anymore with a woman.'

My laptop chimed with an email. 'What *now*?' I glanced at my inbox. 'More love letters from Council?'

I clicked on the message.

I'm working down here in Auckland, but I want to come work for you. I liked what you said on that Facebook video, about women supporting each other. My auntie's up in Whangārei and I'd like to come back there, slow things down for a bit. I'm attaching a photo so you can see what I look like. The name that I work with is Grace.

I opened the attachment, and the three of us peered at the screen. *'Holy shit,'* I breathed. 'Hello, PSWG.'

Grace was, in a word, a knockout. Standing in front of a full-length mirror in a white crop top and silver hot pants, she held her phone out in front of her. Her face was obscured by a heart-eye emoji, but it was her *legs* that caught my attention. 'She's a perfect size six,' I said, 'I'm sure of it. And those legs are about ten miles long.'

Amber squinted at the selfie. 'Zoom in on her legs, will you?' she said.

'*Why?*' Karli asked. 'She's *stunning.* Ring her up! Ring her right now!'

I zoomed in on Grace's bare legs. 'Okay, she's got lots of mosquito bites. But we can Photoshop that out, no problem!'

'Hmm.' Amber looked skeptical. 'If you say so.'

'Anyway.' I counted her cash and filled out her pay stub. 'I should call this girl. Don't forget you have Ravi Bow Dick tomorrow at eleven, and Jimmy Poetic at twelve-thirty.'

'I like Jimmy,' Amber said, tucking the cash in her purse. 'He always reads me his love poems. So I'll see yous,' she said over her shoulder, as she left the office. 'Let me know how you get on with Grace.'

'The traffic analysis won't be too bad,' the consultant told me over the phone. 'We can probably get through that for seven grand. But if they want you to upgrade the drainage and sewage, that could come in rather dear. You could be looking at twenty, thirty thousand dollars.'

'The . . . drainage and sewage?' I repeated, swerving around a chicken as I drove down my driveway the following morning. 'Why's it on *me* to upgrade the sewage? And why would I *need* to? It's not like men come to The Bach for the toilets.'

'It's about the numbers, really,' he explained. 'If you're getting multiple clients using a room in one day, whereas before it would have been one or two, then Council can claim that's more wear and tear on the pipes, and they can require an upgrade. But I wouldn't worry, because we can—'

'You don't *understand,'* I cut the guy off. 'I don't have thirty thousand dollars. I don't have a spare *seven* thousand dollars. If they want all that, then I'm finished. The business is going to close.'

'Ah,' he said. 'Yes, I see. Well, give us a bell if there's anything more we can do.'

Grace came in for her pictures that morning, in skinny jeans and a jade silk halter top. '*So* glad you made contact,' I said, shaking her hand. 'I think you're going to *own* this town.'

Grace was as gorgeous in person as she was in her selfie, with her lithe dancer's body and mile-long legs. Her jaw looked tight when she smiled, but that was probably just nerves. She tucked her blonde hair behind her ear.

'It was bad there,' she said, 'down in Auckland.' She fiddled with the strap on her silver handbag. 'The place where I worked? It was run by gangs. I got into some bad stuff, so I thought maybe if I came up here, I could . . . you know, calm it down. Get healthy.' She was biting the inside of her lip. 'So where do you want to do this? Here in the office, or . . . ?'

'We'll go to the service room,' I told her. 'Room 6.'

I could have asked her to give me more details. The 'bad stuff' she got into in Auckland, or what she meant by 'calm down' and 'get healthy'. I could have asked about all those mosquito bites. But when we got to Room 6, she pulled a pair of white platform heels out of her bag, with straps that crisscrossed and laced up her ankles. And when she put them on, her legs became truly sensational.

I had time to ask her a lot of things, while I was taking her photos. But I had Council on my ass and six kids to support. And all I could think was: *cha-ching!*

—

With Grace on our team, we had a real business, and the phone rang so often we gave it a nickname: we started to call it the Batphone.

Booking with the youngest and the thinnest please

Anyone young slim and good looking?

Any slim size 6 ones today?

Yes! I texted them back, and for once it was true. All of Grace's photos were stellar, with her legs in those white platform heels, but there was one where she was draped across the bed, in a pink bustier and transparent undies, where she could have been a model in any top magazine in the world. I sent that picture out, and no man ever said no.

Besides which, that girl was a worker. She was used to being on shift in the brothel, so she came in each day for the Now Right Nows. She saw Andy Giggly, who tittered nervously in his bookings, and Neville Magic Fingers, who could actually give a girl a real orgasm with just his hands. She saw Carl Computer, a nice, lonely IT professional in town, and Sean The Sensual Brit, one of the few who was any good in bed.

'I'm on *fire!'* she declared one day with Karli, when she'd made five hundred dollars and was cruising toward six. 'I love these days! I'll just take all the bookings, because you don't know when they'll stop, but they also might keep going and going and I can't wait to get the chakras tattooed on my back.'

'Pardon?' Karli asked. 'The what, sorry?'

Grace stopped herself, looking confused. 'That wasn't what I meant to say.'

'What did you mean to say?'

'I . . . can't remember. That happens to me sometimes.'

'Okay, well let's get you started on a Dream Bag.' Karli tactfully changed the subject. 'It's probably best if you don't carry around so much cash? So we can put a bag in the safe here, with your name on it and all your accounts, and then you can save up for whatever you like. Chakras, chocolates . . . whatever!'

'Was she high?' I asked Karli later.

'I don't know,' she confessed. 'I can't tell. Like maybe she's just so excited? To finally be making some money?'

'If she is and we ask her she'll lie,' I said. 'And I don't want to be the hard-assed bitch who's handing out drug tests.'

'So we'll just keep an eye on it!' Karli chirped. And we decided to leave it at that.

It was the beginning of March, and we were entering our third month at The Bach. I'd just weaned Matisse so he could stay home with Patrice, and now I had plenty of new energy for the business. With seven women on board – Amber, Haley, Ruby, Queen Bee, Sabra, Piper, and now Grace – The Bach was making more money. I still wasn't paying myself a salary, but the pile of invoices started to shrink. One afternoon Karli texted as I was cooking dinner.

$700 so far . . . getting pretty fast at making this bed!!

And the next evening, on my shift, I shut down a second motel room so we could service two clients at once. That night I texted Karli.

$870 as I write this and one more booking to go . . .
we might have an actual business here!

The contact list on the Batphone started to grow: we had Ronnie Chicken Legs, Troy Let's Do It, and Jack the Panty Thief, who somehow made off with Sabra's lace knickers. There was Gerald The Shy Farmer, a lonely man too timid to make any friends, and Cruz the Clit Nibbler, who we had to remind not to bite. Piper saw a client named Ronald, and when he pulled up in his truck, it took him several minutes to get out. When he did, we saw what the problem was: he must have weighed four hundred pounds.

'He didn't want to have sex,' Piper reported. 'I don't think he could have done, anyway. He just wanted a girl to be nice to him, you know? Like he asked me to hold his towel while he showered, then he asked if I would just dry him. I don't think anyone touches him, like *ever.* Not unless he's willing to pay.'

One week after the *Herald* article, an email came through from a stranger:

Hi Antonia, thank you for your statements in the NZ Herald the other day. I think you are right, we live in a society that refuses to acknowledge and validate that men may have strong needs for intimacy, attention and loving care. And for many, this translates as a need for sex. If more men could afford your services in a comfortable and ethical context, I believe it would have a significant impact on mental health. Thank you.

'THAT'S what I'm talking about!' Karli crowed when she saw it. 'It's NOT about shagging and sex. People are stuck behind their computers all day – and not only they're not being intimate, they're not even *touching!* People need touch, they have a *skin hunger!*'

'Skin hunger,' I repeated. 'I like that.' The Batphone buzzed.

Would you take a 9inch up the ass??

I jabbed out a reply.

You first, buddy.

'On the other hand,' I said, 'it is, sometimes. Just about sex and a shag.'

Brothel in a motel, motel in a brothel. Escort agency and brothel. I turned those words over in my head at night, on my long drives back to the farm. The family was usually asleep when I got there, Patrice and the baby curled up in our bed. Patrice would leave out a plate of dinner for me, sometimes with a bottle of wine. I'd heat up my meal and pour out a drink, then stream some dumb show on my laptop until I wound down enough to find sleep.

But one night I pulled up Google instead, and searched for the Prostitution Reform Act 2003. I hadn't read the text of the law for six years, since I'd first learned about decriminalization. Stamped with the seal of New Zealand, the law was both boring and dry: 'This Act (other than the provisions referred to in subsection (2)) comes into force on the day after the date on which it receives the Royal assent . . .'

Blah, blah, blah. I scanned on ahead. 'The purpose of this Act is to decriminalise prostitution (while not endorsing or morally sanctioning prostitution or its use) . . .'

Yes, yes, you don't approve. I get it. Nobody does. I took a bite of risotto and read on.

'"Brothel" means any premises kept or habitually used for the purposes of prostitution; but does not include premises at which accommodation is normally provided on a commercial basis if the prostitution occurs under an arrangement initiated elsewhere—'

Say what? I went back and read that again. 'Does *not include* premises at which accommodation is normally provided on a commercial basis *if the prostitution occurs under an arrangement initiated elsewhere.*'

'SON OF A BITCH!' I pushed my chair back with a loud scrape, which brought Patrice shooting up the stairs to check on me. He was bleary with sleep, a bath towel held loose at his waist. '*Ça va? Tu t'es fait mal?* Are you hurt?'

He noticed the laptop in front of me. '*C'est les salauds* over there at the Council? They're trying to shut down your brothel?'

'No,' I told him, 'they can't. *Because I'm not running a brothel.* Or an escort agency.' I leaned back, lacing my fingers in triumph.

'You're not?' Patrice was confused.

'*No.* I'm running a motel. Where prostitution just happens to occur.'

'Here's what we need to do,' I told Karli, when I saw her at the motel the next day. 'We move the office.'

'You're joking,' she said with a frown. 'To *where?*'

'To that junky garage, under Gavin's apartment. That way the bookings won't be made from the motel. The *motel* will have sex work happening in it, but we can't be called a brothel.'

'So no traffic study? No resource consent?'

'*No nothing.* We're just two nice ladies in the garage, getting clients for the sex workers next door.'

'Oh my God,' Karli breathed. 'I *love* it.'

Moving the office ended up solving two problems, because we could rent out Room 1 as a motel room, which covered more of the motel's expenses. Then I got a $30,000 bank loan, using the motel income as collateral. That took some of the pressure off, and it gave us some money to do up the garage.

'We'll carpet it black,' Karli mused, standing in the raw cement space. 'And do the walls in a dark, luscious red. We'll have the lounge room right here as a hang-out space, and the girls can make coffee and tea. Then around the corner, over there,' she picked her way over the raw cement floor in her heels, 'we'll have the dressing room! It's actually going to be *so cozy.*' She rubbed her hands together. 'Like a *Batcave,* except for sex workers!'

'Perfect,' I said, 'but if it's all black and red, I think we should call it the Dungeon.'

'The only thing is . . .' Karli hesitated.

'Yes?' I asked.

'Aren't we supposed to not go into debt? Like, when it comes to consent?'

'No one's in debt,' I said, 'as far as I know.'

'But *you are,* right? I mean, to the bank. And don't you think that might maybe push you . . .'

'To what? '

'To make not-so-great choices? To pay back the bank?'

'*Pfff,*' I said. 'I'll be fine! I'm just thrilled to have all this legal shit sorted!'

—

I thought the loophole I'd found was a good one, but I needed a lawyer to confirm. 'Call Bridie,' said Diana at the NZPC, when I called her to ask her advice. 'She does a lot of work for the industry. She'll write a letter to Council for you, and she'll probably make this whole thing go away. Reckon she won't charge you either; she's like that.'

And as if by magic, it worked. We moved our office to a building fifty meters away, and a wonderful lawyer named Bridie drafted a letter to Council.

Overnight, we stopped being a brothel.

—

'Grace is taking money out of her dream bag,' Karli warned me, the next week on Thursday. 'And she's been driving down to Auckland on the weekends. She told me she needed to buy trousers, so she took the whole eight hundred dollars she had saved. But who needs eight hundred dollars for trousers? I mean, it's her money, but—'

'Come on,' I broke in. 'Are you buying that?'

'Nah,' Karli sighed. 'Pretty sure she's on the gear.'

By that point, it was already too late. The next day, Amber stopped answering her phone. But she'd always been a party girl. We figured she was probably drinking a lot, and we knew she'd left town to pick up a used car. On Friday, Bee's phone went to voicemail. And Grace was nowhere to be found.

She was supposed to come back on Sunday, and Karli was in charge of the phones that day, so I texted to see if she'd shown.

Grace isn't back yet. She's been texting and calling all day. Says she doesn't have money to buy petrol to get home. Wants to borrow money. 😃 👊

DO NOT GIVE HER MONEY

But you know that.

I know. Now she's calling on my other phone. She's been texting Bee all day too . . .

WHY IS SHE TEXTING QUEEN BEE?

To go in halves with her. On drugs.

Sorry I don't have better news.

—

The next day, when I got into work, a new message was waiting on the Batphone.

Well CRACKHEAD

YOU LOST IT ON THE METH

WHERE IS THE MONEY YOU OWE???

You done the same thing as in Perth spent it on meth

pay what you owe or ill try your trick and send the police round to bust you

Pay what you owe CRACKHEAD

The mention of Perth was a giveaway. It wasn't just Grace who was back on the pipe. Amber was back on drugs too. And now her crack dealer was threatening me.

I have notified the police about your texts. I have nothing to do with drugs or methamphetamine. Please stop contacting me.

Then I blocked his number, and hoped that the problem was solved.

Chapter 11

But it turned out my problems were only beginning. In the space of a week, I lost half my staff to meth. From what I could work out, Amber and Grace spent their money on drugs, and they got into debt with their dealer. To pay the guy back, they figured they'd buy a bunch of meth to start selling – so Grace asked Queen Bee to invest. I called up Bee to find out how that went.

'Nah that ain't even ON,' she snapped when she got on the line. 'I put that shit behind me *years* ago. I'm out here trying to create a life I don't want to escape from, and that bitch tryin' to drag me back in. I told her to check herself and fuck off with her pipe and her drama, clear?'

'Clear,' I said, my guts twisting. Then I called Grace, and told her to come in and pick up her things.

'I know you're on drugs,' I said when I saw her. 'And you tried to get Bee to buy some with you. She put that life behind her, and she's a single mother with two babies – and you want to get her on *meth?*'

Grace said nothing, but she looked sick to her stomach.

'I don't think you're a bad person,' I told her. 'I think you're good. But you're making bad choices because of the drugs. You can't work here anymore. You need to get help.'

It took her about a minute to collect all her things, two pairs of high heels and her snacks from the fridge.

'Is there anything you want to say?' I asked.

'I'm sorry,' she said, in a little girl voice.

'Have I been unfair?'

'No,' she said. 'You've been lovely.' And she turned and walked out the door.

'I think . . . I'll just work on my own for a bit,' Haley said when I called to check in. 'Karli told me about what happened down there, and . . . I'd rather steer clear of the drama.'

'That's Grace and Haley gone,' I reported to Karli. 'Bee says she wants some time off to think, and Amber won't pick up the phone. Not that I'd let her work anyway, since she and Grace were the ones who started this mess.'

'You don't want her anywhere *near* here.' Karli poured boiling water in the French press, then got out two mugs from the drawer. 'She's deep in the drugs. I heard she got evicted from her flat? For painting the walls of her room black? And now she's livestreaming videos of herself on Facebook, giving herself these awful tattoos.'

She handed me a coffee and I sank into my chair. 'It's *March,*' I groaned. 'The Bach has been open two months, and Grace only started *four weeks* ago. Did *we* do this? Did *we* get them back onto drugs?'

Karli considered this. She looked paler than usual, and I noticed she wasn't wearing much makeup. 'No.' She shook her head. 'Because look at the other ladies we have. Bee was on meth in the past, and she's already made more than a grand here. Grace was calling and texting her, and I'm sure she was tempted, but she didn't get back on the gear. And Ruby – she got done for drink driving, but it's not like she's spending her money on the piss.'

'Well, she isn't *making* much money, to be fair.'

'No, but it's more than she made at the call center. I think the addicts went back to drugs 'cause they're *addicts*. And the rest . . . are just trying to get by.'

'Yeah, speaking of that.' I hesitated, choosing my words. 'I think . . . we need to lower our prices.'

Karli sucked in air through her teeth. 'Are you *sure,* Antonia? 'Cause three hundred bucks – it's already not much, especially when you count GST and expenses.'

'It's a lot for Northland, though,' I argued. 'Down in Auckland, you can charge four or five hundred. But men just don't have that kind of money up here.'

'So what were you thinking?'

'Two-forty an hour for full service. That's twenty percent off. Keeps us much more expensive than the Velvet Lounge, so people will know we have quality. And at that price, I think we'll bring in more bookings.'

'Are you sure, though?' She bit down on her lip. 'You know once we lower our prices, we can't just bring them up again.'

'I'm sure,' I said, though I wasn't at all. 'Now that we're legal, we need to start filling up. *And* we need more women. So let's get flicking on Tinder.' I got out my phone and pulled up the app. 'We need some all-natural hippie girls. Organic vegans who won't touch the meth. Here, how 'bout this one?' I showed Karli a photo of a tall, slender woman, hiking through the bush with a pig on her back. 'Okay, she's probably not vegan. But if she hunts, she's gotta be fit, right?'

I swiped right.

—

On top of the methamphetamine crisis, there was always more drama at home. Peter used his payout from the house to buy himself a creaky old boat to live on, which he kept tied to a pile mooring, rowing back and forth to shore in a small plastic dinghy. 'How's that safe for the kids, when they come out on Saturday?' I asked him over the phone. 'Neither of them can swim, and Silas could have a seizure and fall overboard.'

'Details,' he said, 'but about that. I can only take Miranda this weekend.'

'You want the normal one but not the *disabled* one? You can't pick and choose who you take!'

'Well, that's how it is,' he said flatly. 'I'll pick up Miranda at four.'

The next day, I got home and Patrice was outside, chopping wood with unusual force. Jabberwocky, our psychotic rooster, was prowling the garden. Named for the Lewis Carroll poem, he had *jaws that bite* and *claws that catch*. And sure enough, when I got out of the car, he hurtled himself in a rage at my legs. Sighing, I kicked him away. 'Fuck off, rooster. What did I ever do to *you?*'

Then I noticed that things were unusually quiet. 'Where are the kids?' I asked Patrice.

'Putain de bordel de merde,' he swore, straightening up with a wince. 'I told them to stay in their room. I do NOT want to see their faces!' He balanced a log on the chopping block, and split it in one savage blow.

When a Frenchman says 'fucking brothel of shit', you know he's not playing around. I put down the groceries. 'What happened?'

'They got hold of some glass from the window that broke, and they used it to cut up the trampoline.' *Chop.* 'Like devilish children *de merde!' Chop.* 'They could have sliced up their hands and their arms!'

'I'll go talk to them,' I said. 'I'll find out what's going on.'

Up in their room, Titou was sitting on his bed, clutching Miranda's turtle as he stared at the wall. Miranda looked up with her chin trembling. 'You guys okay?' I asked. 'Why are you trying to murder the trampoline?'

Miranda stuck out her lower lip. 'My tummy hurts,' she whimpered.

'It does? You think you might need to throw up?'

'And also my head.' She put both her hands on her ears. 'And also it's here.' She moved one hand to her chest. 'I just feel so *sad*, Mama,' she sobbed, and the tears finally spilled down her cheeks.

'Oh, honey,' I said. 'About what?'

The words came out in a blur. 'Papa's not here and he doesn't want Silas, and you're always gone, and Titou and me got in trouble, and now the trampoline's broken, and Patrice is mad and also . . .'

'Yes?'

'Sometimes I'm so sad, I feel *sick.*'

'Okay,' I breathed, sitting down on the bed beside her. 'You know I have a business, right?' Across the room, Titou didn't turn around, but I saw his back straighten. He was listening.

'Yes, Mama, and it's called The Bach, but what *is* it? That girl Aimee at school says it's a *sex club* where people do *sexing,* and—'

'Hey.' I put my arm around her. 'I don't know what Aimee heard from her parents, but The Bach is an *escort agency.*' Now Titou turned around, still hugging the turtle. He wasn't even pretending not to listen.

'Well, what's that?' Miranda sniffled.

'It's a place where ladies do dress-up, and they make lots of money, and they give men kisses and cuddles.'

'It is?' Miranda wiped at her eyes. 'That's not so bad.'

'No.' I gave her a hug. 'No, it's not.'

—

At least one person was feeling good about life: our brand new superstar, Piper. Sabra couldn't work during the day with her nursing program, so Piper started coming in early, applying her makeup with expert precision. One day her three-year-old son had a sniffle, so she brought him with her to work. She set him up on the couch with his coloring books and crayons, and put headphones on his ears so he could listen to music. Then she pulled out her portable speaker and started pumping Beyoncé's '6 Inch'.

'She's *literally* singing about me right now! *I'm* stacking money!' Piper rummaged around in her makeup bag. 'I got this cherry blossom mist from Sephora. It says to hold it eight inches in front of my face. Is that more than eight centimeters, or less?'

'More,' I said, holding up two fingers. I glanced at the boy and lowered my voice to a whisper. 'Like the length of a really nice dick.'

'Oooh! Okay!' She spritzed her face, admiring herself in her hand mirror. 'D'you know Hot Raj told me he'd buy me diamonds if I'd be his girlfriend? He told me he'd take me to Paris. Ha! What a liar.' She ran her makeup brush over her cheekbones, dusting them with a glittery sheen. 'I'll buy my *own* damn diamonds, thank you very much.'

'You'll be able to soon,' I flipped through my log from the previous month. 'You're making almost a thousand a week here.'

'I know! Men love me 'cause I'm little and cute.' She held up her cell phone, snapping a selfie of her finished face. 'I do the sweet and innocent thing, and they eat it up. Ha! What idiots.'

My phone buzzed with an unknown number.

Is Piper available for sensual massage?

'You want to do a sensual?' I asked her. 'It's a new guy.'

'Sure!' she chirped. 'When's he want to come in?'

I jabbed at my phone. 'Half an hour. Hang on, he's got a few more questions.'

Is it until I cum?

It's until the end of the time you have booked.

Up to you if you'd like to come.

Will she lick the cum?

'Gross!' I showed Piper the screen.

'I mean. Does he come strawberries and chocolate?' Piper rolled her eyes. 'Then *maybe.*'

She ended up taking the booking, and while she was up there, I tapped the boy's knee. 'Manaia?' I asked, and he put down his black crayon, looking up at me with huge dark brown eyes. His lips were a perfect rosebud, the same beautiful feature I'd noticed when I first met his mother.

I lifted the headphones from his ears. 'Did you want a snack? It's almost morning tea time, I think.'

He nodded gravely, and I went to the refrigerator, pulling out ham and bread, butter and blueberries. I fixed him a sandwich and cut off the crusts, then filled a little egg cup with berries. He came to the table and sat in a chair, his chubby legs dangling in the air. 'I have a block set, if you want.' I waggled my eyebrows. 'D'you want to see if we can make a super-tall tower?'

He placed a blueberry in his mouth, then furrowed his brow. 'Can I crash it?' he asked.

'*Absolutely,*' I said. 'Do you think you can make it go to the ceiling?'

Manaia and I played for the next twenty minutes, stacking our blocks into ill-fated towers. We were destroying our fourth or fifth structure when the timer rang out on my phone. I sent Piper a text.

Time's up! You all good?

I'm awful

Can you come up here?

DONT BRING MANAIA

Sure no problem I'll get Debra to look after him

One sec

'What's *wrong?*' I asked when I burst through the door. 'Did he hurt you? Was he terrible?'

Piper was slumped on the couch, weeping as she looked at her phone. 'What? No, he was fine. He was lovely, actually.' She held up her phone. 'It's my *shit* of an ex!'

'What happened?' I sat on the sofa beside her.

'He found out I work here! And now he wants to take Manaia away.' She sobbed, tears smearing her mascara.

'But . . . how did he find out?' I asked. 'You haven't told anyone, have you?'

'Snapchat.' She sniffled. 'That day when I made all that money with Fuckwit, I put up a picture on Snapchat. Of my money, all fanned out on the bed, and me . . . and I guess he recognized the painting in Room 6? Or someone he knows did. *And he screen grabbed it!*'

'Oh, *shit.*' I rubbed my hands on my thighs, thinking. 'Tell you what. You have a shower and take a deep breath. I'm just gonna make a call.'

She shuffled her way to the bathroom, and I called the lawyer who'd helped us with Council. 'Bridie?' I said when she picked up the phone. 'Can the courts take a woman's kids away, if they find out she's doing sex work?'

'Depends,' she replied. 'Is she working from home?'

'No, she's one of ours.' I explained what Piper's ex had threatened.

'No way,' Bridie said. 'Anything like that would get thrown out of court. I know it, because I've seen it tried.'

Piper came back, drying her hair with a towel. I waved her over. 'Really?' I asked. 'Could you say that again? Hang on, I'm gonna put you on speaker.'

'As long as she keeps it away from her children,' Bridie repeated, 'doing sex work cannot be used against her. In fact, it could be seen as a *net positive,* because she's working to benefit the child.'

'Thank you,' I said. 'That's wonderful news.'

I tapped out and smiled at Piper. 'You see? He *can't* take Manaia. This is legal work. You're working to *benefit* the child.'

'Really?' she said. 'Are you sure? Who was that?'

'A lawyer,' I told her. 'Not some random. This woman really knows all her shit.'

My phone buzzed.

Jus wondering how much for Piper for
15mins penetration.

I tapped out an answer.

Piper's done for the day, but Sabra and Ruby
can see you if you like. Our shortest booking
is a 30 minute GFE, $180.

'Okay,' Piper's voice sounded shaky. 'I'm gonna get dressed and go get him from Debra. Thank you for that.'

I nodded and let myself out of the room. My phone buzzed again.

Whose cheapest penetration?

I took a deep breath. *Don't cut the guy's nuts off,* I reminded myself. *He just doesn't speak fluent English.* I could tell from his syntax that he wasn't a native speaker. I just hoped that he wasn't South Asian. Months ago, I'd heard the ladies of Reddit talking about those clients online:

queenvagine
unpopular take but I don't service Indians. Do you?

territor!al: personally I think it's racist to blanket ban a whole group of people like that. I've seen plenty of nice south asian men and anyway how can you tell if he's bangladeshi or pakistani or what?
queenvagine: it's the accent. if he wasn't raised in the west it's too risky. i don't think they're bad but they don't know about consent
MadamAntonia: what do you mean?
queenvagine: I don't think they get sex ed over there. And then they'll be like can I have multishot and lick boom suck ball and i'm like SIR I AM NOT A VENDING MACHINE
MadamAntonia: what's multishot?
territor!al: coming more than one time. JFC **u/MadamAntonia** are you a madam or what??

Now, after four months at The Bach, I definitely knew what multishots were. I'd also experienced those cultural differences. I tapped out a reply to Penetration Guy:

> Our prices are standard, and our ladies give excellent service. And we prefer to say 'full service' or 'sex' . . .

penetration is something you do with a drill.
Would you like to make a booking for this evening?

—

'The whore gods are smiling,' Karli sang out, when I saw her the next day at the office. 'That girl with a pig on her back, on Tinder? She swiped right. She's coming in at eleven to talk to us.'

'Oh my God, that's *incredible* news.' I put my bag down and flopped on the couch. 'Because Ruby just texted; she's moving to Oz. So now we're down to only two girls.'

'There's *more,'* Karli told me triumphantly. 'We got an email from another one. Single mum, late thirties. Usual story, two kids and no man. She wants to come in at twelve.'

I got up to pour myself a coffee, trying to shake the cobwebs from my head. I'd been awakened last night with a violent thump, when Silas had a seizure and fell out of bed. I found him on the floor of his room, still asleep. Patrice had to help me lift him and change him, then I turned him on his side in the recovery position, so he wouldn't choke if he had another fit. By that time, six-month-old Matisse had realized he was alone in our bed, and he'd started to howl in dismay. It took another half hour to settle him, and by that time I was fully awake, staring at the ceiling and worrying about Silas.

The seizures had started three years ago. 'They're common in cases like these, I'm afraid,' the neurologist had said. 'We can give you some drugs to control them, but they may still happen now and again. It can be quite dramatic, but he's unconscious during the fit. You can't do much but protect him from falling and from hitting his head. And you'll want to time the seizure as well.'

'Time it?' I'd asked. 'Why?'

'It can't last more than five minutes. If it does, give him a dose of Midazolam. And then you'll have to take him to hospital.'

'What for?'

'Past five minutes, it's status epilepticus. That's when the seizure gets dangerous. And there can be a slight risk of death.'

'I think that's her,' Karli was peering at the security camera feed. 'She says she wants her name to be Ivy.'

I pushed back the thoughts from last night. 'Okay, great. I'll go let her in.'

Ivy was standing at the motel reception, a thin, tall European woman in jeans and a beat-up old army jacket. Her long brown hair was tied back in a ponytail. 'Oi,' she said with a wave. 'How ya going? I'm the one you hit up on Tinder.'

Back in the Dungeon, she made herself comfortable, shrugging off her jacket to reveal a faded black AC/DC shirt, a botanical tattoo up one forearm.

I gestured to it. 'That's a nice design. Where's it come from?'

She held out her arm so I could inspect it. 'Harakeke. It's native flax. Grows everywhere, out where I live. I like to weave it, make bags and that.' She settled back on the couch and stretched out her legs. She had on big, burly hiking boots that she hadn't bothered to lace up all the way.

'I live out in the bush,' she said. 'Out by Kaikohe. There's fuck all jobs out there, and I need to provide for my daughter. Got a veggie patch and that, and I like to hunt. But then there's school uniforms, and shoes, and camp . . .'

Ivy squinted, taking in the red walls of our dungeon. Karli had brought in a riding crop and paddle from her sex shop, and we'd put them on the wall for decor. 'You do . . . that shit?' Ivy asked. 'Caning and flogging and that? Because that's not my deal, not really. More of a meat an' two veg girl, myself.'

Karli laughed. 'Oh, I *wish!* But the men in this town are quite basic. It's kissing, shags, and massage. No one asks for fetish or spanking.'

'That pig you were hauling on Tinder,' I said. 'Did you kill that thing yourself?'

Ivy looked proud. 'Did, too. Filled the chest freezer for six months. You do what you have to, to get by. Plus it's a bloody good time.'

My phone buzzed with a text from Queen Bee.

Heeeeey don't know if I'll be in again – my sista
found out what i'm doing, and now she's all drama
with the whanau.

Ouf. Sorry to hear that.

Nah dont even
The day her opinion earns me an income is the day
I'll give a fuck what she say
Loooool #talkischeap

Three little dots, then she texted again.

Im sending you one of my besties, she want you to
call her Alicia.

AMAZING. At what time?

Fuck should I know. Hit you up if i get the karere but that girl move at her oooown pace

Thank you!!

No worries

Gaaaaaaamon!! 💪💪💪

'Sorry!' I said, looking up. 'Could I just ask you a sort of weird question? We're running a drug-free establishment here. So you don't . . . I mean, do you ever . . . have you ever smoked any P?'

'Me? Nah, I don't touch the stuff. That shit's poison.' Ivy laughed. 'Jim Beam for me, all the way.'

'Great.' I breathed a sigh of relief. 'Then let's get you sorted with paperwork. Looks like we have two more ladies to see!'

'I'm not a slut,' Alicia said when we met her. 'I mean, some of my mates are *way* sluttier than me. And they're out there giving it for free! I reckon at least I should get paid.' She slipped off her ballet flats and perched cross-legged on the couch, her big blue eyes wide and friendly.

'Any kids?' I asked.

'Yeah, nah.' She patted her big, heavy bookbag. 'Working on my nurse's diploma right now. Just started. And the student allowance is *crap.* I've been living at home 'cause I can't even pay for a flat! But maybe with this place I could save.' Her honey blonde hair was back in a long, heavy braid, which she twisted between her thumb and first finger. 'Plus, Bee says it's the *easiest* money ever. Half the time she says she doesn't even have sex with them! Just gives 'em a gobby, or twerks!'

'Well.' I held a hand up. 'Bee's special.'

'I reckon it's all a performance, right?' She picked up her braid and curled it into a top knot, spearing it with a pencil from her pocket. 'You make 'em feel like king shit. That's all any of them wants anyways – you have a quick root, you pocket your money and *done.* It's what we do all the time with boys anyway! Like, *please,* tell me about that *cool as* motorbike you've just got, or how *big* that crayfish is, or *how many* drinks you necked last night? They're all a bunch of drongos here anyway, might as well get paid to chat 'em up.'

'Drongos?'

'Yeah, you know. Munters. Bogans.'

'Unsophisticated boys from the country,' Karli hissed at me.

'Who's that on your security camera?' Alicia jerked her head at the monitor. 'Someone else coming to see you?'

Karli glanced at her phone. 'Shit, it's nearly twelve! That'll be Danielle. Another Bach lady who's coming to interview. D'you mind going round the corner to the dressing room?' She gave Alicia some forms and a pen. 'You fill these out, and we'll have a quick chat to Danielle. That way, everyone stays discreet.'

Alicia stood up, but she still looked confused. '*I* don't care if she sees me here.'

'But it's about *you* seeing *her,* just as much,' I explained. 'Unless you both decide to work at The Bach, I'd rather keep everyone's secrets.'

Alicia nodded, ducking around the corner as I went to get Danielle, a tall, curvy woman with her long auburn hair swept up in a clip. 'I'm forty,' she said, 'with two girls to support. I just recently tried to start dating again, and you wouldn't *believe* how bad it is out there. They don't even pay for your dinner! You split the bill, then you go home to bad sex with a guy who's watched too much porn.'

'Are you working right now?' I asked.

'Yes, and I have a good job, too – I'm actually a tertiary level instructor, if you can believe it. But you can't pay for a family on one income. I've tried and it just isn't working. Plus, I love sex,' she said with a grin. '*And* I'm good at it. Plenty of men have told me. Why not make the most of my assets?'

'She's *does* have assets,' Karli confirmed, when Danielle had filled in her forms and gone out. 'Forty! Wish I had skin like that. And no tattoos! She doesn't look a day over thirty.'

'What about those boobs!' I cleaned up the coffee table, collecting the mugs and the spoons. 'Men are going to go nuts for that body. She looks like a Playmate!'

'What do you think she teaches?' Karli wondered out loud.

'I'll tell you,' Alicia came back from the dressing room, handing Karli her filled-out forms. 'She teaches Beginning Anatomy. She's one of the tutors in my nursing course.'

'NO,' I protested.

'*Yes,*' Alicia said. 'I could tell right away from her voice.'

'Let me get this straight,' I clarified. 'So not only you can't make it as a student in this town, or as a young single mum with two kids – but you also can't make it as a *senior nurse and a tutor?*'

'The struggle is real,' Alicia said, smiling. 'Shit's expensive.'

—

'I can't believe I just got paid for that,' Ivy declared, coming out of her first ever booking. 'The guy's seventy-three years old, right? And he *just wanted to do oral on me!* I came three times and no joke! And I didn't even have to have sex with him!'

My phone buzzed with a text from Bruce 73.

> Your Ivy is an angel! I thought multiple climaxes were a myth. Now I see the myth is true!!

'Well, you certainly made *his* day,' I said, reading the rest of the text. 'And get this: he wants to book you for *three hours* this Friday! Can you come back in? I know it's a drive . . .'

'Shit yeah,' Ivy said, pulling on her old beat-up army coat. 'I'll come in for $360. Not sure what we'll do for three hours, though. Might need to bring in a board game. Otherwise, I don't think I'll keep up!'

Alicia's first booking was with Shaking Sammy Sikh, and when I heard his accent, I was on high alert. But she came down with a bright, happy smile on her face, her cheeks flushed and warm from the shower.

'He was *so* nervous, ay!' she reported. 'Shaking and quaking in his boots. Don't think he's had much experience. Don't think anyone's taught him anything! *Hard out* . . . he asked me where the clitoris was, so I got out my anatomy textbook an' I showed him! Fuckin 'ell, he thought it was way up *inside!*'

'You gave him an *anatomy lesson*?'

'Takes up the time, doesn't it? Then I asked him about the scarf he wears on his head, and he told me all about his religion. D'you know he has to wear special underwear? *And* he wears his turban in the shower. It was so interesting, and I learned so much *stuff!*'

Danielle saw Fuckwit Wants It Right Now, and when it was over, she told me his real name. 'It's Rahul,' she said. 'And you guys shouldn't call him Fuckwit anymore. He was actually really passionate, great in bed!'

'He didn't get crazy with the licking?' I asked.

'I *loved* the licking. And he loved my tits. Got a bit bitey on my neck, though. Gave me a hickey.' She kicked off her heels and sat down to pull on her boots. 'It's hard to believe – I'm making money, *and* I'm getting sex. What more do you need?'

Piper saw Sweet Little Ken, a virgin who'd just finished high school. When Don High Blood Pressure called, I put him with Sabra – I figured it would be good for her nursing training. Ivy was delighted with Kyle Lovely Forestry, a guy who worked out in the bush – they screwed for ten minutes, then talked about pig hunting. And Danielle, it seemed, was insatiable: she took all the bookings that came for her, and then called in to ask for some more. Her favorites were Marco Big Dick Milan and Travis Fucks Your Brains Out, until she met up with Roy Cucumber, who told us he had a thirteen-inch dick, and described it 'like a very large cucumber'.

As for Alicia, she snapped up the South Asians. 'I think she's the white girl ideal,' Karli commented, taking a look at her bookings. 'Blonde hair, blue eyes, perfect skin. But still with the hips and the boobs.'

'She asks them about their culture, too,' I said. 'They love it! She put on Bollywood music in a booking the other day, and she danced for the guy mid-screw!'

'Who was that?'

'Hamid Happy Cuddly,' I said. 'And she did it for Vikram Exceptional Young Indian, as well.'

'That girl's a phenomenon.' Karli shook her head in awe. 'She's going to build her own brand.'

As the business got more demanding, Karli and I split up our shifts, no longer spending hours in the office together. We alternated work days so we each had time with our kids, but I'd usually check in at the office on her days.

One evening in June, I was soaking up some quiet at home. Patrice's children were all with their mother; Matisse had been fed and was sleeping; and Silas had had a seizure on the bus ride from school, so when he got home, we'd put him straight to bed. It was only the three of us for dinner: Miranda, Patrice, and me.

'I'm going to make you this salmon dish,' Patrice said, whipping up a glaze in a stainless-steel bowl. 'It's soy sauce, honey, and sesame.'

'Honey on *fish?*' I wasn't sure about that.

'Do *I* have to eat it?' Miranda asked. She was sitting beside me at the dining table, drawing an underground cave full of crystals. 'How many bites do I have to eat?'

'C'est une tuerie,' Patrice told her. *It's a killer.* 'You'll see. We sold thousands of these at the restaurant.'

'Do you think I should take Silas to the doctor?' I sipped a glass of red wine as he cooked. 'He's been having a lot more seizures lately. I wonder if we should change up his dose.'

'I think so, yes.' Patrice put the salmon in the oven. 'The bus driver . . . I think he was terrified.'

'Yeah,' I agreed. 'But that could have been the rooster. That little asshole started pecking his legs today.' I sipped my wine. 'Either way, I don't think it's what he signed up for, when he started driving children to school.'

'Well, it *is* scary, Mum!' Miranda put down her pen. 'Silas goes AAAAAOOOOOH and then he shakes like he's been electric-ated!'

'Don't make that noise,' I said. 'Please. It totally freaks me out.' Each time Silas seized, he let out a loud groan, which sounded like horrible pain. The doctors had explained it was involuntary, the sound of air being forced out of his lungs, but each time I heard it, I panicked. If he was standing, he'd collapse on the floor, where he'd twitch for a minute or two, usually wetting his pants. The longest seizure so far was two minutes. But I knew they were starting to get longer.

'A table,' Patrice said, coming over with three plates of food. 'Let's eat. I'm telling you, this salmon will change your life.'

Miranda pushed away her drawing to make room for her dinner, then grimaced when she saw her plate. 'How many bites, Mama? Because this fish is *brown* and there's *seed* things on it, and—'

'Sesame seeds,' Patrice corrected.

I picked up my fork and my phone rang. Patrice looked affronted. 'It's *dinner time.*'

I glanced at the screen. 'But it's Karli. I have to take this real quick.'

Getting up from the table, I slid the glass door open and stepped out on the deck for the call.

'Antonia?' Karli was out of breath, like she couldn't take in enough air.

'What's wrong?' I asked. 'What happened?'

'Ah . . . it's *really bad.* This guy texted, and he wanted the youngest and the thinnest, so of course I said Piper, 'cause she's just nineteen. He's real cute and young, and he wanted PSE, and you know how she loves to put on a show . . . but then he got rough, and she asked to stop – but he wouldn't! He just . . .' She took a shuddering breath. 'He – *held her down,* even when she said no, then he finished and jumped in the shower. That's when she called me. I tried to get up there right away, but I had four kids in the dungeon, and it took me a minute, and—'

'Who was it?' I demanded. It had to be a new client. It couldn't have been any of our regulars. I *knew* them, and they knew my rules. *None of them would do that.*

'Ricky.'

'Ricky *Come on Titty*?!'

'Yeah. Him.' She hesitated. 'I . . . I thought it would be okay, since you'd already warned him. What do I do?' she asked, her voice small.

'He can't do that,' I said. 'Call the cops.'

Chapter 12

I went back inside and sat down to our dinner. Patrice gave me an inquiring look.

'What's wrong, Mama?' Miranda wanted to know.

I switched to French, which we used when we didn't want the kids to understand what we were saying. 'A client got too rough with one of the girls. Then he held her down and kept fucking her while she said no.'

Patrice frowned. *'Ça va pas, ou quoi?' Is there something wrong with the guy?*

'I don't know.' A wave of nausea hit me and I looked down at my meal, the salmon slick with soy glaze on my plate. I couldn't eat. Instead, I texted Karli.

Let me know what the cops say. Do you need me?

I'll come out there if you need me.

Seeing the look on my face, Miranda sounded nervous. 'What happened?' she asked me again.

'Nothing. I . . . Someone got hurt at work.'

'And do I have to eat any more fish? Because I had three bites, and Patrice said—'

'Just get an ice cream,' I told her. 'It's fine.'

I stepped out on the deck and called Karli, hoping to get some more detail.

'So, he got too rough. And he kept going even when she said no. Did he hurt her?'

'Yes.' She sounded miserable. 'I have to go. The cops are here.'

I went back inside, my head spinning with questions. *How long did it take? Why didn't she scream? How could he do that, with cameras all over?*

Patrice had left my plate at the table when he cleared, probably to tempt me to eat something. Miranda was upstairs, the water running.

I lifted the fork to my mouth, then I stopped. 'Ricky,' I said.

'That's his name?' Patrice asked. 'The guy?'

'Ricky Come on Titty . . . DO NOT TAKE BOOKING. I think . . . No, I *know* – I'm ninety-nine percent sure I changed his name in the phone to Ricky Do Not Take Booking. Because he was incredibly rude, he thinks he's too good for the rules, and no one wants to see him, and he gets too rough with the ladies. And he tried to take his money back last time, with Ruby. I'm sure I changed it. I *think* I'm sure.' A sick feeling rose in my throat. *Did I forget to change his contact details?*

'I'm going to go take a shower.' I didn't need a shower. I needed to work it all out in my mind. *Are the cops going to shut us down now? What about Council – will they start up again with the resource consent? All those people who think we're dirty, who say sex work is all about violence and harm. Are they right?*

The hot water pummeled my body, and once I'd finished washing I turned around, letting the stream pound hard on my lower back. I leaned my forehead on the vinyl of the shower stall.

That motherfucker, I thought. *We were trying to provide a safe place.*

But it wasn't safe, was it?

I failed.

I stepped out of the shower and saw I had a missed call. I dialed Karli, dripping warm water on the floor.

'They got him,' she told me. 'Down the street, they picked him up. He's in jail.'

I exhaled. At least we could count on the cops. 'And we're going down to Wellsford, to see the medical examiner.'

'Wellsford? But that's an hour away! What's he doing way the hell down there?'

'Dunno.' Karli's voice was flat. 'He's out there doing another investigation. We need to see him now, tonight. They think if they can find signs of trauma . . . it's evidence.'

'Do you need me?'

'No.' This time she sounded more like herself. 'We've got this.'

'Okay,' I said. 'Please keep me posted. Is Piper okay?' *Stupid question.* 'I mean, as okay as she can be?'

'Yep. She's a strong girl. I'll call you when it's all over.'

I went upstairs and did the bedtime routine, reading Miranda a story about a king who wanted to trap all the soap bubbles in his palace. The king's plan didn't work. All his bubbles popped, leaving a sticky mess on the floor.

Turning out the light, I went down to the living room, where Patrice was strumming his guitar.

'I can't think,' I told him. 'I need to talk. I can't calm down.'

'Do you need to go out there?' he asked.

'I can't now. They're down in Wellsford, getting a medical exam.' Looking down, I realized I was wringing my hands. 'Did I do this, Patrice? Did I put this girl in *danger?*'

'The guy is an asshole.' He shook his head. 'That's it.'

'Ricky Come on Titty. No one wanted to see him, because he wanted it rough, and he was obsessed with women being skinny and young, and . . . *clean* somehow. Like, he always wanted to be their first booking.'

'Let's hope his jail cell is clean! How d'you like that, *connard*?'

I smiled, but I couldn't laugh.

'Come to bed,' Patrice coaxed. 'We can watch something stupid on Netflix, change your ideas.' I followed him, but I didn't bring my laptop. We lay there together in the dark, and Patrice rocked me until I fell asleep.

At one-thirty, my phone rang. 'We're on our way back,' Karli said. 'You want to talk to her?'

I ran my hand through my hair, trying to wake up. 'Yeah, I'll talk to her.'

'Hang on – I'll put you on speaker.'

'Piper? Are you okay?' *More stupid questions.*

But her voice was surprisingly strong. 'Yeah,' she said. 'I'm all right.'

'I am so, so sorry,' I told her. 'It's our job to keep you safe. And we let you down.'

'No, you didn't,' she said, 'and Karli really saved the day. She came in when he was still in the shower, and I was so scared – I couldn't move! She kicked him out, and then she called the cops. I was still shaking!'

A few more empty questions, a few more replies, and we ended the call soon after. Everyone was tired, and there wasn't much more we could say.

The next morning I was too sick to eat. And I couldn't stop thinking about the Batphone. *Had* I remembered to mark him as 'Do Not Take Booking'? It was months ago now. *Did Karli override it without telling me? Or did I just forget?*

When I got to the office I pounced on the phone, fumbling it in my hands so it fell face down on the concrete. I picked it up and the screen was a spiderweb of cracks.

That's when I started sobbing. I didn't care about the iPhone. The world was telling us we were doing something dirty and shameful, and maybe the world was right.

When the tears stopped I swept my hand across the screen and brought up the message history. There he was, 'Ricky'. I could tell it was him from the text conversation about a PSE booking with Piper. There were my notes in the contact: *Huge ego. Good looking, but he thinks he's God's gift. Too rough with Ruby in a PSE. Very rude. Tried to take back his money. Most of the girls won't see him, more trouble than he's worth.*

But on the contact itself, the name was just 'Ricky'.

So I did forget to write 'DO NOT TAKE BOOKING'.

I flopped back in my desk chair, heart sinking. *Or did I?* It was unusual to just have a first name in the contact, especially for a client who'd seen us more than once. He would be 'Ricky Respectful' or 'Ricky Giant Cock'. Never just 'Ricky'.

So there were two possibilities. Either I forgot to change the contact – or Karli overrode it, then deleted my note. And it wasn't hard to guess why. A girl crying uncontrollably, cops on their way.

The first thing they'd ask was to see was the phone. How would it look if the contact name said 'DO NOT TAKE BOOKING'?

She must have panicked.

I called Piper, but her phone went to voicemail. Then I called Diana at the NZPC, but she couldn't talk. Piper breezed in after lunchtime, apologizing for missing my call. 'I was with my therapist.'

'You saw your therapist today? That's great!'

She plopped down on the couch and opened her giant handbag, taking out various tubes and compacts, sorting out crumpled receipts and making a pile beside her. 'Yeah, we were already working on some of these things. From before. And I – I'm glad it happened to me, you know? Instead of one of the other girls.' She seemed entirely consumed with her purse.

'Because . . . you feel like you can handle it?'

'Oh, it's happened to me before. I'm used to it.' Her breeziness took me aback. *What's happened before?* I wanted to ask. *Getting held down? Getting forced?*

'And I want to come back to work! Karli said I'd have to wait at least a week, 'cause the doctor gave me meds for possible STIs, but I want to come back.' She opened her wallet and pulled out some notes. 'Look at my money!' She fanned out the cash and admired it. 'It's *so great* to have money. I've caught up on all my bills, my rent . . .'

She looked fine enough, but I hesitated. 'Well, as far as work goes, ultimately it has to be your choice.'

'You know what he said when he saw me? "You're so little," he said. "You're so tiny." *Fuck him!* I might be little, but he's an arsehole. And he can't take away my right to work!' She took a break from the contents of her handbag, leaning back on the couch to consider. 'He really loved me, you know. Even when he was holding me down, he said "I want you for longer." Can you believe it?'

'Well, you are very lovable,' I told her. 'But that doesn't mean he can violate your right to consent.'

'He thought he could!' She nodded vigorously. 'He said, "I can do whatever I want, I paid for it!"' She picked up her wallet again, unzipping a side compartment. 'Oooh, more money! Look, here's more money I forgot about!' She waved the notes at me then added them to the rest of her stash. 'I bet Karli I can earn two thousand five hundred in a week. Wouldn't that be amazing?'

She tucked her wallet back in her purse. 'So when can I come back to work?'

After our chat, she went out to buy makeup, and a few minutes later, Diana called back. When I told her about the altered contact name, she drew a sharp breath. 'No matter how much you want the money, no matter how much you want the booking, you've got to trust those instincts,' she said. 'And your off-siter needs to know it as well. You get a bad client in a restaurant, your server might get yelled at. You get a bad one in a booking, it can get a lot more dangerous. Well. I don't have to tell *you* that.' She paused. 'So what did she do, when it happened?'

'Well . . .' I hesitated. 'She's so small and he was on top of her. I think she went limp out of fear.'

'That happens a lot, actually. More than you'd think. Fight, flight, or freeze – most of the time, it's survival. It's like, *maybe if I don't fight back he won't kill me*. And what about the cops? How are they proceeding?'

'They've got him in jail. They're taking it really seriously. They got testimony from the victim *plus* Karli, and with the bruising they think they can prosecute.'

'Yes, yes, yes!' she cheered, but then her tone changed. 'That's great, but I have to warn you, it may all come to nothing. It could be a slap on the wrist and he'll be walking the streets next week. It's hard to get a conviction, even now.'

'But he left marks!' I protested. 'And Karli will testify! How could they not put him in prison?'

'It's better than it used to be,' she admitted. 'With sex workers, they used to just say she's a slut, so it's her fault. Now it's possible to convict, but it still isn't easy. People are so set in their ways.'

I hung up the phone, feeling like I'd walked through the looking glass. I'd lived my life as a well-spoken white woman. I'd always assumed the system would protect me, and if anyone hurt me, they'd be sent to jail. How naïve that seemed now, and how stupid. Piper had been held down, there was physical evidence, Karli backed up the story, and still: Diana thought he could get off because she was a sex worker. When you're in this business, society's safeguards don't apply.

Late that afternoon, Karli came in, her face looking gray. She lay on the couch with her phone and a notebook while I tapped at the calculator, each of us trying to work out the accounts for the previous day. The cops had taken the cash from the booking to analyze it for DNA, but that wasn't the problem. We were both in a fog, too stunned to add and subtract.

On the fifth try, we finally made the numbers work out, and Karli even cracked a faint smile. 'I knew those cops were straight up. When they nabbed him, he was crouching in the bushes, and he came out whingeing about how he paid for it. You know what the lady cop said? "You didn't pay to *force* a woman, mate." She was so great. At one point I started to lose my shit, and I said to her, "When do you give up? When do you stop fighting? For women to make money, for men to have intimacy, to stop all this shame around sex?"' She swiped at her eyes. 'I thought she'd tell me to get stuffed, but she didn't. She said "You *never* give up. Oh, *please* don't give up."'

I didn't want to upset her, but I knew I had to ask. If I didn't, it would poison our friendship.

'Ricky . . .' I hesitated. 'I could have sworn I changed his name in the Batphone to 'Ricky DO NOT TAKE BOOKING'. Did I forget to do that?'

Karli shook her head. 'No. You didn't forget.'

'Look,' I said. I took a deep breath. 'I want you to know. Just in case it's eating at you. I probably would have taken that booking as well. If it was a really slow day . . . I never would have thought he'd try something so fucked.'

She nodded, unconvinced – and I didn't blame her. Because I wasn't telling the truth. I was saying the words I thought she needed to hear, but I'd known that Rick was bad news. That's why I'd banned him. And even though Karli made an honest mistake, that wouldn't turn back the clock. We could never again say The Bach was completely safe, or that no one had ever been hurt. Like Diana said, Piper could have been killed.

Karli still looked miserable, so I tried to distract her. 'There were . . . what, *four* kids here last night? Your two boys, and Danielle's two girls? I think maybe we need to rethink the childcare thing.'

'But that was our *thing!*' Karli protested. 'To take care of the women, and have a safe place for their kids . . .'

'I wanted to offer free childcare, and I still do, but I think we should hire a nanny.' I looked at her square in the eyes. 'Do *you* think you can keep four kids and all the ladies safe at the same time? You're not Wonder Woman. How are you supposed to do that?'

That's when Karli's face crumpled. 'I was taking care of the babies!' she sobbed. I got up and hugged her, feeling her shake in my arms. Crying together would have been a relief, but my eyes were dry.

Instead, I felt a shuddering breathlessness, a razor wire binding my heart. I'd had that feeling before, when I was pregnant and Peter said *you broke us,* and *how could you do this,* and *I can't even look at you* and *you disgust me.*

I was scared. With everything that had happened in the past twenty hours, I was afraid of what would come next.

Chapter 13

Every time the Batphone buzzed with a new number, I braced myself to hear from the cops, or Council. Piper was violated in my motel, while she was working for me. Did that make me legally liable? Forget about legal, did that make me *morally* liable?

'Did you hear about the Warehouse in Dargaville?' Karli had the *Herald* spread out, her heels propped up on the desk. 'Someone robbed it at gunpoint; tied up the workers and bound them to chairs. Then they took off with a whole load of jewelry and watches and that.'

Gun violence is rare in small town New Zealand. 'Did they shoot anyone?'

'No, but I'll bet you those people are traumatized. It's not totally unlike Piper, if you think about it. Two guys pulled a gun while they were doing a robbery, but no one's taking the Warehouse to court.'

The Batphone buzzed. *Shit.* I looked at the screen.

Come to New Plymouth please.
It's so hard to find sexy as women who take it in the ass here

'*Ugh.*' I showed Karli the text. 'Doesn't your heart weep for him?'

'With a mouth like that, it's no wonder he can't get any action!' Karli wrinkled her nose. 'I wouldn't drive six hours for that.'

I shrugged. 'At least he said *please*.'

In the end, I did hear from the cops, when they came by to drop off the cash from the booking, after they'd finished their analysis.

'Sorry about that,' the cop said. 'It's how we do things. Could you just sign the docket right here?'

If Piper had given up at that point, I might have shut everything down. I couldn't feed my family with money we earned from her trauma. But after her one-week stand-down, she insisted on coming to work. 'It's my *right* to earn money!' she said on the phone. 'And do what I *want* with my body! Fuck that guy, he's got no say!'

So we got back to work.

The first thing I did was hire a self-defense instructor, a guy who Karli had known back in school. Greg was a tall, athletic Māori guy who seemed perfectly at ease in any setting – even a room full of sex workers. Up in Room 6 the next Friday, Karli set out two packets of cookies, and the girls traded stories as Greg got set up.

'Saw Adam the Awesome Dairy Farmer Tuesday,' Alicia bit into a Mallowpuff. 'He's such a sweetie! Had him for sensual, and d'you know what? He *really* just wanted a massage! Works hard on the farm and his legs were so tired.' She shrugged. 'He said, "If I'm gonna pay for a massage, might as well get a naked chick to do it," and you know what? He's probably right!'

'Ugh, you're lucky,' Ivy grumbled. 'I got a date with Nick Smelly Dick. Do they use soap in the shower, or just look at it? Do they actually even know what it is?'

'I didn't go through with one last week,' Sabra said. 'I had this guy Eric, and when he pulled down his pants there was a *lump,* like the size of walnut, right there on his groin, by his dick!'

'Eeeew!' Piper squealed. 'What *was* it?'

'Could have been a cyst,' Danielle offered. 'Or an inguinal hernia.'

'Whatever it was, I wasn't going there!' Sabra held up her hand, palm out. 'No, thank you! I put on a glove and gave him a hand job. He left with a big smile on his face, and I made him promise to go see his GP.'

'Don't worry,' I said. 'He's in the phone as Eric Lump on Crotch now. He can't come back till he gets it removed.'

Greg had finished setting up his white board. 'Ladies,' he said. 'Shall we start?'

'Remind me to tell you about Arjun Poppadom,' Alicia hissed at Piper with a nudge. 'He brought a whole bag of poppadoms into our booking!'

'I love it when they bring snacks.' Piper sighed, reaching for a handful of iced animal cookies.

'Ladies,' Greg repeated. 'We only have an hour, so d'you think we can start?'

'Sorry!' Alicia crossed her legs and tried to look serious. 'I'll be good from now on, I promise.'

'Okay.' Greg wrote three words on his white board and underlined them.

<u>MEN ARE PREDATORS</u>

'That's something I want you to take away with you today,' he said. 'We just are; it's a biological fact. So even though a man may *seem* quite reasonable, you've *got to be prepared* if things should go off the rails. Now. What should you go for, if he starts to get aggro?'

'His balls!' Ivy called out, from her chair in the corner. 'Smash him one right in the balls!'

'You'd think so, but it's not really true,' Greg explained. 'You've got to be real close to the guy to get him there, and if you're that close, he might grab your arms or pin you against the wall.'

I shot a look at Piper, but she seemed unfazed, munching on her small stack of cookies.

Greg held up his hand, fingers spread. 'You make *the claw,* like this. Fingers spread out and bent, you've got five points of contact, then you *rake* your hand into his eyes. Once you've injured his eyes, he's distracted, and *then* you can go for the balls.'

'What about weapons?' I asked. 'Like pepper spray?'

'You can't use it, unfortunately,' Greg said. 'Not here. Or your girls could get done for assault.'

'But what if it's not a weapon, necessarily? Like a screwdriver?'

'You'd have to prove that you had the screwdriver out anyway, like if you were doing a DIY project. You can't just keep one right there by the bed.'

Danielle raised her hand. 'I used to work in a mental health ward, and they taught us different ways to deal with a violent attack, depending on if you're standing or lying down. And if you're flat on your back, I think what you want to use is your legs.'

'Yes.' Greg pointed at her with his marker, then wrote STRENGTH IN YOUR LEGS on the board. 'Get your knees under him if you can, then push him with everything you've got. That's where your power is, as a woman.'

He turned back to face us. 'HIPS. That's another one.' Greg wrote it on the board. 'You're strong enough to birth a baby there, so you're strong enough to shove a man off in a pinch. If he's on top of you, jerk your hips *up* to chuck him off balance. If you can get out an arm, grab a bicep – *not* a fist. That's where the full strength of his blow is. Here, shall we practice?'

We split into pairs, and ran through some scenarios. I *think* we learned something – at least, I hope we did. There was an awful lot of giggling and some tossing of cookies.

After Greg's class, I kept the girls back, so we could talk about calling for help. I pulled out my phone, and noticed I had a missed call from Peter.

'It's clear we can't count on our phones,' I said, 'if it gets bad and you need to get help. If you have to unlock it, that's five or six taps, then pulling up the phone app and finding the number for the Batphone – it's way too much work. It's too complicated.'

'I know!' Piper burst out. 'And my hands were shaking *so bad* when it happened, I kept tapping the wrong thing and then I'd just have to start over.'

'That's not your fault,' I told her. 'It's *Rick's* fault. And my job is to make *fucking sure* it doesn't happen again.' I pulled out a black clip-on beeper. 'I'm putting a wireless alarm by the bed. You slam the button, and the beeper goes off on my belt – or Karli, whoever's in charge. One click and you're done. No more screwing around with your phone.'

'Also,' Karli chimed in. 'I found a child minder. She'd like to have a little bit of notice, so if you need her for a booking, try to let us know in advance. But she's at uni and she's living at home, so she's usually pretty available.'

'Sounds good to me!' Piper stood up, brushing the crumbs from her legs. 'But sorry, guys, I have to leave early. We're doing a party for my granddad tonight, and I have to go pick up the cake.'

When she left, the mood got more somber. 'She *seems* fine,' Alicia ventured, twisting her braid with one hand.

'Better than fine,' Danielle said. 'She seems cheerful.'

Ivy shook her head and stared at the floor. 'Yeah, but how *fucked* is it, he can do that to her, and she's not even that bothered 'cause it's happened that many times before?'

'Quite fucked,' Karli said, 'you're not wrong. But this is her way of dealing with it. And if we're about consent, and she wants to work, then we're not going to tell her she can't.'

That's true, I thought, *or that's what we're telling ourselves.* But Greg's words kept rattling around in my head: MEN ARE PREDATORS. Was it really enough to tell them where to park, to insist on politeness, to put in an alarm? The first time, it happened in seconds. If we got another bad client and the alarm went off, how would I even get there in time?

On the other hand, I'd had the right instinct about Rick. That's why I'd banned him from The Bach.

Once the girls left, I pulled out my phone and called Peter. 'I have Silas,' he said. 'Picked him up early from school. I gave him his meds, and—'

'What, *what?*' I cut in. 'It's three in the afternoon. He doesn't have his dose until bedtime!'

'Yeah, well.' I could practically hear the guy shrug. 'I wanted to see my son. And I thought I'd get the meds out of the way. So anyway—'

'We changed his dose,' I snapped. 'Did you know that? No, of course you didn't, since you haven't *seen* him for the past six weeks.

He's been having more seizures, so we changed up his meds. And now you've given him *the wrong dose at the wrong time.*'

'Hey, you wanted me to spend time with him, right?' Now Peter was getting annoyed. 'So I'm spending more time with my son. Why do you have to be such a *bitch* about everything?'

'I . . .' The Batphone was buzzing. 'I have to go. Let me know when you're bringing him back.'

I pulled out the Batphone, and saw a text from an unknown number.

Do u use condams baby

u do not with me

me very clean

We always use condoms. They protect your health, the health of the ladies, and they're required by New Zealand law.

Cn I have bj with no condm please

im really clean babe

'Jesus fucking *Christ,*' I muttered to myself. 'Did I *stutter?*' I took a deep breath, willing myself to find patience.

Can you call me, please? We prefer to talk to new clients over the phone.

The Batphone jingled its tune. 'Is this The Bach?' asked a man with a South Asian accent, and I felt myself tense. I know it wasn't fair – in fact, it was racist – but those women on Reddit were right. When men spoke with that accent, we could be pretty sure they hadn't learned about consent.

'Hi,' I said. 'What's your name?'

'I am . . . Sanjay.'

'Okay, Sanjay. Let me make something quite clear. *All* sexual contact with our ladies requires the use of a condom. That's both sex and oral. That's a *legal requirement,* and if I *ever* hear you try to push for no condom, you will be *permanently banned* from The Bach. Is that clear?'

'Yes, mam.' He sounded contrite. 'I didn't know this.'

'Well, now you do.' I listed the ladies who were available that night, recommending Alicia, because I knew she could handle him. Then I hung up the phone and I called her.

'He might try to ask for no condom,' I said. 'But I told him if he does, he'll be banned.'

'Cool beans,' she said, 'I can do it. I'll just pull out my phone and show him the pictures.'

'Wait,' I said. 'Pictures of what?'

'Gonorrhea sores on a penis. I've got some *real* juicy ones saved up! That usually calms 'em right down.'

'Okay, you're brilliant. I love that.' I sent Sanjay a confirmation. Three little dots, and then he replied:

Yes mam

Cn you ask her 3shorts suck ball kiss lips and boobs

oral with condam and shower

I sighed.

Yes, I'll ask. But as far as multishots go, it's at Alicia's discretion.

Then I put his name in as 'Sanjay 3Shorts Suck Ball WARNING'.

—

When Peter brought Silas back home on Sunday, he rolled down the window to talk. 'Got a delivery from Aussie to Fiji,' he said. 'Might be gone two months, maybe more.'

'Two *months?'* I repeated. 'Is it really that far?'

'The boat needs some work,' he said. 'Haven't seen her yet. And then we'll have to wait for a weather window. And I might spend some time up there, sailing around.'

'What about the kids?' I asked.

'What about them? If you want child support, I have to make money.'

'BUS!' Silas hollered beside me. 'BUS-ah-bus-ah-bus. WHORES!'

Peter backed up the truck and Silas yanked on my hand, pulling me away toward the house. 'BUS!' he declared. 'Bah . . . ah . . . baah . . .'

Peter leaned out the window. 'He's been doing that,' he said. 'He's been losing the "S" sound in "bus".'

Well, if you didn't fuck up his medicine dose, I wanted to snap, but there wasn't much point. I followed Silas back inside the house.

Miranda was on a quilt on the floor with Matisse, reading him a book about bugs. 'This is a spider,' she pointed. 'And that one's a fly. But flies can make maggots, and maggots are *gross.* Hi, Silas,' she said, looking up.

'HIIIIIII!' Silas crooned, making his way to the couch.

'Was that Dad?' Miranda put down the book, and Matisse seized it and shoved it into his mouth.

'Yep.' I sat down with them, and Matisse dropped the book, lifting up his arms to be held. I breathed in the smell of his fine, silky hair.

'Why didn't he come in and say hi?'

'I don't know, baby,' I told her. 'He says he's doing a delivery to Fiji, and he might be away for two months.'

'Two *months!* How many *days* is that?'

'Sixty,' I said, 'maybe more. He needs to fix the boat first, over in Aussie.'

'Where's *Fiji?'* she asked in despair.

I pulled out my phone and brought up a map of the South Pacific, holding it away from Matisse's sticky hands. 'About three thousand k's,' I said. 'Not too far. A lot closer than sailing to America!'

'Is the blue part the ocean?'

I nodded.

'But it's so *big!* What if he falls off the boat and he's drownded?'

'He won't fall,' I told her, reaching to give her a hug. 'Your dad's a very good sailor. I promise, Miranda.' I pulled back and looked her square in the eye. 'It's going to all be okay.'

But will it? Even with five girls on staff at The Bach, I still wasn't making a salary. I could pay the rent and the business expenses now, but at the end of the month, there was nothing. I was living on that business loan, and week by week it was just getting smaller. I knew that couldn't go on forever.

On Monday I checked in at the office, where Karli was engrossed in her screen.

'We got an email,' she said, 'from this submissive named Joel. He'll be in town for three weeks on business. He wants *everything.*' She picked up her notes. 'Sensual massage with teasing but no touch, then we're supposed to force him to wear satin undies. He wants chastity? Like, his dick in a cock cage? Plus cock and ball torture, and then *pegging!* Oh!' She clapped her hands. 'This is going to be *so much fun.* And you know? I even have the cock cage. Never did sell it, when I had my shop. I think it scared people away.'

'What do you think we should quote?' I read the email over her shoulder.

'Here.' She showed me a page full of notes. 'Six hundred a week is how I figure it, so eighteen hundred all up. And half of it's *ours!* I'm gonna meet him next week for a coffee, then we'll work out the details from there.'

On Tuesday I came into the office and was greeted by a text that came through in the night.

20 min multishot + anal

'He must have thought he was being direct,' I told Karli when I showed her. 'But warm me up a little bit, you know? Maybe start off with *hello.*'

'That's the thing about this business,' she sighed. 'Some of them are legit disgusting, right? But even when they get to the point, it sounds gross! They talk about us like a collection of body parts.' She pitched her voice low to sound like a man. 'Size six blonde please, long legs and big tits. *Pfff* – they wouldn't know a size six from a size eight waistline if it came out and bashed them on the head, but they've heard people say it in the movies or whatever, so they think that must be the best.'

But in the weeks that followed, they weren't all gross – and some of them tugged at my heart. Including one from a man called Charles:

> I'm a lonely old widower. The missus has been gone for five years now. I'm too old to muck about with those dating apps, they're just confusing. I'd like to meet a nice girl for a cuddle, and then we'll see what transpires.

Danielle met him at the door in a low-cut black dress, over turquoise and purple lingerie. 'Got him into the shower and I lathered him up,' she reported, 'then he lasted about a minute in bed. And we just cuddled! He told me about the nuts and the citrus he grows. We actually have some things in common – we talked about rock and roll and motorbikes. Charming guy!' she said. 'A real gent. A lot better than some of the *real* dates I've had.'

Phil was another new client:

> I'm a physics professor. Retired now, 65 years old. My wife has Huntington's Disease. She doesn't really know who I am anymore. Do you think I could see one of your ladies? And (sorry to ask) but could she possibly wear sheer black stockings?

I asked Piper, and she practically choked. 'Sixty-five?! No way, that's *so old.*'

'Yeah, but . . .' I paused, considering my words. 'Piper, you're *twenty.* Everyone's old to you!'

'And hairy,' she pointed out. 'And he'll probably smell like old man.'

'But think of it like this!' I smiled encouragingly. 'He's smart, he'll be grateful, plus he's experienced. It could be the best shag of your life!'

Piper hesitated. 'The *best* shag?'

I nodded. 'There's a lot to be said for years of practice.'

'All right then, I'll give it a crack.'

One hour later she was back in the office, flashing a hundred-dollar tip. 'Couldn't believe it,' she said. 'He was so *kind,* like what do you call it? Court . . .'

'Courtly?' I asked.

'Yeah, that one! He held up my towel for me after my shower, and dried me like I was a princess or something. Shit, *boys* these days.' She shook her head as I wrote out her pay stub. 'No manners. No respect! *And* no skills.' She lowered her voice to a whisper. 'We didn't even shag in the end, but he gave me the best head of my life.'

When Dan made contact, his text was a first.

> I'm white, 48, and I'm straight. I should say that I'm missing one leg below the knee – an accident I had on the farm. I've got an odd kink and I hope you can help. I love dressing up in women's clothes, but I find it hard to do my own makeup. Do you have anyone there who can help me?

'HELL, yes!' Alicia clapped when I told her. 'I LOVE doing other girls' makeup!' When Dan the One-Legged Crossdresser saw her, she spent an hour composing his face. 'Foundation, concealer and blush. Then I have this pearlescent highlighter I use to really bring out the cheekbones. I told him he needs to exfoliate though, if he wants to get a nice, healthy glow. And moisturize! ALL men are hopeless at moisturizing.'

When she was done I gave her a ride home, and I asked how she was liking the work. 'I love it!' she said. 'I'm so confident now, and I'm learning so much about bodies.'

'Like what?' I flicked on my signal, turning left off Riverside Drive.

'Dicks are all different! And bodies. I think it's good training for my nursing actually, 'cause— *Shit.'* She ducked down in her seat.

'What?' I glanced over, and saw her pressed down by the door. We passed a cop car at the side of the road. 'Alicia? What are you doing down there?'

'Nothing!' She bounced up again and smoothed back her hair. 'Just didn't want to get snapped by the cops.'

'Why . . . not?'

'Nothing!' She waved me off. 'Don't worry about it. It's just silly.'

I had to get back to The Bach for a booking with Ivy and Bruce 73, so I dropped it. I figured she was being dramatic.

At the end of the night Ivy pocketed her cash and pulled on her big, bulky army jacket. 'You know?' she said, 'you're the best boss I've had. No fines, no room fees, no bullshit. Plus I don't even need a man now. Not like I was looking for a boyfriend, but . . . we have needs. And now I get everything I need right here.'

The following morning when the Batphone rang, I was surprised to hear the voice of a woman. 'Hello,' she said, 'my name's Tammy. But I'm calling on behalf of my son. He's twenty-two now, and . . .

it's hard for him. Ethan's had cerebral palsy from birth, you see. He's in a wheelchair, and he's got sensory issues as well. He's on disability. He can't work and he lives at home with me. He's been saving a bit from his checks every week, and he'd like to see one of your girls. D'you have anyone there who would be sensitive? And not be offended? Or scared?'

'*Absolutely*,' I told her. 'Yes. I have the perfect woman in mind.'

I knew Sabra would be a great fit for this guy, and when I called her she didn't even hesitate. 'Of course I'll see him,' she said, 'that sounds fascinating. When's he want to come in?'

'Thursday night,' I told her. 'Early, like 6.30pm. I'll shut down a motel room, 'cause he can't use the stairs. His mum's driving him. She's the one who called up for the booking.'

Tammy's van pulled up right on time, and I watched her push out a young man in a wheelchair. He rolled over to Room 5 and knocked, and after thirty minutes, he wheeled himself out again.

When Sabra got back to the office, she was crying.

'Oh my God!' I jumped up from my desk. 'Are you okay? What *happened?*'

'Yeah,' she smiled. 'He just *touched* me. He was so lovely and kind. He said that I looked like an *angel*. He kept touching my hair, and—'

'Yes?' I sank down in my chair, relieved.

'He was so true, so . . . *real*. He actually touched my heart. I felt awful taking his money.'

Later that night, an odd text came through. Karli wasn't there, but I told her about it over the phone.

'New client,' I said when she answered. 'He wants to nurse.'

'He wants to nurse?!' she repeated. 'Like a *baby*?'

'Yeah,' I told her. 'I googled it. Apparently it's really a thing. It's called erotic lactation.'

'Oh my God.' Ice clinked as she sipped at her drink. 'I just *love* that this is my work call.'

'I know, right?' I sighed. 'But I don't think we can service him. None of the ladies have babies.'

'Could we *fake* it?' she asked. 'With a bottle?'

'No,' I shook my head. 'This guy wants it straight from the source.'

I went out to clean up Room 6, which hadn't been used since Ivy's booking with Bruce, toweling down the shower and changing the sheets. When I was finished, I fluffed up the throw pillows on the sofa, and I found a small card, peeking out from under a seat cushion.

I picked it up. It was one of our business cards. The front said 'The Bach, Northland's Finest Escort Agency'. I flipped it over. There was our motto, 'Ready When You Are', and our contact details, but they were crossed out. Beneath that, someone had written 'Ivy', with some numbers.

I pulled out the Batphone and checked. It was Ivy's personal phone number.

Chapter 14

'I just don't think I can do this anymore,' Danielle was telling me over the phone. 'Ever since what happened to Piper – I can't let it go.'

'Yes, but it's *not going to happen again.'* I held out my phone and glanced at my timer. Alicia was ten minutes into a one-hour booking with a new guy named Abhi South Asian. I'd told her to text me if he pulled any nonsense.

'Look.' I put the phone back to my ear. 'There's an alarm now. And Karli and I have new rules. For the madams, and for screening the clients.'

The conversation between Karli and me had been blunt. 'The number one rule between us, which can *never* be questioned or broken,' I'd told her, 'is if one of the madams puts DO NOT TAKE BOOKING on a client, then *we do not take that booking.* Ever.'

'We should tell him then, probably – shouldn't we?' Karli asked. 'So he fucks off and doesn't ring back?'

'No.' I shook my head. 'If he knows he's banned, he'll just change his name, and call back from another phone. Men are sneaky like that, especially the ones who don't like the rules. If a bad client is banned, then the girls are just busy. We tell him that no one's available.'

'Anyway,' Danielle was saying, 'I might come back later, but don't want any more bookings for now. Probably best if you take me off the website.'

'Okay,' I told her. 'I'm sorry to hear that, but it's always your call.'

My phone buzzed with a message from Alicia.

He wants a refund

What?? But you've only just started your booking. Why?

Cos he came 15 minutes into the hour. And now he wants a refund for the rest.

Tell him to call me please.

'Let me explain something to you,' I said when Abhi got on the line. 'When you book an hour with one of our ladies, you pay for an hour *of her time.*'

'Yes, mam,' he stammered. 'But I—'

'But *nothing.*' I told him. 'You had the choice to sit down like a gentleman. Have a cold drink, and maybe get to know her first. But *you* wanted to get right down to business. And now you want your money back? Forget it.'

'Yes, mam,' he said. 'I am sorry. But next time—'

'*Next* time, you can book thirty minutes with Alicia. If she'll even see you, which she probably won't.'

A text message came through and I hung up with Abhi, then tapped at my screen.

Can Sabra work on Saturday

I wanna experience bum bum

Excuse me? What's bum bum?

lol fuck the anus

If Sabra will see you, then Greek is $100 extra, at her discretion. And please don't use that kind of language with me. Sabra is a human being, not an anus.

Then I clicked out and set up a contact for him: 'NEW CLIENT Wants Bum Bum HANDLE WITH CARE.'

Alicia came down with the cash from her booking, her wet hair pulled up in a twist. 'He paid for it all, *and* he gave me a tip! Said to say sorry again.' She laughed. 'I think you scared him, Madam Murphy!'

'Just doing my job.' I filled out her pay stub. 'Scaring men's a big part of my job.'

My phone buzzed and I looked at the message.

Sex

Sex

Sex

?????

'And teaching them,' I added, as Alicia walked out the door. 'Since these guys' mommies never taught them any manners.'

Welcome to The Bach. Would you like to make a booking with a beautiful girl?

He didn't reply, so I put him in the contacts as 'NEW CLIENT Sex Sex Sex Weirdo'.

That evening, I texted Piper.

Do you want one more? Known client. White, 40s. Reasonably fit, average looks. Called Brad I Love You.

Why's he called that?

He wants the girl to say 'I love you, I love you' during sex. I don't think anyone's really said it to him before. Probably just lonely.

I'll take it. No problem. I'll make him think I'm in LOOOOOVE!

'But apparently she wasn't convincing enough,' I reported to Karli the next day. 'Because when she turned around to put her clothes on, he grabbed all the money and ran.'

'No way!' Karli gasped. 'He did a runner?! Where was she keeping the cash?'

'Out on the table, I guess. Obviously I paid her out. So instead of making $120, we lost it.'

'What a *dick,'* Karli said. 'I love you, my arse. No *wonder* he can't get someone to say it for free. But also . . .' She shot me a pointed look. 'That girl's a liability.'

'Piper? What do you mean?'

'I think she winds people up with the tiny and cute thing, so men try it on 'cause they think they can.'

'It's not her fault that guy held her down.'

'No, of course not,' Karli conceded. 'But she *does* something to men, with that baby doll act. Keep a sharp eye out. It could happen again.'

—

The next morning began with the usual chaos, ushering six kids out the door. At 6.30 I woke up Miranda and Titou, then went into the bedroom next door to get Silas. I opened the windows and sprayed air freshener around, then gently shook him awake. As always, he greeted me with a wide, sunny smile, delighted with the giant poop in his pants. I lay him on the bed and stripped off his pajamas, trying my best not to breathe. Moving quickly, I noticed how much weight he had lost: his knees now looked wider than his thin, bony legs. I cleaned him and bagged the nappy to hold in the smell, then eased him into his school clothes. His pants fell down now, since he'd lost so much weight, but Patrice had found braces in a two-dollar shop. I clipped them in place, and they made Silas look especially dapper. I completed the look with his ubiquitous gum boots – practical in the country, and they didn't have buckles or laces.

Before I walked him downstairs, I went to the six-year-olds' room. 'Get out of bed NOW and get dressed or there's NO SCREEN TIME!' I threatened, and instantly they shot out of bed.

'I wanna dress in the closet!' I heard Titou declare, then Miranda: 'YOU had it LAST TIME. And ANYWAY—'

Ignoring this, I helped Silas downstairs. Nova was dressed and packing her lunch, a container of couscous and raw, grated carrots.

'*Mais enfin, Nova,* don't you get hungry?' Patrice had Matisse in his lap, and he was feeding him a bottle. 'Take some protein. Take some *meat.*'

'No, I'm fine.' Nova put a slice of bread into the toaster. 'I don't get that hungry during the day.'

'Would you put in a toast for me?' Maris was hurtling down the stairs in a stretched-out man's T-shirt. 'Has anyone seen my uniform top? Ugh, *and* I have squash today!'

'*Pas mon problème.*' Patrice put down the bottle, patting Matisse on the back. 'You girls need to organise yourselves; you know this.'

'HONEY!' Silas tugged at my arm.

'Oh, whoops! Sorry, Silas.' I glanced at the clock. He had fifteen minutes before his school van arrived. 'I'll get you an Ensure.' Even though Silas was refusing most solids, we were trying to pack in as much food as we could. That meant high-calorie meal replacements, and purées fortified with butter and cream.

'I WANT THE SPINNIEST STOOL,' Miranda announced, sliding down the banister with Titou right behind her. 'And toast in the toaster with butter and salt please!'

I was crushing Silas's epilepsy medicine between two spoons. 'Don't you want an egg?' I suggested. 'Or some fruit?'

Climbing up on the stool, Miranda shook her head firmly. 'Toast in the toaster with butter and salt!' she repeated. I squeezed honey in the spoon, and popped the medicine in Silas's mouth.

'Could I have an egg?' Titou looked hopeful, climbing on the stool by Miranda.

I checked the pantry. 'Sure, but you'll have to go find it, because I think we used them all for the quiche last night.'

'But they're *hiding* their eggs!' Titou protested. 'Last time I found one in the artichoke bushes! *And* it had poop on it,' he finished, looking grim.

'*Plus* there's the rooster.' Miranda pointed out. 'C'mon, Titou, let's do it together.'

The six-year-olds ran out the sliding glass door, and I saw Titou grab a length of wood from the deck. 'But your . . . toast?' I asked lamely, a piece of bread in my hand.

'I'll take it!' Maris snatched the bread from behind me, popping it into the toaster. 'Papa, I *don't* have a clean uniform shirt and I don't know what to do.'

'Put it in the dryer.' He lifted Matisse and sniffed at his bum before putting him down on a quilt. 'That's what I did as a chef, when my pants weren't always so clean.'

Maris opened the fridge. '*God,* they ate all the hummus?! *Who* ate the hummus?'

Patrice got up for more coffee. 'It's in the kids' lunchboxes. *Qui va à la chasse perd sa place!*'

Maris rolled her eyes. 'What's *that* supposed to mean?'

'You lose your spot if you go hunting,' I explained.

'What's *that* got to do with *hummus?'* she protested dramatically, then flounced down to the laundry to deal with her uniform.

I looked out the window. 'There's your school van, Silas! Let's get you outside.' I walked him down the stairs, passing Matisse on his red quilt, who was smiling and chewing a rubber giraffe.

I got Silas in the van, then I went up to pack for work, at which point screams of panic rang out from the vegetable patch.

'LET US IN!' shrieked Miranda, sprinting for the sliding glass door. Right behind her, Titou was fending off Jabberwocky, brandishing his stick like a sword.

They both rushed inside, then I slammed the door shut just as Jabberwocky body-slammed the glass, all talons and furious beak.

'We got *six!'* panted Titou, shoving his hand in his pocket. It came away dripping with egg slime. 'Uh . . . maybe five?'

Miranda triumphantly pulled three eggs from her pockets. 'You should have been more *careful,* Titou,' she scolded. '*I* carried three, and—'

'Okay, that's enough,' I cut in. 'We have to get going. Do you want an omelet? Or scrambled or fried?'

—

I rarely had time to eat in the morning, just packing a couple of hard boiled eggs or some fruit in my bag. With six kids, a farm, the motel and the agency to run, Patrice and I split up our schedules with neurotic precision. Once Matisse was six months, we put him in crèche for half days, then divided the duties at home and at work. Three days a week, I ran The Bach and the motel, and Patrice did the housework, the cooking, and baby care. The other three days, I stayed home and did admin, while Patrice went to town and helped Debra with the motel. Sundays were supposedly our one day of rest, but with half-a-dozen kids aged six months to seventeen, 'rest' was a fanciful concept.

That day, it was my turn to manage The Bach, so once the younger kids had left on their school buses, I loaded up the teenagers and Matisse in my car.

By 9am, the kids were dropped off at their schools, and I arrived at the motel. I opened Room 6 and started warming the coconut oil, then brewed some coffee and sat at my desk. As usual, I opened my emails. *Bills . . . bills . . . disgruntled motel guests . . . more bills. Hello, what's this one?* I clicked on it and started to read:

> *I'm 29 years old, NZ European. I'd like to work for you, but I live up in Russell. It's a long drive, and I'll need to put my young son in care. Do you think I could just work two nights a week? Do you think I could make any money like that?*

'I don't know, darlin',' I said to myself, salting a hard-boiled egg.

I clicked on the photo she'd sent, and I practically spit out my breakfast. '*Holy* mother of God.' I swallowed and enlarged the photo.

Mia, as she would come to be known, was a classic PSWG. Except instead of being a size eight or a six, this woman was *tiny* – maybe a size two or a zero. She had long, white blonde hair and a symmetrical face, but with that figure she'd blow up the phones. I jumped on my laptop. *Absolutely you can work two days a week! And I think you'll make a lot of money. Would you like to come in for a chat sometime?*

Alicia had a prebooking with Ravi Bow Dick at 10am, and at 9.45 she burst in. *'Shit,'* she muttered, 'I'm late. And I still haven't put on my makeup!'

'That's fine,' I said, still engrossed in my screen. 'You've got perfect young skin! Just slap on some lip gloss and go!'

'But what about this?' she asked, and I turned. There was a large, purple bruise underneath her left eye, and the flesh there looked swollen and sore.

'Jesus,' I said. 'What happened? Did your boyfriend—'

'Yeah, nah.' Alicia flopped on the couch and dug around in her handbag, pulling out a tube of concealer. 'Girls are just bitches, you know?' Taking out a mirrored compact, she went about painting her face. 'Went out with me mates last night and got snapped, one of them called me a dirty whore. So I punched her in the face. Tequila, ay!' She folded her compact. 'You never know what might happen. And you know what's crazy?' She bent her head down, attacking her thick hair with a brush, then flipped it back up with a grin. 'Those girls are bigger sluts than I ever was! They're on Tinder every day, ho'ing it up!' She pulled her hair into a topknot, then snapped an elastic in place. 'Least I'm gettin' paid, bitches! Least I'm gettin' paid.'

The next day Mia came in for an interview, smartly turned out in a dark pencil skirt with a fitted knit top. 'I lived in the UK for years,' she explained when I asked. 'Born in Northland, but I married an English guy. We had a good life out there, too. He's a property developer – we had a real big house and flash cars.'

'So, what are you doing in Russell?' I asked. 'You've come a long way from Britain.' About an hour north of Whangārei, Russell's a gorgeous, beachfront community – but it's mostly full of tourists and retirees.

'He started hitting,' she said in a quiet voice. 'And I had to get my little boy away. I'm from Russell, and my mother helps out when she can. But now he's fighting for custody, 'cause he hates paying child support – it's not like he *wants* our son – and each time, I run up my legal bills. I'm $40,000 in debt right now, and he can just afford to keep paying. I can't.'

'No offense, but your ex-husband sounds like an asshole,' I said.

'You've got that right!' She gave a dry little laugh. 'But it is what it is, and now I need money. So, tell me, how would this work?'

'We'll take some photos of you,' I told her. 'Sexy pictures, in nice lingerie. No tattoos or faces, I edit that out. And if they come out as well as I think they will, you'll be making as much cash as you want.'

She hesitated. 'Is something bothering you?' I finally asked.

'It's not the sex that I'm scared of, that's easy,' she said. 'But what if they're not . . . satisfied?'

'What are you talking about?' I was incredulous. 'You're *gorgeous.* They're going to go nuts for you.'

She had a pained look on her face. 'I'm afraid I'm not tight enough. You know, after kids. And then they won't like what they get.'

'Believe me,' I told her. 'They'll *love* you. And they're gonna be *lucky* to book you.' But I couldn't help thinking about the men that we serviced – the ugly, the boring, the fat. How none of that affected their confidence – they still strode through the world and showed up on my Batphone with **which one is the best** and **can i have a discount** and **will she suck with no condom for free?**

And here was this beautiful, educated woman, offering the most intimate service, who any man would be *lucky* to be with. Worried that her pussy wasn't tight enough.

Women. We always know how to put ourselves down.

'I *hate* them,' Mia said, when I sent her the pictures. 'I look trashy and slutty and gross!' Karli had photographed her in a selection of lingerie, and I thought the pictures were dynamite. She was so thin that the angle of her hip bone was evident – and I knew it would drive the men wild. 'Can't we take some *classy* shots?' Mia complained. 'Like with me in a skirt, and an elegant blouse? Wouldn't *that* bring in the bookings?'

'Unfortunately not,' I said. 'Maybe in Auckland or Wellington that might fly, but the men here are pretty darn basic. Some of them *will* want to talk to you, and they'll love it – but most want to see what they're paying for.'

'So my tits and my ass,' Mia said sourly. 'They just want to see what they're buying.'

'Men are very visual,' I tried to explain. 'Most places make you sit in a lounge in your undies, or do a line-up whenever a client walks in. With us, you do one set of pictures and forget it. We put them online, and the bookings roll in.'

'I know,' she sniffed. 'I just wish it could be . . . you know, *classier.*'

'Think of it this way,' I said. 'It's a character you're playing. It's not you, and it's not your real name. You just play this role for two nights a week, then pocket your cash and go home.'

'All right then,' she agreed. 'Put the photos up. I'll be in Thursday at four.'

That Thursday she was visibly nervous, practically shaking as she entered the Dungeon. 'I wasn't sure what to wear,' she said, 'so I figured I'd dress like I was going on a date.' She had on a pale pink mini dress, with a white headband and white beaded heels.

'You're perfect,' I said. 'You look beautiful *and* classy. And I've booked you with only known clients. You've got Yann The Cute French Guy, Colin Easy Asian, Neil Vanilla, and Tony Quick to Come. They're all nice, safe guys, and Yann's actually *hot.* Like you might want to date him for real.'

'That sounds okay.' She smoothed back her hair with both hands. 'I'm just so nervous, you know?'

'There's no need to be. Just remember, it's only a boy.'

'Only a boy.' Her voice was unsteady. 'Okay. It's only a boy.'

Her first night, Mia made five hundred bucks, and drove home with a grin on her face. 'See you next Tuesday!' she sang as she sailed out the door. The only hiccup came the next morning, when the phone for motel reception rang.

'This is Doris,' a woman said, 'from Room 7. And I think you should know there's *prostitution* going on in your motel.'

'Really?' I kept my voice calm. 'And what makes you think that's the case?'

'The SEX! There was *so much* SEX! From next door – in what's that, Room 6? All night long, they were coming and going, and the *woman* was having *loud orgasms.*'

'So let me ask you,' I said, 'how much is too much?'

That took her aback. 'How much *what?*'

'Sex. How much sex is too much sex?'

'Well,' she made a choking noise in her throat. 'It was going on until one or two in the morning, I can tell you that much!'

'No, it wasn't,' I said.

'It most certainly was! How would *you* know?'

'Because the last booking was at eight o'clock.' I sighed. 'I know, because I made the booking. She's an escort who works in my agency.'

There was sharp intake of breath.

'And prostitution is a legal business in New Zealand,' I told her. 'And she finished at nine, so . . . maybe invest in some ear plugs?'

Click. Doris hung up the phone.

'A new girl made contact,' I told Karli. 'Or *woman,* really, since she's about 40.'

'Oh yeeees?' Karli waggled her fingers in delight. 'PSWG?'

'No,' I said, 'not at all. But there's something about her. She's Māori, with a pretty face. Long legs, and massive, big boobs. She hasn't got the world's flattest tummy. And she's *totally* covered in tats.'

'Kids?'

'She's got two, she told me. One of them's actually a teenager, and the other one's around seven. And she's already picked out a name, because she's worked before. She wants to be called Tonya.'

'So what's the problem?'

'I don't know . . .' I considered. 'There was just something off with the vibe.'

What Tonya had actually said in her interview was that she couldn't get enough sex. 'I'm pansexual,' she announced. 'I love *everything* in bed. Kink, fetish, tie-and-tease, you name it. I just love men's bodies, you know? All bodies, actually. Women's, too. Really, I just love to have sex.'

'So when d'you think you might be available?' I asked, pulling out a schedule.

'Anytime, really. Day and night. And I'll see all sorts. Ugly ones, hairy ones, fat ones . . . even last-minute ones, 'cause I only live ten minutes from here.'

'Good to know,' I said, but that worried me. All the women had *some* kind of boundary. Tonya seemed too eager to please.

But she wasn't lying about her kink experience, and soon she was taking more challenging clients. Randy Scarred had an old, ragged wound from his groin down his thigh, a long line of twisted red skin. When Sabra didn't pick up her phone I called Tonya, and the scar didn't faze her a bit. 'I've worked as a caregiver,' she told me, 'at hospice. Believe me, I've seen a lot worse.'

One night, I was working alone in the Dungeon when a soft-spoken American man called up. 'Do you . . . do you know what ASFR is?' he asked.

'I think so,' I said. 'Is that when people listen to whispers?'

'Uh . . . no, not that. Can I send you a link?'

'I think he wants you to be an android somehow,' I told Tonya once I'd seen the web page. 'It stands for Alt Sex Fetish Robot.'

'Oooh, that's a new one,' she said, perking up. 'How does it work?'

'I think you just lie there, like on a massage table. Just limp, and you let him . . . manipulate you.'

'Sounds *hot,*' she said. 'When's he want me, eight-thirty? Sure, I can get there in time.'

'I booked Tonya with Wes Kinky Childhood Trauma,' Karli told me, the next week in the Dungeon.

'Haven't heard of him,' I said. 'Who's that?'

'He's new. It all happened on Tuesday. We were texting back and forth all day long. He said he was sexually abused as a child, so anything intimate triggers his PTSD. He wanted to see a professional, and try it with a blindfold and earplugs.'

'And?'

'I thought he might like the gimp hood. You know, the one from my shop. Tonya took the booking, and it sounds like it really worked for him. Like, he was in tears by the end.'

'So maybe I was wrong about the vibe,' I said, 'if Tonya's our new in-house kink specialist.'

'It's not just the youngest and the thinnest,' Karli shrugged. 'Sometimes, it's about being *kind.*'

Despite all our progress, and our growing team, Karli was pulling away. She started closing up early on her days, then going home to have dinner with family. 'You can't do that,' I said. 'We're open till nine. What will clients think, when we don't answer the phone at eight-thirty?'

She shrugged. 'I don't know. And anyway, the Batphone was dead. What am I supposed to do, just *sit* there?'

'You could reach out to some of our regulars, see if anyone's wants to come in. Work the phones a little, flirt with the men. See if we can get them interested in a booking.'

I couldn't say much to convince her, though. I think she thought The Bach would be a fun little laugh, an easy way to make a thousand a week. But then one day, the cops got involved. And she saw that sex work could also be dangerous.

One day I came in and looked at the logs, and saw Karli had made zero bookings the day before. She'd hired the babysitter to take care of her sons, then she'd closed up the office at seven – leaving me a $60 bill for the sitter.

'What's this about?' I held up the scheduling sheet. 'Not even *one* booking all day?'

'What do you want me to do?' She threw up her hands. 'They wanted a white girl. And Alicia was on, but she's ghosting. I can't pull a girl from thin air. And I can't force the clients to call.'

'But if they don't call then I can't pay you. And we can't know if they called if we're closed! Look.' I took a deep breath. 'I think we have to structure this differently. Instead of a flat weekly pay, I'll pay you a quarter of the take on the days when you're working, plus a hundred-dollar bonus if you clear a grand. So, if you hit a thousand a day, you're actually making *more* money. But if there's no booking, we both take the hit.'

She thought about this. 'You've changed, Antonia.' She looked down at her long, sparkly nails.

'Yeah.' I nodded. 'I probably have. But I have to make sure we survive.'

I could tell Karli resented the change, but it made all the difference. At the end of July, when I'd paid the bills, there was money left over in the bank. *Did I forget to pay a big invoice?* Rent was covered, utilities, water, our ad fee at New Zealand Girls . . . and there was still money left in the account. I pulled up the banking site on my laptop. And for the first time, I paid myself a salary.

That night, I was stirring a pot of chili on the stove as the family swirled all around me. 'NO FAIR!' Titou yelled. 'That's the spinny stool!! You got the spinniest stool!'

'I got here first!' Miranda spun herself around on the best kitchen stool, though they both looked identical to me. 'And you got it for breakfast so I get it for now!'

Matisse was now a chonky, eight-month-old baby, in a white knit cap with little ears sewn on the head. He was squeezed in his big safety seat on the counter, gumming a hunk of baguette. He watched his two spinning siblings with wonder, dribbling wet clumps of bread down his front.

'WHORES!' Silas yelled out from the couch. 'HONEY!'

'Hang on!' I called out. 'I got it!' I lowered the heat on the chili and whipped out some peanut butter and bread. Peanut butter and honey sandwiches were the one solid thing that Silas could still eat, and we tried to feed him as often as possible.

Once I had Silas in front of a sandwich, I turned back to my chili and tasted it. 'Why don't you guys go feed the chickens?' I said. 'Go see if you can find any eggs.'

Miranda crossed her arms over her chest. 'But what about Jabberwocky? He tried to *get* me last time!'

'Just use a stick,' Titou boasted. 'I'm not afraid of a *bird*.'

'I'm *not scared.*'

'Are *so*. *I'm* getting the eggs.'

'ME FIRST!' Miranda launched herself at the sliding glass door.

'RACE YOU!' howled Titou, dashing out right behind her.

I stirred the pot. In that moment of quiet, it hit me: *I bought this meat and these beans with my pay from The Bach. The tomatoes and the spice and the onions. The wine in the glass that's beside me. My business is feeding my family.*

Peter had been gone for a month already, on his delivery from Australia to Fiji, and his support payments were infrequent and small.

But that didn't matter. *I can support us, with this agency I started from scratch.*

I know what the world thinks about prostitution. But I thought about Sabra and Ivy, who'd finally caught up on their bills. Mia had just hired a custody lawyer. Alicia had moved into a flat. Yes, something awful had happened to Piper, but she was pressing charges. She was fighting back.

I searched my heart, and I tried to find shame or regret. But I couldn't. It just wasn't there.

'You're not going to *believe* who made contact,' Karli said, the next time I checked in at the office. She was practically buzzing with glee. 'Look at this girl.'

She clicked on the file attached to an email from someone named Livia. And up popped a photo of the most beautiful woman I'd ever seen in New Zealand. It wasn't just that she was slender, long-legged and tall. She had exquisite bone structure with high, sculptured cheekbones, the kind of thing you'd expect on a runway in Paris, not in small-town Whangārei. Full breasts and hips, a perfectly flat tummy. And the kind of striking green eyes that can trap you.

'She offers Greek!' Karli squealed, unable to contain her excitement. 'And get this . . . she has a BABY!'

'No!' I couldn't believe it. It was all too good to be true.

'Yep!' Karli snapped her fingers three times in the air. 'Erotic lactation, baby. It's a brand new extra at The Bach! Thank you, whore gods!' She clasped her hands toward the Dungeon ceiling. 'You have blessed us, though we don't deserve it!'

'I'd just like to get back to work,' Livia said, when she finally came in for a meeting. 'But it's not easy with a baby, you know? It's complicated. I need to be able to make my own schedule.'

Livia was even more gorgeous in person. I shuffled my forms and tried not to stare. 'You've got that here,' I told her. 'A flexible schedule, one hundred percent. Every booking is your choice to take.'

'That's great.' She breathed out. ''Cause my husband's just training as a locksmith, and his pay packet's quite low. So everything's been really tight.'

'Will you keep it secret from him?' I asked. 'Working here?'

'What? Of course not!' She laughed at the thought. 'I tell him everything. He supports me, if I want to do this. And where I was working before . . .'

She trailed off, and I waited.

'It was dairy farming. A pretty good one too, but each day it just broke my heart. They'd induce the cows, so they gave birth to these tiny baby calves. And they'd just get put in this pile, and get killed at the end of the day.' She shuddered. 'But there are *live baby calves* shivering in the rain, standing on dead calves, waiting to be killed. And I just would cry about that every day. So anyway . . .' She waved her hand, casting the memories away. 'That's probly more than you wanted to know. But what I mean is, *that* work was degrading. *That* work felt wrong to me. But this? I'm sure I can do it.'

'I'm sure you can, too.' I looked down at my lap, thinking how I might broach the subject. 'Since you have a baby . . .' I started, 'we've had an odd request. There's a guy down in Auckland who . . . is interested in erotic lactation.'

'Erotic lactation?' Livia blinked. *'Oh,* you mean breastfeeding. Like with a man.'

'Would you consider offering it?' I asked. 'I mean, as an extra. All the money would just go to you.'

'Sure, that's no problem!' She shrugged. 'I mean, as long as I can save enough for my son. My husband's done it before, just to try. Is it really that popular?'

I held up my hands. 'Couldn't tell ya. To be honest, I learn new things every day!'

Livia's photos came out exquisite, no surprise to Karli or me. I didn't need to retouch a thing – her skin was flawless, and she had no tattoos. My favorite was one in a red basket thong, with a red-trimmed halter top and matching high heels, her bum in the air on a bed.

'But that's not the one that the clients are noticing.' Karli pulled up our website. 'It's *this* one.' She clicked on a photo with an odd composition, Livia on her back on the bed. She was wearing a plain pair of black undies, and she was covering her breasts with her hands. 'See the rib cage?' Karli pointed with a pencil. 'She's kind of sucking her air in, and her rib cage is so obvious?'

'It's not the prettiest one,' I said. 'It actually looks kind of weird, like she's starving.'

Karli sat back in her chair, chewing the tip of her pencil. 'That's what they love,' she said. 'Swear to God. I sent out that picture and they went *ballistic.'*

'Pretty, skinny white girls,' I said.

'Yeah, but it's *more* than that. They want them delicate looking, and fragile. That's why Piper does so well, and now Mia.'

'You'd think they'd want a woman with meat on her bones. I get the slender thing, but don't they want boobs?'

'Not necessarily.' Karli shook her head. 'I think they want a girl who makes them feel big.'

'Should I buy myself a wedding ring?' Piper was stretched out on the couch, waiting for her booking with Gordon Nice Belly.

I looked up from my laptop. '*No.* Why would you do *that?* Save your money for something useful, like going to college, or buying a house.'

'It's just . . .'

'What?'

'It's not about having a sparkly ring so much. It's more about how people treat me. Like when I go to WINZ, right? And I'm little and cute and so young, with a child – *plus* I'm Māori – then they just treat me like *nothing*. Like some Hori teen who got preggo too young, and they might as well chuck me in the bin. But if I dress nice, with jewelry and stuff, and I do my makeup, then they start taking me seriously.'

'Ah.' I took a breath. 'Hadn't thought of that. That sucks that you have to deal with that.'

'That's okay,' she shrugged. 'Least I'm *buying* my jewelry, instead of—'

I gave her a sharp look. 'Instead of *what?*'

She sat up on the couch and leaned in. 'Okay, I probably shouldn't be telling you this, but it's juicy goss and I can't resist.' She paused for dramatic effect. 'D'you know the Dargaville Warehouse that was robbed last month?'

'Yeah . . .'

'*Alicia's boyfriend was one of the robbers.* And he's keeping his share out at her flat! Like, diamonds and watches and things!' She cocked her head. 'Now I think of it, maybe I could get *him* to sell me a ring. I mean he's got to get rid of it somehow.'

'Do *not* buy a stolen ring off Alicia's boyfriend. Jesus, that explains why she's not picking up the phone. And why she didn't want to get snapped by the cops.'

'I know, right? Makes sense.' Piper jumped to her feet. 'Well, gotta go! Gordon Nice Belly and me have a date.'

—

Mia was booked solid on the nights she came in, taking home five or six hundred each time. 'I took my son shopping for trainers,' she said, after her first couple of months at The Bach. 'I told him he could have anything he liked. I've never been able to do that before.'

Livia got as much work as she wanted, fitting it in around her baby's schedule. 'I'm so much more confident!' she sang out, wiggling into a white leather miniskirt. 'All these men telling me I'm beautiful and gorgeous all the time. But d'you know what the best part is?' She shook her breasts into a tight floral halter top. 'This work has released me from the daily grovel!'

'The daily . . . grovel?' I repeated. It was an odd choice of words.

'Yes, you know – just the worrying, all the time. And thinking about money. I can think about *other* things now! Like yoga, and going on a bike ride with family. *And* I took everyone to the dentist. It's so expensive to go, before it wasn't even a priority. And it feels so good, to take care of our teeth.'

Our pig-hunting bush woman Ivy was still with us, and by August she was coming in for whole days at a time. She liked to sit in the Dungeon and wait for her clients, next to a pile of flax leaves. She'd pass the time in deep concentration, weaving kete, traditional Māori flax bags. 'Keeps me busy,' she said, 'then I flick 'em on TradeMe. But only if they're perfect. If they're not, I won't sell them.'

She was creative in other ways, too. One day she brought in a set of black leather lingerie, that she'd designed and sewn by herself. 'I want to take new photos with these on,' she announced. 'It's more my style than any of that lacy shit.'

The new photos were incredible, her confidence radiating out of each frame. We showed them to Bruce 73, and he just about lost his mind. 'She's my heavy-metal angel!' he raved to us over the phone.

'Did you see this?' I showed Karli the message. It was her day to manage, but I was checking the phone. She seemed distracted, poring over a textbook called *Bookkeeping Made Easy.*

'Hmm?' she asked, looking up.

'What's that you're studying?' I pointed at the book. 'It would be *amazing* if you learned about bookkeeping actually. Do you know how much I pay our accountant? I could pay *you* inst—'

'This?' She marked her page and closed up the book. 'It's more for my husband. You know, with his business.'

'Oh,' I said, frowning. 'Okay.'

At the end of September, Ivy abruptly disappeared – and my calls went to voice mail. 'It's probably drugs,' Karli said when I told her. 'It usually is, when they ghost us like that.'

'She said she didn't *do* drugs!' I held up a woven flax square. 'She *made* this for me! Said I was the best boss she's ever had.'

Karli shot me a look. 'You do realize that everyone lies about drugs? What's she going to say, "Yes, Madam, I *do* like to get high on P"?'

I put down the square. 'No . . . I guess not. But I really *liked* her, goddammit.' And of course, this was what Lacey had warned, back at the very beginning. *The whole business is built on lies. Illusions and lies. Your clients are lying to their partners. The girls are lying about their identities. And everyone's paying in cash.*

'Anyway,' Karli said, 'I won't ghost you. But I do need to give you some news. I think it's time for me to move on from The Bach. Spend some more time with my boys.'

'You're *quitting?*'

'I'll give you four weeks to find a replacement. But yeah, I think this place has changed. You've *definitely* changed.'

She was right about that. Because now that The Bach could pay all its bills, and I could draw down a salary, we had a profitable business on our hands.

And yes, I had changed. Because I wasn't just a recently divorced mother anymore, struggling to support a family on my own. Sure, I was all those things, but now I was something else, too: I was a real, live pimp.

Chapter 15

ESCORT AGENCY MANAGER

The Bach, Northland's premiere escort agency, seeks a manager. Known as 'The Ethical Brothel', we pride ourselves on operating a high-end, discreet and professional business, and providing a supportive environment for our workers.

As manager, you will work 10am until 10pm and often later, three days per week (Monday, Wednesday, Friday.) Your responsibilities will include:

- Promptly responding to client calls and texts
- Calling escorts into work
- Supervising bookings: ensuring girls are prepared comfortable and safe
- Ensuring service rooms are clean and topped up with supplies

- Cleaning rooms between bookings
- Working social media to promote the business.

The successful candidate will have:

- Excellent oral and written skills
- A friendly disposition
- A talent for sales
- An open mind with regard to sexuality and sex work
- The desire and ability to speak to the media
- Fluency with social media (Instagram, Snapchat, Twitter).

The Bach is a new company (founded January 2017) and we are growing steadily. This is a commission-based job with performance bonuses and plenty of room to expand your earnings.

'I'm gender non-binary,' Wren said when I met them. 'I use they/them pronouns. Do you think that will freak people out?' They'd come to their interview in a clean T-shirt and jeans, short hair combed close to their scalp. Their face was chiseled and delicate, and I'd just assumed they were queer. But *gender non-binary?* That was a new one. (Remember, this was 2017.)

Seeing the confused look on my face, Wren jumped in to explain. 'Sex is the bits that you're born with, but *gender* – how we identify as male or female – is a performance. I don't take either side. I move in between.'

'And so are you . . . gay?' It probably wasn't legal to ask that, but this wasn't an ordinary interview.

Wren laughed. 'My partner's assigned male at birth, but she's transitioning female. So yeah, you might say it's complicated.'

'Well . . .' I considered. We were up in Room 6 on a quiet afternoon, and I'd just finished explaining the madam job. 'I have no problem with any of this. I have a close friend who's trans and I grew up in San Francisco. I'm about as open-minded as you can get with this stuff. But this is small-town New Zealand. I'm not sure how the ladies will take it.'

'Yeah.' They looked down at the table. 'That's why I've been out of work for a year. This town doesn't know what to do with me. Plus, I was born in the States, and raised up in Canada. So I'm an outsider that way as well . . .' They trailed off.

'And before that you worked as an actor, right?'

'Yep. I write and perform when I can.'

'And also as a . . . dominatrix? Is that what you said in your email?'

Wren twisted their lips. 'Yeah. I do that now and then. And I've never managed a brothel, but domming is all about consent. And keeping things safe. Which I figure is a big part of the job, right?'

I nodded. 'Absolutely. I'm just not sure what the girls will think.' With the exception of Mia, who had lived abroad, all of our ladies were from Whangārei. Of course there were gay people here, and very likely trans people as well. But there were also about two dozen churches, many of them evangelical. There were hardly Pride parades storming the streets. From my experience, most openly queer people in New Zealand lived in the cities.

Wren seemed so cool and collected, but now I heard a tremor in their voice. 'The women might surprise you. This is a place of no judgment, where we can all be ourselves. Maybe that'll extend to me, too?'

They had a point. 'You know what?' I said. 'There's one way to find out. If you want the madaming job, it's yours.'

'Awesome,' Wren said. 'I'll take it. Only "madam" is . . . kind of femme for me. Is there another title I could use?'

I thought about that. 'When you're managing this place, I'm usually not here. And you're the one who's in charge. So why don't we call you . . . Boss Wren?'

They grinned at that. 'Boss Wren,' they repeated. 'I like it.'

'Then we've got a gender non-binary, North American dom on the team,' I said. 'Welcome to The Bach. I'll tell you one thing about this job: it's *never* boring.'

'Can my sister come in for an interview?' Livia asked on her next day at work.

'You have a sister?' I said. 'Well, *shit,* is she as gorgeous as you?'

'I think so,' Livia nodded. 'She's fairer. With blue eyes, and dark curly hair. Well, she's bleached it at the bottom, but it's dark on top. She's a little bit wilder than me.'

'And she needs a job?'

'No, she's *got* a good job. She's an anesthetic technician, like for surgeries and that. But she has a lot of student loan debt, and once they take that out she's left with like twenty dollars an hour. Plus she's on her feet eleven hours a day. I think she's wanting a change.'

The next day at five, Tara perched on the couch, a tall, curvy woman with masses of multicolored curls on her head, from platinum, to bronze, to a deep, rich mahogany. Elegantly dressed in a black leather skirt and trim matching crew neck, she put on a pair of wire-rimmed glasses to examine our paddles and riding crops. 'I *love* BDSM.' She gave a mischievous grin. 'I've played with my husband for years, and I think I could do it for money.'

'We can help you with that,' I said. 'We just hired a professional dom as a manager, in case you ever need any tips. But tell me – Tara, right? That's what you want to be called? What makes you want to work at The Bach?'

'The *money*.' She ran her hands through her curls. 'I knew my sister was earning heaps here, but then she showed me her pay stubs. And I went, *holy crap,* have you counted how much money you've made? And she said no, she just kept putting it in the safe. So I went and added it up.'

Tara slid her glasses down her nose, then peered at me over the top. '*My God,* I told her. You're on track to earn more than ninety grand this year! And you're working ten hours a week! So what the fuck am I doing at hospital? All that training, for twenty dollars an hour!'

'That's messed-up,' I agreed. 'They don't pay you enough.'

'*No,* they don't. And the nurses are bullies. Plus they say I have an attitude!' She flicked her hand in annoyance. 'But honestly, when they're putting the line in wrong, how am I supposed to *not* say anything?'

My phone buzzed with a text from Bruce 73.

Madam Murphy, will you please ring me for a chat?

Ignoring him, I handed Tara some forms. 'Here's the basics on how we run things, plus the prices for each of our services. You only do what you're comfortable with – Greek, fetish, tie and tease – all that's extra. And let me know when you can take pictures!'

'Oh, I can't wait!' Tara stood up and collected her bag. 'This'll be *heaps* more fun than surgery!'

I showed her out, and my phone buzzed again.

How old is Mia and what nationality

Can I eat her pussy and her arse before I fuck her 😉

Sighing, I sank into my chair. *Don't blow up his phone,* I reminded myself. *Educate the guy, don't castrate him.*

Please don't talk that way. Firstly, you'll need to be a gentleman and respectful if you want to come to The Bach. But to answer your question, Mia is 29 years old and NZ European. Yes you can perform oral on her, but rim jobs are $50 extra, at her discretion. So you can ask. Nicely. 💋

Then several more messages popped up on my screen:

Hi ivy what's yur cheapest price

Ivy is no longer with us, but the lovely Livia is! And Mia is available on Thursday. Our least expensive booking is a 30-minute sensual massage, $120. Or a 30-minute GFE for $180. 💋

I could be interested in half an hour.

Would you be keen to do some lines of mdma and fuck?

No, The Bach is a drug-free establishment. If you mention drugs to me one more time, you will be permanently banned.

Any no condom?

No.

By the time I finished dealing with that nonsense, I'd forgotten Bruce 73. He'd texted again.

Are you available Madam?

Whoops! I'm so sorry. What can I do for you, Bruce?

I'm such a damned fool, such an old silly fool.
Do you think you could meet with me?

I'm sure you're not foolish. I can meet you. The cost will be $100. I'm free tomorrow at 10 if that works. I'll be the lady in black!

I wouldn't let him come to the Dungeon, of course. I told him about a bench I knew, under a tree by the river.

I'll be there. Grey hair with a checked blue shirt,
silly old fool Bruce

He actually turned out to be reasonably handsome, with grey hair cropped short, and laugh lines crinkling the corners of his eyes.

'It's Ivy,' he said when I joined him. 'I'm sorry, Madam Murphy, and I'm *really* sorry now, but I broke the rules.'

'And did what?'

'I started seeing her privately. It was *her* idea, she said she would give me a discount, but I ended by paying much more.'

I thought back to that card that I found in Room 6. *I should have known this would happen.* Out loud, I said, 'What do you mean?'

'It was smaller lots of money at first, a thousand to stay over all night. Then I bought her a new truck.'

'You bought her a *truck?*'

'She said hers wasn't safe! And she needed it to drive out and see me in town. One day I paid her a thousand for an overnight, and she came back and said she was robbed! So I—'

'No you didn't.'

'I did! I went straight back with her to the bank machine, and took out another thousand! Then she wanted her daughter in private school, and I've always put a value on education. So I paid her daughter's tuition.'

'You paid her *tuition?* How *much?*'

He let out a long, shaky sigh. 'Twelve thousand. She said we were in love . . . and I believed her. You know how it is, or maybe you don't. We were intimate. It felt so *real.* Then I rang up the school, when the last payment was due, and they'd never heard of the girl.'

'So she just took the money.' Bruce nodded. 'How much is she into you for?'

'Fifty thousand,' he murmured. 'Or thereabouts. More than I can afford to give up. So what should I do, do you think?'

'You should block her,' I said. 'Now. Block her number. Block her on social media. If you don't, she'll keep coming back for more.'

'But it's been *ages* since she asked for money!' he said. 'More than a week, at least. What if it could have been something? What if she just wants to talk?'

'Bruce.' I tried to sound gentle. 'What we sell at The Bach is a fantasy. When you thought it was love, she was doing her job. You should never have seen her privately, but you know that. And you're not going to get that money back. But right now, you need to protect yourself.'

'I know.' He took out his wallet, and pulled out a hundred-dollar note. 'I just thought we might be together, you know? And I wouldn't end up so alone.'

'You *charged* him to talk?' Wren asked, back at the Dungeon. 'After she stole fifty grand?'

'You're new at this.' I held up my phone. 'You have no idea how much men ask for. And how many want to chat up the madam. See? Look at this.' I showed them my most recent text exchange with a client we called Jim Take No Crap.

What're the chances of seeing Livia for $100?

Zero.

Daaaaaaamn.

The phone buzzed again.

Does it get cheaper if iv been once b4??

'What would you do with that?' I asked Wren. 'Remember, we never bargain.'

They took the phone and tapped at it, a wicked little smile on their lips. 'How's this?' They gave me the phone.

Does the dentist get cheaper after you've had a cleaning?

Depends how many teeth they have 2 clean . . . thot id ask . . . sorry

There's no discount. Ever.

'You know what?' I said, pocketing the phone. 'I think you're a natural.'

Robyn came in at the end of October, in tight jeans and knee-high black boots. At forty-five she was older than most of our girls, but with her thick black hair and long, slender legs, I knew we could get her some bookings. 'I need to save up,' she said, 'to get away. My partner . . . he's been getting real rough. But whatever I earn, it's got to be cash. That way he won't see it in the account.' She leaned back on the couch and rolled out her neck, her movements slow and considered.

'Are you a dancer?' I asked.

'What?' She shook her head. 'Not me. No, I train German Shepherds, and other big dogs. That's why I live way out in the country, so I can work with the breeder. I'm also a trained massage therapist. D'you think that would be useful at this job?'

'Are you kidding?' I said. 'It's all agriculture here. We have *tons* of farmers who need a massage.'

Peter had come back from Fiji in September, but then he took more deliveries, and he'd only seen the kids once or twice. Then suddenly, one day my phone buzzed with a text:

I can take both the kids for a week starting Sunday.
My girlfriend can help me with Silas.

Nice of you to join us, I thought to myself, then I called him and made the arrangements. 'Silas needs three Ensures a day to keep up with his calories,' I explained. 'Then I blend up what we're having for dinner. Add cream if you've got it, or a big chunk of butter. He's been getting way too skinny. I'm worried.'

'So what about *food?'* Peter wanted to know. 'What happened to peanut butter and honey?'

'I don't know,' I said truthfully. 'Most of the time, he won't eat it. I'm thinking it might be a sensory thing.'

There was a pause on the line. 'Well, he was eating just *fine,* the last time he stayed on my boat.'

'But that's the thing,' I said. 'That was *months* ago now. A lot of things have happened since then.'

'How'd that new girl get on?' Piper asked, painting her nails while she waited for a booking.

'Robyn?' I sipped at my coffee. 'She's fabulous. I put her with easy guys for her first few bookings. Nico Nice, Rhett Babyface, Chris Kind Respectful and Honest. They're *raving* about her massages. She's older, but that makes it easier. There's less drama with more mature women.'

'Oh my God.' Piper blew on her nails. 'Speaking of drama. Did you hear what happened to Alicia?'

'Have you heard something?' I was starting to worry about her. 'I haven't heard from that girl in *days.*'

'It's her boyfriend. He got done for the Dargaville robbery. And now he's home on remand. Has to wear an ankle monitor and everything!'

'And Alicia's *with* him?' Piper nodded, engrossed in her nails. 'What the hell are they doing all day? They must be so bored, if he can't leave the house.'

'Mm.' Piper closed up her nail polish with the pads of her fingers, then waved both hands in the air. 'I'm sure they're finding *some* way to pass the time. 'Kay, I have to go up to this booking. What's this guy's name again? Kasey?'

'That's what he told us. Watch your step, he's got an Indian accent.'

Kasey had booked two hours with Piper, and when she came back down she was winded and rosy-cheeked, like she'd just got back from the gym. 'Daaaaaaaaaamn,' she sang out when she entered the Dungeon. 'That boy eat the booty like groceries!'

'Rim job?' I asked, taking notes in the phone. We always made a profile for new clients, as soon as they had their first session.

'For forty-five minutes!' She collapsed on the couch. 'At *least.* Which was fine, 'cause he did the work. And he's a manager at KFC, too! So he'd already been on his feet all day. I was *dying* though,' she confided, kicking her heels off her feet.

'Why?'

'Because I had to fart *so* bad! And I was holding it in the whole time! When he finally left I could let it all go, and it was the most marvelous fart of my life!'

'Okay then, I guess that's his name.' I pulled up his contact. 'So the ladies can all be forewarned. Kasey who works at KFC, I now christen you . . . "Kasey KFC Eats Ass Like Groceries".'

—

By November, we were closing in on our first year in business, and Room 6 was often booked out. 'I think we could start a new service room.' Wren was flipping through the logs from the previous weeks. 'I've had to turn away business, even when we had ladies who wanted to work – because the motel was already full.'

'I've been thinking about that.' I put my feet on the coffee table. 'Room 5's just under Room 6, and we can watch them both from the same camera. Let's close Room 5 down for the next week or so, and see if we can fill it with Bach clients.'

'Also? The commission system works fine for me, but I think we should start closing later. We're getting calls from guys who want to come in at eleven or twelve, and I have to turn them away.'

'You'd stay that late?' I wasn't sure about that. Late-night bookings seemed riskier to me.

''Course I would!' Wren laughed. 'I'm *loving* this job. I get to talk about sex all day, and slap down the boys when they step out of line. Plus, in case you forgot, I'm American.' They puffed on an imaginary cigar. 'Assigned capitalist at birth, baby!'

And that was the thing about Wren: they were astonishingly good at their job. The commission structure, which Karli resented, worked well with Wren's natural hustle. They made three or four hundred a day, upselling the men, and closing later and later each night. Not only that, I'd been wrong about our ladies: they couldn't care less that Wren was gender non-binary. Sometimes they used the wrong pronoun for them, but Wren just corrected them without making a big deal, and everyone took it in stride.

Now that we were busy, I no longer sat at my desk, worrying and hoping for business. A day at The Bach had a pace of its own, and it was fun to be the woman in charge. I'd picked out a uniform that I wore every day, because it was comfortable and it made me feel strong: black jeans, black T-shirt, cropped black leather jacket, and a pair of knee-high black boots. The boots had thick, sturdy soles for running up and down stairs, and I could kick someone hard if I needed to.

When it was my turn to manage, I turned on the Batphone, checking the messages that had come through overnight. Men who texted after one in the morning weren't serious – they were usually just horny and high. Here's one we received at 1.46am, from an unknown number:

free tonight
Greek

I didn't bother responding to that one, but I did put him in the phone as 'Middle Of The Night Greek Guy', so we knew what he wanted if he called again.

Then I'd take a look at the scheduling sheet. On the best days, we'd already have three or four bookings reserved in advance. Wren would have noted which women were available, and I loved it when we had a good mix: Livia or Mia (the PSWGs), Robyn (our expert masseuse), and Tonya or Tara (who specialized in kink.) Sabra and Piper could always get bookings, so if one of them was on I knew we'd be busy.

I'd look through the Batphone and start to text men. *Would you like a date with a beautiful girl today?* Some men didn't want to be contacted, and some of them asked me to text them in code: *We have some great specials available today; would you like to know what's in stock?* Of course, there were never any specials – Bach prices were all non-negotiable – but it was a way to keep things discreet.

Sometimes the first booking was at ten in the morning – we had one guy who travelled to Auckland for work, and he liked a nice orgasm before the long drive – but most of our clients started calling at lunchtime. There was often a lull mid-afternoon, and then it got busy at night. That's when the job was more physical: tramping up and down stairs with clean towels and sheets, fresh drinks to stock up both fridges. At the same time, I could be texting three or four clients, chatting with one guy who wants **GFE + Greek with Livia at 9**, another who wants to know **what girls are available? can you describe them?** and some jerk pushing for **no condom? u do natural?**

Then there were the complicated conversations, the ones that took a little more time.

Do any of the girls do bats 4 a bj

Bats? 🦇

Chuff

What's that in English?

Meth

Now I understand what you are saying. No, we are not that kind of business. If you would like to take advantage of the drug addictions of vulnerable women, I suggest you call somewhere else.

Asshole.

OK thank u . . . finally some girls with some morals

At the end of the night was my favorite part: after I'd cleaned up the office and laundered the dresses, washed up the coffee and tea cups – that's when I counted the money. I always felt like a badass, taking out the fat purse from the safe, then sorting the notes into piles of hundreds and fifties, twenties and tens. We never made so much money that we needed an automatic counting machine, the ones drug dealers use in the movies, but on a good day I ran out of room on the coffee table. And that always gave me a thrill.

As the holidays loomed, The Bach started cranking, and sometimes my attention would slip. I used to carry two cell phones at once, the Batphone in my right back pocket, and the motel phone in my left. That way, Debra could take care of the housekeeping, and I could help her by answering the motel phone.

One morning, still yawning from the previous night's shift, I pulled out a phone when it rang.

'Yes please, I would like to know what's available?' said a male voice on the line.

'Sure!' I cooed, in my best madam voice. 'We've got Sabra and Piper till three, then Tonya and the beautiful Mia's here this evening. When were you thinking of coming?'

There was a pause on the other end. 'Uh . . . I was wanting to book a motel room. This *is* Marina Court Motel, yes?'

'Whoops, yes of course!' I corrected, realizing I had the wrong phone. 'What day were you wanting to join us?'

When Alicia finally made contact, I dove for the Batphone. 'Where have you been? I was worried!' Of course, I knew where she'd been since Piper had told me, but I wanted to hear what she'd say.

'Just dramas, ay,' she said. 'Boyfriend got snapped by the cops. And now he's back home with me. And I want to save up for Christmas! Get some prezzies for him and his kids! D'you think I can I come back to work?'

'What will you tell him?' I asked. 'Does he know you're working?'

'Won't tell him!' she said. 'It's fine. Cool beans! But do you think you could text me in code? Like, pretend you need me for baby-sitting an' that?'

'Okay . . .' This was giving me an uneasy feeling. 'Lord knows, there's plenty of work for you.'

With eight women on board, we had no lack of clients, but the men started to change as the holidays approached. A lot of them didn't have family to visit, and they were lonely, so they drank or did drugs.

One of our holiday clients was Chad P Cooked and Drunk, a shell of a man who ran a successful business in town. 'He's so lonely and *sad*,' Sabra said the next day. 'And he kept booking ladies to *talk*. I think he must have seen four of us! All night long he was here! And he was way too drunk to have sex.'

She was right. I had a look at the schedule. During Wren's shift, he'd spent almost a grand. Just to have someone to talk to.

A lot of men asked to trade drugs for sex, including Matt DO NOT TAKE BOOKING, who asked if we'd accept a mixed payment.

'What's that supposed to be?' Wren wanted to know.

'Mixed,' I said. 'A mixture of cash plus drugs.'

Wren rolled their eyes. 'Well, since money, sex, and drugs are all equal, maybe *we* could fuck the drugs, and he could just pay the rent.'

We had some good laughs, but the truth was more serious. That first holiday season of 2017, the nights were funny and thrilling and ridiculous . . . and they also felt out of control. Like we were all in a car accelerating, shooting into a curve at top speed. Almost always, when men came to The Bach late at night, they were high or drunk, sometimes both. Sometimes we had three rooms running at once, but only two had alarms. We screened our clients, and we had self-defense tips, but could we really subdue a drunk rapist?

How would we ever do that?

By spreading our fingers and making a claw?

Chapter 16

'I've been thinking . . .' Wren said. 'It's perverted, but just hear me out.'

'Oh, *this* should be good.' I sat down to listen.

'Livia and Tara are sisters, right? They're both super hot; all the men love them. So why don't we do a new special? A straight double with sisters! We could call it . . . the Sexy Sister Double.'

'Oh my God,' I breathed. 'You sick genius.'

'Why, thank you. And I bet we could charge through the nose for it. If a regular double is $360, then we could price the sister double at . . . what? Five hundred?'

The door to the Dungeon flew open, and Alicia and Tonya burst in. 'I *love* working here!' Tonya threw out her arms, inked in full sleeves of Māori tattoos. 'There's *so many* dresses and heels!'

'So true, ay?' Alicia tossed her bag on the ground and they both pranced past us, heading back into the dressing room. 'Have you seen the new black mini dress? It shows off my boobs? And it's cut so I look *super* fit!'

Tonya's voice again: 'This place is my *family*; it's like my new home!'

Wren and I exchanged a look. *Family? What is she talking about?*

I got up and poked my head in the dressing room. 'Alicia? It's ten in the morning. Aren't you usually in class now?'

She was meticulously picking through the hangers, checking out the new underwear sets I'd just bought. 'Ah, I quit!' she chirped, not looking up.

'You quit the whole nursing program? Why?'

Tonya yanked open the supply closet. 'Oi, these boxes of condoms are all in a mess. Can I sort them out?'

'Yeah, sure,' I told her. 'How come you quit the program, Alicia?'

''Cause those bitches who snapped me in the club the other night, they started spreading rumors at school. And I just couldn't take the bullying, ay? And anyway my boyfriend needs me at home.'

'For what?'

'Well, he can't leave the house 'cause he's got an ankle monitor, so someone's got to bring him food and that. That's why I reeeeally need work. So can you please pimp out this booty, madam? 'Cause I really, really need some cashola!'

'Sure,' I said. 'Just keep your phone on. I'll tell you if something comes in.'

She finally stopped fiddling with the lingerie. 'Actually, do you think you could get an 0800 number? 'Cause I never have credit on my phone.'

'You mean a toll-free number?' I asked. 'I can't—'

'You should really have a *system* for organizing the condoms,' Tonya interrupted, making piles of boxes on the floor. 'And what's in this carton?'

'Vibrators,' I said. 'I bought us a whole bunch of bullet vibes.'

'Oooh!' Tonya started pulling off the packing tape. 'Can I open them? I *love* bullet vibes!'

'Sure,' I said. 'Knock yourself out.' Then I turned back to Alicia. 'Look, I want to help, but you need two basic things to work here. A cell phone with credit, and a functioning car. So I'm not going to get an 0800 number.'

'All goods,' she shrugged. ''Cept my car's munted as well. I think it needs a new clutch! Adulting, ay? It's the worst!'

The Batphone buzzed, and I ducked around the corner. Wren mouthed the words *Are they high?* I shrugged and held up both hands, then I looked down at the phone.

Hey what's on offer today?

Are you mistaking us for a sandwich shop?

1 ham and cheese with extra avocado and do u still do those custard squares?

The lovely Tonya and Alicia are here right now. No custard squares. Tonya is buxom and kinky, Māori with stunning body art . . .

Yeah thanks but I'm more into white girls sorry

Then why not visit Alicia? She's 20 years old, size 8 and a full DD . . .

'You want a Now Right Now?' I called out to Alicia. 'He's a new guy; I'll find out what I can.'

'Cool beans!' she replied. 'I *love* this lingerie set. It's white so I'll look like a virgin!'

The client was texting again.

Can I pay with drugs?

You must be out of your goddamned mind. We are not that kind of business. Fuck off and never contact me again or I'll call the cops.

I put him in the contacts as 'Can I Pay With Drugs DO NOT TAKE BOOKING'.

'Never mind!' I told Alicia. 'Looks like he can't make it.'

'Aaaaaw, what happened?' She came out with one hand on her hip, decked out in the new white lingerie.

'Good Lord,' said Wren, covering their eyes with their hands. 'Put that away. You'll blind me.'

'I don't know,' Alicia sucked in her tummy, inspecting herself in the mirror. 'I'm so *bloated*. I can't go to the toilet, but fresh veggies are all so *expensive* . . .'

'I'll get you another guy,' I told her. 'Don't worry. That one was kind of an asshole.'

Staying open until two or three in the morning meant our days could be eighteen hours long, and though Wren and I each worked just three days a week, it could still be a punishing schedule. 'There's a woman who applied in the first round,' I told Wren. 'I chose you since you know about kink. But she's worked at a rape crisis center, and I'm starting to think we could use her.'

'Call her up!' Wren encouraged. 'I could *definitely* use some more sleep.'

The new woman asked to be called Moneypenny. 'I just got back from the UK,' she said, settling herself on the couch. She was a fiftyish woman with bobbed grey hair, in jeans and a faded Sonic Youth shirt. Her accent was difficult to place.

'So are you English?' I asked.

'No, I'm from here, but I moved out there with a boyfriend who turned out to be no good. Got violent. Now it's twenty years later, and I have a small son. I thought it would be better for him here, growing up.'

'And why do you want to work here?'

'To keep women safe,' she said right away. 'I think it's fascinating, what you're doing here. I worked at a domestic violence refuge in the Midlands, so it was a similar thing, staying discreet and keeping it safe. And the men could be such *fucking wankers*.'

'How d'you mean?'

'If they found out where we were! They'd try to break down the door, drag the women back home. So I know a thing or two about maintaining security, if that helps.'

'It could,' I said. 'And we've had a few wankers, but most of our men have been fine. Lonely guys, men whose wives don't want sex. Or they're working so hard they can't find a girlfriend. Or they're disabled, or sometimes just shy.'

She raised an eyebrow. 'Or selfish narcissists wanting to cheat?'

'A few of those,' I conceded. 'And some who don't know about active consent. But mostly, they just want to be touched.'

—

'Are *all* Mediterranean guys hung like donkeys?' Sabra had just finished her booking with Kostas. 'I've seen *two* of those chefs from that café, the Olive Branch? And both of them are rocking these *snakes.'*

'No idea,' I said, putting him in the contacts as 'Kostas Epic Long Shlong'. 'Was he gentle, at least?'

'He was fine,' she said. 'It's not *his* fault. But I'll tell you, Madam, at this point I don't even need the money. I just come in for the D! I was in there on my hands and knees, right?' She got down to demonstrate. 'And I looked back and saw this *ginormous eel* aimed at me! And I started crawling away from it, little by little, 'cause how's *that* gonna fit inside *me?'*

'But you handled it?'

'All sweet.' Sabra got back to her feet. 'He was actually quite good, if I'm honest. Maybe I should have a holiday in the Med!'

The Batphone rang. 'The condom broke!' Alicia had just finished an hour with Hot Raj. 'Prosty fail!'

'Oh, *shit,'* I said. 'Call the Prostitutes Collective. They'll give you Plan B for free.'

'I should have checked it had the little air bubble thingy at the end! But he kept saying "Let's hit it" like he was in *such* a massive rush!'

'It happens,' I soothed. 'It's okay. But *please* take care of your health.' And I changed his contact to 'WARNING Raj Hit It'.

Later, Piper was in the Dungeon getting changed into her street clothes after her booking with a new client named Tim. The Batphone buzzed, and I tapped at the screen. 'Everything all right, Tim? Did you forget something?'

'I thought the lady using toys was a part of it?' He sounded miffed. 'Part of a . . . a GFE?'

I looked at Piper. 'Yes, a toy show can be part of the service, as long as you ask politely.'

'Well, she wouldn't touch it. She actually *refused.*'

'He brought his own dildo!' she whispered. 'It was crusty! Like it literally had white flakes on it.'

I nodded. 'Yes, but Tim? You can't bring your own toys for the girls. We have no way of knowing they're clean. Would you borrow a toothbrush from a stranger?'

'Well . . . no,' he conceded reluctantly.

'There you go! We have some lovely new dildos in stock; next time let us know and we'll have one ready for you.' I updated his contact to 'WARNING Tim Crusty Toys Literal White Flakes OMFG'.

Dale drove up from Auckland for erotic lactation, and he called me after as well. 'Livia only let me nurse for ten minutes!' he whined. 'And I paid for the hour, with extras! So why did she have to stop so soon?'

'Because, Dale,' I gathered my patience, 'Livia has an *actual baby*. She needs to save something for him.'

The Sexy Sister Double was ready to launch, and Livia and Tara couldn't wait. They were so excited to work together and make extra money that their first set of pictures came out far too sexy. Wren sent them in, and New Zealand Girls wouldn't run them.

'Let me get this straight.' I sat down on the couch when they gave me the news. 'They said the pictures were "too revealing"? This website sells *sex work,* with photos of escorts, and our Sexy Sister Double's too *sexy* for them?'

'I *know.*' Wren finished a text and looked up from the Batphone. 'There's this one where I had them both standing with one foot on the vanity, in corsets and G-strings? They said they saw labia, but *I* didn't see labia, and believe me . . .' They jabbed the screen to send off their text. 'I *know* about labia.'

'So send them the other one, with the sisters on the bed on their tummies,' I suggested. 'That one's just bum bums; they can't be offended.'

'Bum bums?' Wren raised an eyebrow.

'Sorry,' I said. 'It's something a client said. Sometimes I think I'm losing my mind.'

Once the pictures were up, the calls just poured in. A new guy enquired when Wren was in charge, and the next day I clicked on the text, laughing out loud when I saw their response:

Hi Sexy Sisters
Do you offer bi double?
What extras do u offer?

Um . . . no. Livia and Tara are actual real life sisters.
Incest is not an extra we offer at The Bach.

The Sexy Sisters started making over a thousand a week, and that was just their base fees: whatever extras they sold went straight in their pockets. Tonya noticed their profits, and she wasn't pleased. As far as she was concerned, the sisters' success wasn't because they were both young and gorgeous. It was because I was giving them more advertising. She started calling and texting all day and night, asking, 'how are the phones going?' and 'how many girls are on?' and 'do you think it will get busy soon?'

One night she called, and Mia was booked solid. I had the phone pressed to my ear with my shoulder, while I tucked in fresh sheets with both hands.

'How busy are things?' she demanded. 'D'you think we'll get a big rush tonight?'

'No way to know!' I fluffed up a pillow. 'The phones could go nuts in an hour or two. But it's Mia's night, you know? So they're all calling and asking for her.'

'Okay, if you say so.' She sounded annoyed. 'I *guess* I'll stay on until ten.'

'Great.' I tapped out of the call and gathered the laundry, heading back down to the Dungeon.

Moneypenny hardly had time to warm up: her first day of work was non-stop. She managed ten bookings that day, and stayed up until two in the morning. Then she left me a note in the manager's group chat:

> There was an incident this evening with Livia and Sweet Sounding John. He is now WARNING John NOT Sweet DO NOT TAKE BOOKING. He tried repeatedly to have sex with her without a condom and at one point he even pinned her arms down. She had to kick him away and was very shaken up. I have sent him a strongly worded text about his behaviour and that he is not welcome at The Bach for the foreseeable future.

'Are you okay?' I asked Livia when I saw her. 'Moneypenny told me what happened.'

'Lolz, it was fine,' Livia said with a shrug. 'Sabra showed me how to get my legs under him, and I just kicked him off! He didn't try it again, that's for sure. Anyway, I'd rather see *him* than Larry Ogre.'

'Correction,' Wren interjected. 'He has a new name now. Larry Ogre Blood Gash Shit Stains.'

'Good *Christ.*' I sat down on the couch. 'I guess I better hear about this one.'

'Two. Cans. Of Coke.' Livia mimed a massive, thick dick with her hands. 'That's what it looks like; I'm not even exaggerating.'

'Is that *possible?*' I gaped. 'That's insane.'

'*And* he's missing an ear. And he looks just like Shrek. So that's why we call him Larry Ogre.'

'But it gets better!' Wren waved their hand. 'When I changed the bed, he'd left skid marks! And bloody stains on the sheets!'

'From an accident,' Livia said. 'He just bashed his leg whilst at work.'

Wren shook their head. 'Could he put on a Band-Aid? And what about wiping his *ass?*'

'Ah,' I said. 'You're new at this, Boss. You will soon learn the truth: *a straight man does not wash his asshole.*'

'Why not?' Wren widened their eyes. 'They all want the ladies to touch it. Don't they *want* to be clean?'

'I think they all think there's a button inside. And if they press it, they'll turn themselves gay.'

Livia burst out with a laugh. 'That explains a lot! But I just hop in the shower and wash them. Poor babies, they can't manage themselves.'

December rushed past in a blur of new clients, the days blending into the nights. One late Friday night a man buzzed at reception, and I went out to tell him we were closed. He kept pounding the door, so I opened it a crack, leaving the chain on in case. 'I wanna see a girl!' he slurred. 'Adda Bach!'

'Well, you can't,' I said firmly. 'We're by appointment only.' I pushed at the door to close it again, and that's when I noticed his foot, which he'd wedged in so the door wouldn't shut. He leaned close and insisted, 'I wanna girl! Gimme a girl for a date!'

I looked in his eyes and they were flat black, the pupil as dark as the iris. I think he saw me as a thing, blocking him from a girl. If there hadn't been a chain, he would have forced his way in.

But there *was* a chain. And this asshole was pissing me off. 'Smile!' I held up the Batphone, recording. 'You're on camera! Now *fuck off* or I'll call the cops!'

That night I got home at 4.30am, then poured myself a vodka on ice. *Wait, is this day drinking?* I glanced at the clock. *No, there's an hour till dawn.*

In the week before Christmas, the insanity mounted. The clients were drunker, sadder, more desperate. Chase Is A Muppet booked Livia in the morning, then he came back again to see her that afternoon. 'You shouldn't call him a Muppet,' she reported after the first session. 'He's a young guy, and he's lost both his parents this year. His mum died of cancer, then his father got in a horrible car crash. Poor guy, he just booked me to talk.'

'Two hours and you didn't have *sex?*' I opened the contact with his notes.

She pulled on her jeans. 'He hasn't got any other family. He's finding it hard, with no one to talk to.'

'Well, I sure had sex!' Alicia came in the side door, tossing her long coat on the couch.

I glanced at the phone. 'But it's only five-thirty. Don't you have another half hour with Kasey KFC?'

She started giggling, and hid her face in her hands, her whole body shaking with mirth. Livia and I couldn't help it – we started laughing, and it was a minute before Alicia could talk. 'You know how I was so bloated?' she said, 'and I'm trying to eat lots of salads?'

'Yesss . . . ?'

'And you know how Kasey wanted Greek?'

I wasn't sure I liked where this story was going. 'Yeaaah . . .'

'Well, he stuck it right in, yeah? With no warning. And I couldn't help it! It happened so fast!'

Livia and I exchanged looks of horror. 'I *shit* on his *dick!'* Alicia crowed. 'It had been so long, and I was so stoppered up! I think he got scared – he just ran to the shower, and I grabbed the money and left!'

'You know what? I bet he *loved* it,' Livia said. 'I bet he would have paid extra for that. He's such a big sicko, always wanting to rim me, then deep French kiss.' She made a face and stuck out her tongue.

I bit my lip to smother a laugh. 'Well, Alicia, at least you're not constipated. Glad things are working better down there.'

Later that night, Robyn brought in her laptop. 'Can I use Room 5?' she asked. 'I have some paperwork that I need to finish.'

I glanced at the booking sheet. 'Sure,' I said. 'It's free until seven. You can work in there for the next forty minutes or so.'

Sabra came in to get dressed for her booking with Jacob Loves Māori, then she leaned on the desk, watching me text on The Batphone.

Alicia seems sexy but her ass and pussy not visible
can you please send me
And the price too

Sorry mate, no pussy shots without a paid booking.

Any for free though

Okay, now you're starting to piss me off. Does Pak'nSave give you groceries for free? Does the bottle shop give you liquor for free? We are an escort agency. We don't give sex for free.

Ok sorry ill message when im paid

Thank you.

Don't suppose Livia works for scallops haha

No. Does your doctor work for scallops?
How about your sparky?
LIVIA WORKS FOR MONEY.

Sabra was reading the texts as I typed them, and at that one, she laughed out loud. 'How do you do it, Madam Murphy? These men! They're all so frightened of you!'

'They're not frightened of me.' I put down the phone. 'They're frightened I'll turn off the sex faucet.'

'The *sex faucet?*'

'Yep. It's an age-old story. There's even an ancient Greek play about it, called *Lysistrata*. The men were at war, right? And the women wanted peace. So they banded together and refused to have sex.'

Sabra widened her eyes. 'The whole town?'

'Yep, all the women in Athens. The whole *city*. And I don't have every girl in town at The Bach, but I *am* in charge of the eight finest escorts. And men know if they mess with me, they get themselves banned.'

'The sex faucet.' Sabra smiled and nodded. 'I never thought of it like that.'

'That's the thing about women. On our own, we don't have much power, but when we band together it's different. So I think of being a madam as . . . kind of like a union organizer.'

Sabra snorted. 'I should tell my family I joined a union.'

'Why? What do you tell them now?'

'Oh, nothing. They'd be all up in my business. Right now, when I leave my daughter with my mother, I just tell her I'm out with a boy. Which is true – it's just that there's lots of them.'

I glanced at the phone. 'Okay, you better head up to 6 for your booking with Jacob. I need to get Robyn out of Room 5.'

Sabra and I crossed the parking lot together, and she went upstairs while I knocked on the door. 'You okay in here?' I asked, stepping inside.

Robyn was on the couch with her laptop, surrounded by piles of papers. 'Oh hey, Madam Murphy,' she said. 'I'm just finishing. I have to have this ready for the lawyer on Monday.'

'What is it?' An X-ray was draped on the arm of the couch, the ghostly shape of a skull and spinal column visible.

Robyn let out a long, shaky breath. 'I might as well tell you. My partner assaulted me, a few weeks ago now. I'm trying to press charges against him, only I have to save money – for the lawyer, and to move out and get my own place.'

'What did he do?'

'It was . . . awful. We had friends over, and we were all playing cards. And he'd been drinking and . . . other things. He got it in his head I was cheating, and then he fell into this *rage*. He threw me against the wall and he raped me. Right there, in front of our friends.'

I gestured at the X-ray. 'Did he injure you?'

'I have ongoing pain in my neck, yeah. That's why I sometimes move slowly. But anyway,' she started gathering her papers, 'you need the room here, and I'm mostly done. I can finish all this in the Dungeon.'

'Sure, okay.' I let myself out and walked back to the office, thinking about what I'd just seen. The piles of paper, a woman trying to mount a legal case while giving men naked massages. The pale shape of a skull and a spinal column, the tangible proof of her pain.

—

Three days before Christmas, Moneypenny was in charge, and I dropped by The Bach to check in. 'Where are the vibrators?' I grumbled. 'There were *six* of them here on the charger.'

'I haven't a clue,' Moneypenny swiveled in her chair. 'I did think it was odd that those cords were all loose.'

'If people steal vibrators, they should at least steal the cords!' I yanked out the now useless chargers. 'They won't be any use to anybody when the battery goes dead.'

'Also the speakers are missing in Room 5,' Moneypenny said. 'There used to be speakers there, right?'

I let out a groan and sank down on the couch. 'What, do I have to bolt everything down?'

Later that evening, when I was at home, she posted a text to the group chat.

I'm so sorry Madam Murphy but the till's light by $120

Do you have any idea what happened?

I paid out Tonya for a booking then left the cash on the desk whilst I went up to turn over the room. Alicia and Tonya were both in the Dungeon, and they swore up and down they knew nothing.

Okay, take a deep breath. Don't stress. We'll meet up tomorrow to discuss.

'We need a new system,' I told them the next day. 'The Bach is growing, and we're staying open late. It's easy to make a mistake when we're tired. So from now on, as soon as possible, the cash goes right in the safe. And I got you these fanny packs . . .'

Moneypenny smiled. 'What?' I asked.

'We call them bum bags. A fanny's what we call a vagina.'

'Well, perfect then. They're our new fanny packs. Or put the money *in* your fanny; I don't care. Just so you keep it on your person.'

Wren put up their hand. 'Mia says she had a brand new cell phone in her bag when I worked last Tuesday. Still in the box and everything. And when she finished her booking it was gone.' They bit at their thumbnail. 'Do you think we should install security cameras?'

I let out a growl of frustration. 'No. Not yet. I don't want to have to be paranoid!'

'The lingerie's looking pretty sparse,' Moneypenny observed. 'And one of the long coats is missing, the ones the girls use to walk across the parking lot.'

'Which one?' I got up to check.

'The big, black puffy one.'

'You're kidding me! That's *my* winter coat!' I walked back to my desk and looked through the drawers. 'And my backup hard drive is missing. And my . . . shoe brush?'

Wren and Moneypenny both shrugged their shoulders.

'*Really?* An old *shoe polish brush?* The cash and the cell phone, I get it. And the hard drive . . . I'll have to change all my passwords. Even the vibrators! We all love vibrators! But a *shoe polish brush?*'

I put up a sign in the dressing room: *Has anyone seen the shoe polish brush from Madam Murphy's desk drawer? It is the only thing I have from my grandfather. If you have it, please return it. No questions asked.*

'My instinct says Tonya stole the cash from the booking,' Moneypenny ventured when I came back in the room. 'She needs money, so she planned to work late – then when the cash disappeared, she was no longer available.'

'Cash is one thing.' Wren narrowed their eyes. 'But random shit going missing? That sounds like drugs.'

'Mmf.' Moneypenny pressed her lips together.

'What?' I asked.

'I don't like to gossip. And this is just hearsay. But the other day when it was slow, I had a chat to Piper.'

'Yes?'

'And she said she looked in Alicia's bag.'

'Why'd she do that?'

'I don't know, she wouldn't say. But she said she found a glass pipe in there. And . . . let's just say it wasn't the kind you'd use to smoke weed.'

'Why do they do this?' I put my head in my hands. 'We're finally taking off as a business, they're all making good money, we're booked out till two in the morning . . . you think it's drugs?'

Wren and Moneypenny didn't answer, but they didn't need to. There I was with my nice leather boots on the desk, my college degree and my talk of Greek plays. With my house and my reliable car. Taking half of the money they'd earned, without ever taking my clothes off. *When you feel ripped off by the universe, you take what you think you deserve.*

'Never mind,' I said. 'Just keep an eye out. I have to go pick up the kids.'

Wren worked The Bach for the rest of the night. On Christmas Eve morning, I came in to take care of the banking, grabbing the cash from the safe. I popped my head in the Dungeon on my way out the door.

And there it was: my grandfather's shoe brush, sitting at the center of my desk.

Chapter 17

'Oh hey,' Wren sat up on the couch. 'Isn't Moneypenny working today?'

'Did you not go *home?'* I went to my desk and picked up the shoe brush. 'Who dropped this off?'

'I don't know.' Wren yawned, pulling their blanket around their shoulders. 'It showed up yesterday while I was cleaning the rooms. So I guess we have a thief with a conscience.' They got up and went to the coffee station, flicking the switch on the jug. 'And no, I didn't bother going home last night. Or this morning, really. We were open till four.'

'*Four am?* That's pushing it hard, don't you think?'

'Probably.' Wren poured hot water over a tea bag. 'Things kind of went off the rails, at the end.'

'Is everyone all right?'

'Well . . . it's Mia. She had four back-to-back bookings last night, and you know how thin she is, right?'

I nodded.

'I think she was drinking beers with the clients, and probably a few in between. At the end of the night, I went up to clean and she was *wasted.* Like, staggering and slurring her words. And then she came at me!'

'What do you mean?' I frowned. 'She got aggressive?'

'No, the *opposite.* She threw herself at me, she tried to kiss me on the mouth, and then she kept saying she loved me. *I love you, I love you,* she said. And *why don't you love me?* It was . . . really uncomfortable.' Wren warmed their hands on their mug. 'Especially since . . . you know, I like girls. And some of them like to rile me up – not just ask my opinion, but put their tits in my face. It gets awkward sometimes.'

'So what did you do?'

'Well, I got her calmed down. Then I had to convince her she couldn't drive home. She's still up there, asleep in Room 6, I think. She'll have a hell of hangover, too.'

I peered at the security cameras. 'Where was she parked? I only see my car and yours out the back.'

'Well, that's that, then.' Wren put down their tea. 'She must have already gone.'

Patrice had made a *coq au vin* with nasty old Jabberwocky, and about a bottle and a half of Bordeaux. Miranda and Titou, who were used to farm life, took turns chasing each other with the gory head.

'I simmered that *petit enfoiré* for hours,' Patrice said. 'Enough to cook off the devil in him.' The kitchen was full of the rich, meaty scent of broth, red wine and herbs.

'MIH!' Silas insisted, holding up his sippy cup, his MP3 player glued to his ear. This time, it was playing *The Book of Mormon,* something cheerful about stuffing gay people in boxes.

'MIH!' he repeated. 'Bus.'

I filled up the sippy cup and handed it to him. 'Miranda and Titou!' I called. 'Set the table for dinner please!' I pulled out my phone and glanced at it. Moneypenny had agreed to work Christmas Eve, and she was still new at The Bach. I wanted to be ready if she had any questions.

'Why don't we have a tree?' Maris wanted to know. 'Can we not afford one or something?'

'Don't ask so much questions,' Patrice told his daughter. 'Serve yourself a drink and come to the table.'

Nova glided down the stairs with a shopping bag of packages, and she knelt to arrange them with other gifts by the fireplace. 'I only just finished making my presents,' she said. 'It took *ages.* Plus, last month was so busy with exams.'

'Don't think I'll do my NCEAs,' Maris announced, referring to New Zealand's national high school finals. 'Maybe I'll go be a stripper.'

I was pouring a glass of wine, and I stopped. 'Why would you go be a stripper?'

'Easy money,' she shrugged. 'Why bother with school?'

'Sex work is NOT easy money,' I told her. 'Take it from me. Neither's stripping. Take your time and finish your education.'

Maris rolled her eyes as if to say *all grownups are lame,* and went to get a glass for her lemonade.

'Titou, *you* put the plates and the napkins and *I'll* put the knives and the forks, and that way it's fair,' Miranda instructed. 'We'll each put down *two kinds of things.*'

'And spoons,' Patrice reminded them. 'We need spoons for this beautiful sauce.'

Miranda was horrified. 'Well I'M not putting down spoons, since that's THREE things, and Titou put down only TWO!'

'You know what?' I told her. 'It's Christmas. I'll take care of the spoons.'

'Bus-ah-bus-ah-bus-ah-bus,' babbled Silas, his music still pressed to his ear. '*Whores.*'

The kids thought we didn't have a Christmas tree, but I knew what Patrice had been working on. After dinner, when everyone was in their pajamas, we called them all to Titou and Miranda's room.

'Ouch!' Nova yelped. 'I trod on a Lego! You guys ought to clean this place up!'

'It's not so bad,' Maris said. 'I've seen worse.'

'That's 'cause *your* room is filled with old cereal bowls! And nasty old moldy coffee cups!'

'*Shh.*' Patrice put a finger to his lips. 'Close your mouth, all you kids. And look out the window.' He picked up a control box that he'd placed on the windowsill, and we all peered out at the dark. Outside, there was a narrow path to the orchard with a tall pine tree, and beyond it the fence for the chicken coop.

Patrice flicked a switch. And the pine tree, all fifteen meters of it, lit up in a blaze of colorful lights.

'WOW!' breathed Miranda.

'SO COOL!' Titou yelled. 'How d'you do it, Papa?'

'Okay, that's pretty good,' Maris said. 'I'll admit it.'

Beside her, Nova nodded and smiled. 'Good one, Papa.'

I held Silas's warm hand in my own, my right arm around Patrice's waist. 'That's beautiful,' I told him, cuddling into his neck. 'You made something magical.'

'Oooh! Kissy kissy!' Miranda jeered, bouncing on her bed.

'Ew, *gross!*' Titou covered his eyes.

My phone buzzed inside my pocket. I pulled it out, and when I saw it was Moneypenny, I moved back to the corner of the room. She'd posted an update to the manager's group chat, which came through to both Wren and me.

Tonight a very drunk man turned up in a cab and let himself into Room 5. I bolted over there to find his gumboots sprawled over the carpet and him pissing in the toilet (as well as the floor). Told him to GET OUT NOW.

He became verbally abusive and insisted he had a booking and I told him he did not and that he could not just turn up and expect to be seen. He said I was a fucking liar and he did have a booking and that it was a fucking whorehouse and who the fuck did I think I was talking to.

I told him he needed to leave.

He told me to go fuck myself and threw a wad of cash on the table and said he had $300 and what did I think of that?

And I said not much. Picked up his smelly gumboots and threw them across the carpark. Then I called the police.

Before I could respond, Wren jumped into the chat.

Fascinates me that these people keep trying to use the whole sex work thing against us like it's a trump card. Hello . . . legal. It's like they can't accept our lack of shame, so it's their shame. Let them have it!

I smiled and tapped out a reply.

Sounds like you handled it beautifully. Merry Christmas, from Madam Murphy and our little fucking whorehouse.

Three days after Christmas, Alicia had an announcement. 'I'm pregnant!' she sang out, bouncing into the Dungeon. 'I'm gonna have a baby!'

'Oh my God, no way!' Piper was back in the dressing room, getting ready for a booking with Johnny the Lonely American. 'How far gone are you?'

'Six weeks,' Alicia said, 'Or thereabouts. I only just did the test!'

I wanted to pour a bucket of ice water on her head, then give her a dose of reality. *If your boyfriend's the dad then he's a real prize, with a criminal record for armed robbery. Neither of you has any training or qualifications. Word is, at least one of you has been spending some time smoking meth. And by the way, when did that condom break, Alicia? Last month, in a booking with Hot Raj? How d'you know your kid isn't his?*

But out loud, I said, 'Congratulations. I'm sure you'll be a wonderful mom.'

—

'And she will be, too!' I told Patrice, that night in bed. 'Just not at twenty years old. *This* is how they end up at The Bach! They're almost all single mothers, who got pregnant too early with some guy who leaves them with kids! She'll quit for a year to take care of the baby. And then he'll take off, because he's a man child – and she'll be back at The Bach, doing sex work just to survive!'

'But you believe in this work,' he said in the dark, rubbing my back in wide circles. 'You say women should have a right to do it.'

'And they *should*. But that doesn't mean it's the *best* option. It's not like these women have surgical residencies they can go do instead. But it's better than cleaning or hospo – which are pretty much the only jobs in a small town, if you don't have a qualification.'

Patrice was quiet for a minute. 'Everyone works, Antonia. Not everyone likes their job. My mother, she worked in a factory. My brother, he – *comment tu le dis* – he *broke rocks* for a living, before he died. And my father and grandfather, they were horse butchers. I don't think they loved their work every day.'

'Yeah but . . . hang on a second.' My phone buzzed. It was eleven at night, and Moneypenny would be closing. Sure enough, she'd updated the group chat.

Robyn's had a bad booking. All I have been able to establish so far is that he pushed her up against the wall, then hurt her breasts by twisting and squeezing them roughly and she was not able to set up boundaries as she was traumatised. She locked herself in the bathroom and texted me, and I ended the booking.

'Oh God.' I let out a long, shaky breath. 'That's just what her husband did.'

'Qu'est-ce qu'il y a?' Patrice asked, propping himself on one elbow.

I shook my head. 'I don't want to talk about it. But this . . . isn't the business I thought it would be.' I breathed out a shuddering sigh. 'If we were in a big city, a place with a university, I could be picky! I'd just take ones who are emotionally healthy, who are trying to pay for school, or save up for a trip. But Robyn, and Tonya, and Piper . . . they're doing this work to *survive.* If I just hired ladies with healthy, wholesome lives?' I thought about the girls at The Bach. 'Well, I'd still have Livia. And Sabra, I guess. But all the others have *some* kind of problem, and that's usually why they need cash!'

'You're helping them,' Patrice offered. 'They're making good money, which puts food in the mouth of their kids.'

'I know, but . . .' I trailed off. Patrice had been raised in public housing, his mother divorced and with no education. He knew more about this world than I did. For the past forty years, my life had been filled with friendly, reliable people. What did I know about smoking meth, partners who rape, husbands who hit? What could I say to Robyn, or Alicia, or Mia, that could possibly help solve their problems?

Nothing. The answer was nothing. All I could do was give them a job.

Lying there in the dark, a memory came, from when I was sailing with Peter. We were motoring across the Gulf of Panama, and the water was glassy and calm. Peter turned off the engine. 'Let's go for a swim!' he'd said. 'You can put a lifejacket on, and I'll put a line in the water.'

I'd looked down into that inky black ocean, and I thought: *I'm not going in there. Could be hundreds of meters to the bottom.*

That's how I felt at the helm of The Bach. I'd thought it would be fun, and a little transgressive. A way to make money and play with convention. I'd jumped in the water with a splash and a giggle, thinking I'd go for a swim. Only now, dealing with dangerous clients and the women's emotional wounds, I felt like I was paddling the surface of the ocean, above an unknowable, dismal abyss. But there was no line, and there was no lifejacket. I felt like I was swimming alone.

—

'I just want to know why I'm not advertised,' Tonya complained the next day in the Dungeon. 'I'm on all day, but I checked NZ Girls, and you've only got Robyn, Tara, Livia and Sabra with ads up.'

'I told you,' I said, 'we've got twenty-four ad slots a week. That's four a day. So I can't put up everyone's ad every day. But when guys call, I tell them you're available.'

Tonya hitched up her skirt and straightened her stocking, revealing the elaborate ink on her legs: a spiraling koru; a fierce, grinning tiki. 'But out of four girls, *three* of them are white. Is that why my ad isn't up?'

'*No.* Look, Alicia's not up! It's just not her turn. I'll put both of your ads up tomorrow.'

The Batphone chirped.

Hi this is Cameron

Do you have a slim DD? For today at lunchtime?

'See?' I said. 'Here's a Now Right Now. And I'm sending him your photo.' Tonya inspected a spot on her shoe, refusing to look me in the eye. The answer came back.

At the risk of sounding crass, my type is white, pretty face, no tattoos, slim with large breasts.

Do you have one that matches that description?

'Sorry,' I told Tonya. 'It's not gonna work. I think he wants to see Robyn.'

'*Because she was advertised.*' Tonya shot me a glare. 'You see? That's what brings in the bookings.'

'Because he wants a white girl!' I protested, showing her the phone. 'And a white girl with no tattoos! Some clients are racist. Hang on—'

I called Robyn, but the phone call rang out. '*Damn it,* she's not picking up.'

'It's just like the other night,' Tonya muttered.

'I'm sorry, what?'

'When I called you, and you said it was Mia's night. And all the men just wanted her. But you promote her! You push all the *white* girls! And the rest of us just get the scraps.'

I put down the phone. 'Tonya, you're excellent at what you do. You handle tricky clients, especially with kink, in a way that I really admire. And I know they do too.'

'That's *right* they do,' she sniffed. 'Tyler Tickle Ties practically *wet* himself when I tickled his balls Friday night.'

'And in some ways, this is where a parlor can be better. Because if men met you in person, they'd be captivated. But when they're going off pictures, there's a certain kind of client who's always going to want the youngest and thinnest, with no tattoos and big giant breasts.'

'I *have* giant breasts,' she grumbled.

'You have beautiful breasts. But this guy wants a white girl with no body art. And if I send you up there, he'll probably cancel, and make some shitty remark in the process.'

'Whatever,' Tonya said. 'I'm getting my coat.'

She went out to the dressing room, and I picked up the phone and called Tara. She wasn't rostered at the hospital, so she was available. 'Can you see this guy Cameron?' I asked when she answered. 'He's a new guy, kind of a body fascist, but he used the word "crass" in a sentence, so possibly not a total moron.'

'Sure,' she said. 'I can come in.'

While we worked out the details, I was dimly aware of Tonya striding past me and out of the Dungeon. I jerked up my head as she left. She was wearing my black winter coat.

—

'I've asked Robyn to stay with me,' Moneypenny said, the next time I checked in on her shift.

'You *found* her?' I gaped. 'I've been calling and calling, and she hasn't picked up for days. Is she all right?'

'Not exactly. Her partner found her wad of cash, and he forced her to say where she'd got it. Then he beat her quite badly, grabbed everything she owned, chucked it on the lawn, and he lit it on fire. She barely got out with her car and her dog, and she's been living in her car ever since. She only just got some credit on her phone, which is how she was able to ring me. Anyway, I don't want her sleeping rough. She can stay over at mine till she gets back on her feet.'

I took a minute to process this. 'He *burned* all her stuff?'

Moneypenny nodded.

'And she's been living out of her car?'

Another nod.

'Well, *shit,* I guess that's why she's not picking up.'

'Well, shit is right,' Moneypenny said. 'But I can help. Remember, I used to do this kind of thing for a job.'

—

The ladies of Reddit felt like old friends by now, even though – apart from Phryne – I hadn't met any of them in real life. Not sure who to turn to, I started a thread:

r/seggs&violence
MadamAntonia
What do you do when it gets really bad? And you can't talk about it because it's all secrets?

bimbobaggins: umm Netflix and a drinking problem?

MadamAntonia: No srsly. A friend's partner just beat the shit out of her.
bimbobaggins: Truth? People hate financially secure women. Especially women who make their own sexual choices.
MadamAntonia: So what should I tell her?
bimbobaggins: Tell her to keep getting that bag.

That made me smile, but panic was pressing down on my chest. Mia hadn't made contact since her drunken night. Alicia was pregnant, and her criminal boyfriend didn't want her to work. Livia had earned so much cash over Christmas that she'd burned herself out, and now she only took clients two days a week. Sabra's nursing program was getting more demanding, and she'd built up a sizable savings – she only came in, as she said, for the 'D.' And the scale of the horror Robyn had endured meant she needed to focus on healing – there was no way we could put her with clients. But that left us with only three women: Tara, Tonya, and Piper – plus Livia, working part-time.

Patrice was the only one who knew how bad it got, late at night when he rocked me to sleep. Thrashing my head back and forth on the pillow, I was tangled in ethical knots. *Robyn wants to work, but we know she's not ready. But if she doesn't work she can't earn. If she can't earn she can't rent a new place to live. But if we give her work, it could traumatize her. But isn't that her decision to make? And what about Mia? She wanted those bookings, so she could make money for Christmas. So why did she get so drunk that night? Was she trying to numb the pain? Pain from the sex work, or the abusive husband, the guy who's pushing her into sex work so she can pay the lawyer to stop him from taking her child? And what about me?*

Am I a feminist, helping women to earn, or am I pressuring them into degrading themselves? Phryne said the women should never be in debt, because it takes away their right to consent. But what about my debt? To the bank, and to Gavin, to pay for the rent on the lease? Do I push women to work when I know they shouldn't, just because I need the money?

I knew one thing: with everything we'd been through so far, there was no way I'd let The Bach fail. Now I had so many kids to support, and Silas would always need care. The Bach *had* to succeed; it had to make money.

The question was: what would I do to keep it?

Chapter 18

'I was Miss Pole Dance Australia two years in a row,' the new woman announced, when she sat down in the Dungeon. 'Plus, I've worked in parlors for years. And I already have a working name all picked out. When I'm here, you can call me Mysteek.'

I couldn't print the paperwork fast enough. Mysteek was six feet tall and built like a dancer, with long, toned muscles and a cascade of thick, Polynesian hair to her waist. In her early forties, she was so in shape she could easily pass for a thirty-year-old. 'I'm Māori. I've been in Australia for years. Got engaged to a big-time businessman, too. Want to see?' She pulled out her phone and showed me a picture of herself, laughing with some balding white guy. 'But then he dumped me, the tosser. Too bad for him, now he's missing out on all this!' She laughed loudly, and I noticed some gaps, where she was missing a couple of teeth. *But that doesn't matter. Just look at that body! And besides, we're down to three girls.*

'When can you start?' I asked, handing her the packet listing our services and rates.

'Today, if you want! I've got nothing on. And you don't need to train me – I'm a pro!' She scanned the papers I gave her, her long purple nail skimming the page. 'What's this "standard pricing" for extras? Isn't that up to me to negotiate?'

'We do things differently here,' I explained. 'There's never any fines or fees, and we don't charge a room rate. We pay for your advertising and we provide your outfits. But the flip side is, our pricing is standard. I want it to be clear for the clients.'

Mysteek arched one eyebrow. 'But this is my business. I'm the one who sets all my rates.'

'Mm.' I tilted my head back and forth. 'Not really. I've invested a lot in this agency, and it costs a lot of money to run. And while I'm sure you're an expert negotiator, some of our ladies here are quite young. They might find a fifty-year-old businessman intimidating, and they might set their rates far too low. This way it's fairer for everybody.'

'Hmf.' She fixed me with a wary gaze, and I noticed how unusual her eyes were – so light brown, they almost looked golden. 'If you say so.'

'But there's other places to work if this isn't your style . . .'

'No, it's fine,' she said. 'I'll do it your way.'

—

'She's got a *killer* body,' I told Moneypenny and Wren, when we next got together for a meeting. 'And she's experienced, so she can handle herself with tricky clients. It's just . . .' I trailed off, and they looked at me expectantly. 'You know when someone's done a lot of drugs in the past? Or they have a history of mental illness? And there's something a little *off* in their speech?'

The two managers nodded. '*I'm* about to have a history of mental illness,' Moneypenny muttered. 'After that holiday season we worked through.'

'Yeah,' I said. 'She's a little bit off. So just keep a close eye out.'

'Robyn wants to work,' Moneypenny brought up. 'She needs money so she can buy some new clothes.'

'Do you think she's ready?'

'I think she could come in on my shifts. She's living with me, so I know when she's in a good headspace. And I could keep an eye on her then, and only give her the easy ones.'

'Okay,' I agreed. 'That sounds sensible. And there's another thing I want to bring up. The late nights, staying open until three or four in the morning? I think we should dial it back.'

'Thank *fuck* for that,' Moneypenny said.

Wren nodded. 'I did notice diminishing returns.'

'The clients we get,' I continued, 'they're not worth it. They're high-risk at that time, and they're all drunk or high. Whenever we had an issue in December, the problems all started late at night. So unless it's a high-value client, someone we know and respect, we go back to closing at ten.'

'Tonya will be pissed,' Wren pointed out. 'She does well late at night, with the drinkers.'

'Well, too bad for Tonya,' I said. 'Safety comes first, and it's not worth the risk.'

'I can work!' Alicia said in mid-January. 'Had a miscarriage, so I can start taking bookings. But I still don't want to tell my partner, okay? So please, can you text me in code?'

'I'm sorry,' I said, though I wasn't at all. 'How are you feeling?'

'Oh, fine,' she said. 'It's no biggie. Probs not the best time to be preggo, what with the home detention and all.'

'Yeah,' I agreed. 'Probs not.'

'I'm not making enough,' Tonya said the next week. 'I want you to get me more clients.'

I picked up the log and flipped through the pages. 'You've been making six hundred a week, more or less,' I said. 'That's not bad, for five hours' work.'

'Yeah but Alicia's been breaking a thousand!'

'Yes but Alicia's twenty years old.'

'And she's *white.*'

'And the Indian clients love her, because she dances to Bollywood. There's a lot of reasons why she does well.'

'Whatever.' Tonya picked up her bag. 'She doesn't even give rim jobs.'

'What do you mean?' I asked. 'Yes, she does. She's got it down on her list of extras.'

Tonya rolled her eyes. 'She lubes up a glove. Then she gets them to turn the other way, and she *pretends* that her finger's a tongue.'

'No kidding,' I said. 'I didn't know that.'

'Yeah? Well, there's a *lot* around here you don't know.'

'They're spending an awful lot of time together,' Moneypenny mentioned, the following day. 'Tonya, Alicia, and . . . that new woman. Mysteek.'

'Really? What do they have in common?'

'Gambling, I think. They go down to the pokies, to gamble and drink. Tonya cleaned herself out the other day, had to borrow off Alicia to buy milk. Then when Alicia didn't have any credit on her phone, she asked me to contact her through Tonya.' Moneypenny chewed on her lip. 'I don't like it, to tell you the truth. And as for Mysteek . . .'

'There's something off, right?'

'You're right, she's got a beautiful body. But *all* the ladies have regulars, even Tonya! And nobody books Mysteek a second time. And nobody ever extends. And Alicia saw a client she'd seen recently, I think it was Jiujitsu Jack, and he said that she seemed "cracked-out".'

'Like, high?'

'I don't know.' Moneypenny raised her eyebrows. 'But I'll tell you what, I don't like it.'

—

'You should stock *Kimono* brand condoms,' Mysteek announced from the couch. 'They're really the best. If you want to be an *elite* establishment, that is.'

I googled the brand. 'Okay, but those are twenty-five dollars a box. Do you have any idea how many condoms we use? And the government gives us Durex for free.'

She sighed. 'You don't have to listen to me. I've only been in this business twenty years. How long have you been doing this? A year?'

'About that.'

'Then let me teach you some things. Like we *really* need bottles of Purell beside all the beds, and clients need to know that if they touch their junk, they don't touch us until they disinfect their hands.'

'Don't you make the guys shower?'

'Yes, but that's not enough.'

I took a deep breath. 'I don't think so,' I said. 'We can't make clients disinfect their hands every time they touch their own dicks. That's just gonna give them a complex.'

She inhaled sharply, so I dialed it back.

'Look, *you* can bring Purell into your bookings if that makes you feel comfortable. But I don't want it to be Bach policy. We're offering a girlfriend experience here, not running a hospital clinic.'

'Then what about rubbish bins?'

'What about them?' I asked. 'There's one in each room.'

'What we used to do at the parlor is have a small bin on the bed with us, with a nappy bag in it, and condoms and tissues could go right in there, then afterwards just bag it up and chuck it.'

I considered my words. 'But *again*, we do things differently here. The whole point is that we're not a parlor. We offer a girlfriend experience, an illusion. Nobody wants a trash can up on the bed.'

She glared at me then. 'Yes, Madam Murphy. Whatever you say, Madam.'

Mysteek started coming in each day at ten, hoping to catch the Now Right Nows. But it wasn't always easy to book her, especially since she refused to see South Asian clients.

'Had too many bad experiences,' she said. 'They're dodgy as, and I won't do it.'

'Okay,' I said, 'I respect that. But please hear me out. We do have some good Indian clients, regulars who have proven themselves to be safe, even charming. If you absolutely won't see them, I'll tell the other managers. But you're cutting off a lot of your earnings.'

Piper came in then, from a booking with a client called Ajay. 'That poor man!' she said, plopping down in the armchair. 'He's Indian, right? Just came over last month. And d'you know what an Indian doctor in *Auckland* told him? Told him AIDS comes from having sex with a lady you're not married to! What a liar! This guy's a virgin, at thirty years old! Well, he's not *anymore,'* she clarified with a grin. 'I told him about STIs before I jumped on him, though.'

'That's unbelievable,' I said.

Piper nodded. 'Yep. Probably just trying to scare him into never having sex!'

I nodded, and updated his contact to 'Ajay Don't Infect Me'.

'Were you in 5?' Mysteek asked.

'Yeah, why?'

'Because people aren't hanging the shower curtain properly, and it ends up dripping on the floor.'

'Oh! Sorry about that.' Piper shrugged. 'I'm always in a rush to get back.'

'Also, when you go to wash your hands, you should just use the *back* of the towel. That way the front part stays dry.'

'Um.' Piper looked over at me. 'Did she just tell me how to wash my hands?'

Mysteek let loose with a loud, throaty laugh. 'I'm telling you how we should do things around here! I'm a *professional!* I've been doing this since before you were born!'

'Okay, I'm gonna go.' Piper picked up her bag. 'I'm available until four if you need me.'

'I'm available all night.' Mysteek turned back to me. 'So why are we closing at ten? That's *so much money* we're leaving out on the table.'

'Because the late-night clients aren't worth it,' I told her. 'Some of the ladies have had bad experiences, and we're trying to keep everyone safe.'

I was adding up all of the bills for the month, and I turned back to my laptop. But Mysteek kept staring at me.

'I'm not an idiot, you know,' she finally said.

'What? I know that.'

'Tested off the charts when I was a kid. I went to a Catholic school and the nuns, they gave me a test, and I had the highest score they'd ever seen. They wanted to send me to this poncy boarding school in Auckland; I even qualified for a full scholarship. It was going to be a free ride.'

'So what happened?'

'Mum didn't want me to go. Didn't want me to think I was better than everyone, and she needed me home to look after the kids. After that I got away, just as fast as I could.'

'That sucks,' I said. 'I'm sorry that happened to you.'

Mysteek pursed her lips and nodded, still staring at me with those light amber eyes.

'She says you're controlling, belittling, and you have no respect.' Wren ticked off the items on their fingers. 'She says no matter what she tries to contribute, it's always *your way.*'

I let out a long sigh of frustration. 'Well, it is my fucking business at the end of the day. I don't see her paying the rent.'

Wren shrugged their shoulders. 'I'm just telling you what she said. You know Kiwis, they're not always direct. And Mysteek and Tonya have been talking . . .'

'What *now?*'

'They think we're not hearing them because they're not white. And I think maybe we should take that on board. You know, as white people.'

I put my head in my hands. 'Oh, *honestly.* They're also both forty years old! Tonya's got full-body tattoos, and Mysteek's missing four teeth! They're comparing their earnings with Alicia and Livia, but those girls are fifteen, twenty years younger!'

Wren tilted their head. 'Just consider it.'

'Hey, Tonya,' I said, 'You want to make more money, right?'

'Why?' She hoisted her bag on her shoulder. 'Did you just get a Now Right Now?'

'No, but check this out.' I showed her a form I'd designed. 'What if I give you a marketing job? Take our cards out to some businesses in town. You could try some hotels, but they might not be cool. Probably bars, and off-track betting places. Or places where tradies are working.'

Tonya frowned. 'You mean like construction sites?'

'Yeah! Just see who you can talk to. Then here on this form, I want you to write in where you went, how many cards you dropped off, and how they reacted. Keep track of your hours, and I'll pay you twenty bucks an hour.'

'Okay, I *guess* so . . .' She slid the cards and the form in her bag. 'It's not like I'm getting any work around *here*.'

The next day was Wren's turn to manage The Bach, and the following day I was on. Wren had left me a note. *Tonya says you owe her $80 for four hours.*

I called Wren. 'Did she give you a form?'

'No . . .' I could hear them sipping their tea. 'Sorry, I'm just waking up. What form?'

'The deal was to keep track of her hours, and fill out a form with the people she saw and the cards she gave out.'

'Nope, there wasn't any form,' Wren confirmed. 'Is it possible she just forgot?'

—

'*What*? I gave out the cards,' Tonya snapped when I asked her. 'Why d'you have to be so uptight about it?'

'I'll pay you this time, but that wasn't the job,' I said. 'I needed to know where you went, and who you talked to.'

'We went to some bars,' Tonya shrugged. 'Me and Alicia, and then later Mysteek. We gave out the cards and we had a few drinks. Why can't you just believe me?'

And that's when it clicked: why Tonya was panicked about money, and probably Mysteek as well. Both women had run out of options. If Tonya couldn't follow basic instructions, how could she ever hold down a job? And as to Mysteek, she'd been a sex worker her whole life. What could she put on a CV?

—

'My dad found out I was working here and he had a massive freak-out,' Livia announced at the beginning of February. 'Screaming and throwing things – he said I was disgusting. Said he couldn't even look at me, now I'm selling sex.'

'Oh no,' I said. 'I'm so sorry.'

'Lolz, I'm not! Besides, it's ridiculous what he said. It's a *joke*. I'm not selling *sex* when I take their money.'

'How do you think of it, then?'

'I'm selling an *opportunity.* So yeah, if they're polite and respectful, I'll consent to have sex, but I can withdraw consent any time. But Dad doesn't get it. Don't think he could ever understand.'

I filled out her paystub and gave her what she'd earned, a stack of crisp fifties and hundreds.

'Thanks,' she said, tucking the cash in her wallet. 'Anyway, I'm used to it when he yells like that. He's yelled at me like that my whole life, even when I was eight years old and just dropped a plate on the ground. But I'm not that little girl anymore.' She smiled. 'I have my own money now, and I don't have to take it.'

'What are you going to do?'

'We're going to move out to Aussie, for a while. My husband can earn better wages in Perth, and I can spend more time with the kids.'

My heart sank. *Not my most beautiful escort.* 'That's fantastic,' I said. 'I'm so proud of you. By the way, have you seen your sister lately? She hasn't made contact since she saw Cameron.'

'I've seen her.' Livia pulled out her phone and flicked on it. 'I think she's just busy at work.'

—

'Tara's disappeared, and now Livia's leaving,' I reported to Moneypenny the next day. 'I'm happy for her, but she's killing me here! That girl can earn six hundred dollars a *night!* She's our last PSWG!'

Moneypenny leaned back in her chair and her blazer slid back, revealing a T-shirt for a band called Blonde Redhead. 'We have Alicia,' she said, 'though she's not that reliable. The other day she nearly crashed on her way to a booking, 'cause her tyres are bald and she skidded out. All while texting and driving, in that ridiculous babysitting code.'

The Batphone buzzed, and Moneypenny glanced at the text. 'This should cheer you up.' She showed me the screen. 'Shall I tell him that you'll be right over?'

Are yous dtf a handsome young man 33 years young and full to the brim with pure white come I have a 2008 alpha romaeo black with leather seats if you want to come for a test drive it's called black stallion 😉

'Pure white come?' I read the message out loud. 'Why did he have to say that?'

Moneypenny stabbed at the screen. 'It's what racists think happens when they ejaculate. What actually happens is a collective shrug.'

Before I could answer, the phone jingled. 'Welcome to The Bach,' Moneypenny cooed. 'How can I help?' There was a pause. 'Yes! . . . oh, that's wonderful!' She swiveled in her chair and pointed at the phone, giving me a hearty thumbs-up. 'Yes, we *are* hiring, of course.

We offer a girlfriend experience at The Bach. Yes, sex, mutual oral, and kissing.'

Another long pause, and Moneypenny frowned, listening. 'But that's what we offer at The Bach. We can't—' The person cut her off, and I could tell they were yelling. Moneypenny put the phone call on speaker.

'You can't *force* me to kiss, that's *disgusting!* Who do you lot think you are! I'll report you to the NZPC and the cops!'

'Okay, you can do that,' Moneypenny tried to cut in. 'But I assure you, our agency's legal. If you're not comfortable with a GFE, you can—'

She looked down at the screen. 'Oh. I think she's hung up.'

'What was *that* all about?'

'She wanted to work! She was keen, and she said she had experience. But when I mentioned kissing, she just totally lost the plot. It's probably for the best, then.' Moneypenny sighed. 'She wouldn't have been happy round here.'

'You don't have to be crazy to work here, but it helps!' Mysteek came striding into the room, in a tight leopard mini skirt and sky-high heels. She helped herself to the black leather riding crop from the wall, then sat herself down in the armchair.

I told her about the call we'd just had. 'What do you think?' I asked. 'Why do you think she flipped out about kissing? Why do so many women who've worked out in parlors think we're just ripping them off?'

Mysteek snapped the crop on the arm of the chair, fixing me with her golden eyes. 'Because,' she said, 'it's like an elephant in a circus. Her leg's chained to a post, and the trainer's always tasering her, hitting her with that big nasty hook.' *Snap.* The crop hit the arm of the chair. 'Pretty soon, she'll stop trusting anyone. And when a human comes round, she'll be ready to fight.'

She didn't elaborate, but I'd heard some stories. About parlors that fed women CD cleaner and juice, because they'd get drunk and compliant for cheap. About the places that hired girls as young as thirteen, or trafficked immigrants and held onto their passports. How can a woman know, when she calls up an agency, that anyone gives a shit about her rights? I'd been open for more than a year at that point, and no one had checked up on me – not the cops, not the government, not the NZPC.

No wonder that woman who'd called us was angry. Who knew what she'd been through before?

—

The next day I was managing, and the booking sheet was empty. No pre-bookings, no follow-up phone calls. *Damn.* I checked the list of available girls. *Mysteek and Tonya, both ALL DAY. Piper 3-8, Alicia 7-9. No Robyn, no Livia. And Tara still hasn't made contact.*

The Batphone buzzed.

3 guys 20mins each 400.

I sighed, then I texted.

Our shortest booking is 30 minutes, $180.
And we never allow more men than women
in the room. Our ladies are sexy and skilled,
and our prices are fixed. 💋

Another text.

Is it possible to get one today and pay Monday

Surely you're joking.

Well Monday is pay day!

We look forward to seeing you at
The Bach on Monday.

And another.

Who's available at 1 today?

Sexy Tonya and the Mysterious Mysteek!
Shall I send you their pictures?

Yes pls.

I texted the pictures.

Sorry nope

'No thank you' would be more pleasant.
Tonya and Mysteek are actual women.
'Nope' is more appropriate when declining
a ham sandwich.

Then I saw I had a message on Instagram. *Hello I am interested in working for you. If you want you can check out my insta, it's @ellacherryxxx.* I clicked on the link, and I blinked. *Is this girl for real?* She had to be a professional model. Her makeup was immaculate, her long, wavy blonde hair expertly blown out and styled. There were pictures of her in tight cocktail dresses, red lingerie, a miniscule thong bikini out at the beach. I looked again at her handle. *ellacherryxxx. She must be a sex worker! Jackpot!* I texted her back right away. *Absolutely, I'd love to meet you! We're quiet this afternoon if you'd like to come in?*

I think so, she said. *Maybe tonight? Like at 6?*

While we worked out the details, the phone buzzed again, this time from an unknown number.

> We're five guys coming up from Auckland for a stag do. Any chance of seeing 5 ladies for two hours each?

I swallowed. *Five ladies for two hours each is . . . $2400. And half of that goes to the house.* Our take for the day, which was currently zero, would jump up to over a grand. I glanced at my list of available women. *Tonya, Mysteek, Piper and Alicia this evening . . . shit. I only have four.*

Then I clicked on Ella Cherry. *Fuck it, she's experienced.* I took a screenshot of her most recent picture, hand on her hip in a low-cut black dress. *Actually, Ella, would you want a job today? It's a stag do with four other women, so you wouldn't be working alone. Two hours, $240 to you.*

Oooh exciting! she replied. *I mean maybe . . . let me see if my mum can look after my daughter.*

I texted the guy with the stag do.

I DO have five girls! Would you like to see all their pictures?

Yes please!

I sent him the pictures of Mysteek and Tonya, Alicia and Piper . . . and the screenshot from Ella's Instagram.

—

'Yesterday was garbage,' I reported to Moneypenny. 'We cleared two hundred bucks by the end.'

'What about that stag do?'

'It didn't go through. Alicia didn't pick up her phone, and that new girl Ella backed out in the end. I don't think she wants to work in a group.'

'She's certainly stunning.' Moneypenny held up the phone. 'I can see here that you took a screenshot.'

'I need to make five hundred dollars today,' Piper came in the side door and went straight to the dressing room. 'I have rent, and my car needs new brakes. So please, madams, pimp me all over town!'

'Well, it won't be this one.' Moneypenny jabbed at the Batphone. 'Another cheap wanker, trying to bargain.' She gave me the phone.

Hey will a hundred dollerz get me anything

A polite refusal. If you think trying to bargain sex services is cute then by all means go to a pox parlour where the floor is sticky and play Russian Roulette with your health. If you want quality, you pay what it's worth. You have the option to give yourself a handjob for free. Will be happy to help when you can afford us.

'Beautifully put.' I handed it back to her. 'Pox parlor with sticky floors . . . delicious.'

'Well, *honestly,*' she clicked at the phone. 'The cheek! And he doesn't even bother to spell.' The Batphone buzzed, and she read the next text. 'Piper!' she called. 'I've got Sonchai Try Hard. He wants to see you for an hour at noon?'

Piper came back out in her favorite dress, cherry red with a tight halter top. 'Ughhh that guy's so weird, though!'

'He is?' Moneypenny looked at the notes. 'Half Kiwi, half Thai. Really into kite surfing and Dungeons & Dragons. He sounds charming!'

'He's soooooo awkward!' Piper wrinkled her nose. 'I never know what to say to him, so it's always cringe.'

'But if you want to make money, then that's how you do it,' I said. 'Just deal with the cringe. Think of it like this: imagine he's just a weird space alien. And he doesn't speak very good English.'

'Okay *fine,* I'll do it.' Piper went back to the dressing room. 'But try to find me a cute one for later, okay! I don't want to just take the weirdos.'

Mysteek flounced in, decked out in a skin-tight white dress with the sides cut out, crisscrossed laces holding the whole thing in place. 'Jesus,' I said. 'You didn't walk across the car park like that, did you?'

'Of course not, *Madam.*' She gestured to the coat on her arm. 'I always cover up, *as you've asked.*'

'I told her I'd take some new pictures of her,' Moneypenny said. 'To see if we can get her more bookings. Actually, d'you mind taking the Batphone for an hour? That way I can work with Mysteek.'

'Sure.' I glanced at the time. 'That's no problem. I don't have to be anywhere till two.'

'Great, thanks for that, cheers!' Moneypenny picked up her camera bag, slinging it over her shoulder.

'Thank you!' Mysteek extended her arms in an elaborate curtsy. '*Thank you* for everything that you do, you beautiful Madam, and I shall look forward to an *exceptionally profitable day.*'

They left, and Piper came out from the dressing room. 'Wow, the *hostility*. Why's she so angry at you?'

'What?' I must have sounded distracted, because I was reading a text on the Batphone.

> Hi it's ella and i want to know who gave my instagram handle to the guy who was wanting a stag do last night? He found my account and now he won't stop texting saying he knows that i'm a prostitute and he's even threatened to out me to my friends irl. I told him I'm NOT a sex worker which is true! I contacted you once and I NEVER worked NOT ONCE. I'm considering taking legal action for harassment.

'What's wrong?' Piper asked.

'Oh, nothing.' I sat down at my desk so she couldn't see the phone. *Stupid, stupid, stupid. Why didn't I crop out the picture? But how can she not be a sex worker? All those pictures in red lingerie!*

Thinking fast, I tapped out a quick lie.

We sent him your picture as you said you were interested in the job, but we made sure to clip out the handle. Is it possible he did a reverse image search? You have quite a few beautiful photos on Instagram, and your handle includes 'xxx.'

I hit send. *I just hope she believes me.*

Chapter 19

By March, we still hadn't hired the escorts we needed to make up for the ones that we'd lost. Alicia was only making contact sporadically, and Robyn was still trying to rebuild her life. 'She bought a cheap car with what she's saved up, and I told her to go have it looked at,' Moneypenny reported. 'But she didn't have the money for a mechanic, so of course it immediately broke down. Plus her phone doesn't work, and it never has credit. So she can only come in when I'm managing. I drive her in and she spends the day here with me.'

'Oh, I found out what happened to Tara,' Wren said. 'You know how her last booking was with that guy Cameron?'

I scrolled through the contacts. 'Yeah, he's in here as "Cam Makes You Come". She said they had fantastic sex, and we haven't heard from her since.'

'That's because they *moved in together*. She even moved her kids into that guy's house!'

'That sounds stable,' I said.

'Or not,' said Moneypenny. 'Either way, we're one more girl down. Also – have you noticed? It seems like we're losing clients.'

'The boys could be bored,' ventured Wren. 'With so few girls working. You know how they all want fresh meat.'

Moneypenny grimaced at that. 'That's not what I've heard. Robyn says clients are pressuring the ladies to go private, offering to pay for their mobile numbers. They're saying The Bach is a great place to meet women who will then see you privately.'

'D'you think that's why Mysteek doesn't get repeats?' Wren mused. 'She turned down two bookings the last time I was in. Said she was sick, and then her car wouldn't start.'

'Whatever happened to that girl, Ella Cherry?' Moneypenny asked. 'Did she end up ringing a lawyer?'

I shook my head. 'No, I haven't heard anything. That was my fuck-up; I feel like an idiot. But did you *see* her Instagram feed?' I clicked on the Batphone and brought it up. 'She's out there in public with her tits hanging out, with "xxx" in her name! Why would you do that, if you're not selling sex? Or at least out there selling lingerie?'

'Don't you know?' Wren gave me a pitying smile. 'It's a millennial thing. She's not selling anything. They do it for *likes*.'

I shook my head in disbelief. 'That makes *no sense*. I mean, I feel awful about it. But she must get harassed all the time! I can't be the only one who thinks she's a pro.'

Wren sipped their tea. 'Well, you messed up. You wanted the job and you made a mistake. We've all fucked up one way or another.'

'*That's* the truth!' Moneypenny raised her hand. 'I sent Professor Phil Black Stockings his client notes the other day by accident.

I was trying to text them to Alicia, and I was in the wrong thread! Thank *God* it didn't say anything awful, like he's got yucky toenails and a tiny, weird dick.'

'There's a saying I use, when it gets slow around here.' Wren put their tea down, then pressed their hands together in prayer. 'The Dick Will Provide. And it always does! So say it with me, ladies.' They bent their head.

'The Dick Will Provide,' we all chanted together.

'Amen to that,' Wren said.

—

I was finishing the night on a Friday when Tonya called me up on the Batphone. 'Client's leaving,' she said. 'And he still owes $750 in extras.'

'Seven hundred and fifty dollars?' I was shocked. Our pricing for extras was standard at The Bach, and most of them cost fifty bucks. Greek was a hundred if the lady consented, but that was the only exception. I wanted to ask, *Did you gold plate your pussy and then fill it full of champagne?* but I bit my tongue. Instead, I just asked, 'How did he rack up so many extras?'

'I don't know,' Tonya said. 'He just did. He was really drunk. And you said you'd pay us out, even if the client doesn't pay, so I think *you* should pay me.'

'That's for the *basic booking fee,'* I corrected. 'Extras are between you and the client. And actually, Tonya, especially if he seemed drunk, you should have taken the money up front. You basically gave him $750 worth of service on credit.'

'Whatever,' she snapped. 'I'm coming back to the Dungeon.'

But back in the office, she wasn't letting it go. 'I know some bad guys,' she said. 'They're in a gang. We can hire one of them to take care of it for us.'

'You want me to *hire* a man to what – break his legs? That's not how we do business,' I told her. I filled out her pay stub for the booking and handed her the money, which she stuffed in the pocket of my winter coat. 'I still don't understand how he racked up those extras – how did you have *time*, in less than an hour?'

'Don't worry about it,' Tonya muttered, opening the side door to go back to her car. 'It's not your problem anyway, is it? That's what you said. It's just all on *me.*'

—

'Oh, I heard about that,' Piper said the next day. 'Tonya told me the whole story. The guy was *super* drunk, so she charged him $400 for a rim job, and $350 for Greek. She reckoned he was too drunk to care! Then when it was over, his card declined, so she got shafted.'

I called Tonya in. 'You can't charge $400 for a rim job. The price at The Bach is fifty bucks.'

Tonya rolled her eyes. 'What about *my* rights? Ethical brothel, *my ass.*'

'You have every right to withhold consent,' I told her. 'That's why we call it an extra. If you don't want to give a fifty-dollar rim job, then don't. But don't charge $400 for it here.'

Tonya blew a short puff of air out her lips. 'My rim jobs are the best in the North Island. There's guys who drive three hours from Auckland, just to get my tongue on their butts.'

'I have no doubt,' I said. 'You're fantastic at what you do. But just like a restaurant takes a hit on the food and makes money on the wine, we're going to have some services that are more profitable than others.'

'Whatever.' Tonya shook her head. 'He was wasted as, anyway.'

'That's another thing. If you feel safe, you can take a drunk client. But I don't want you ripping him off.'

'I told you, I'm worth it!' she snapped.

'Then charge $400 for rim jobs,' I said. 'But not at The Bach. No one is forcing you to work here.'

—

'The rumor mill's in overdrive,' Moneypenny reported. 'Mysteek and Tonya have a little whispering campaign going on.'

'Are they back on the overpriced rim jobs?' I asked. 'I thought that I'd made myself clear.'

'*And* it's spreading to Piper. D'you remember the other day, when she saw Sonchai Try Hard? She's saying you pushed her into taking the booking.'

'She said I – what? *Pushed* her? She said she needed to make all that money!'

'I know,' Moneypenny said. 'But she's young. And maybe you don't realize how much power you have, since you're so much older than her. *And* the boss.'

I considered this. 'Maybe you're right. I'll talk to her. But meanwhile, how do we fix this?'

'Might be good to work it out with a kōrero. That's a Māori word for an exchange of ideas, a conversation. I can bring in some food if you like. And we just give the ladies a chance to be heard.'

The next day at noon, we all got together: Mysteek, Tonya, Piper, and all three of the managers. 'Robyn's had a bad night,' Moneypenny explained. 'She wanted to sleep in. Alicia's not answering her phone, no surprise. So these nibbles will be just for us!' She passed around the plates that she'd brought, one of hummus and raw vegetables, the other of warm, homemade lemon squares.

Wren gestured at me. 'Madam Murphy, do you want to start?'

'Sure.' I looked out at the ladies, who were busy distributing lemon squares. 'I know there's been some . . . unhappiness with our prices, and I'm here to listen to your concerns. Also, I understand that someone felt pressured into a booking the other day.'

'Yeah, that was me.' Piper put up her hand. 'With that weirdo Sonchai. I told you I didn't want to see him, and you said I should anyway! And it was cringe. Just like I expected.'

Wren swallowed the carrot stick they'd been crunching. 'I have a little experience with this, from when I was a dom. Why don't we make up a kind of safe word. Like . . . *hard no?* We all joke about the clients, call them weird or whatever, and some of them literally shit the bed. Which is gross. Some ladies can handle that, and some ladies can't.'

'And sometimes you're just having a day,' Moneypenny added.

'Exactly. So if you say *hard no,* then the manager drops it. We tell the client that you're not available, and we don't bring it up ever again.'

'And if you *never* want to see him, then tell us that too, and we'll put it in his client notes.' Moneypenny said, helping herself to a lemon square. 'Does that work?'

'Yeah,' Piper nodded, looking down at her lap. 'That works.'

Mysteek took a notebook out of her bag. 'Well, *I* have a list.'

'Pick the first three,' Wren suggested, 'and we'll take it from there.'

'Doubles bookings prices are too low, and so are couples bookings. *And* I want to negotiate my own extras.' Mysteek tapped her pencil on her pad.

'Okay,' I said slowly. 'We've been talking about some of those things as well. We'll raise the prices for doubles to $450 – that's $150 for each girl, and $150 for the house. Couples will go up as well. We'll move it to $400, split half-and-half with the house.' I took a deep breath. 'But extras pricing needs to stay standard.'

Mysteek scoffed. 'Well, I don't consent. This is my business, and you have no right to tell me how to run it.'

'But it's *not* your business,' I explained. 'This is not a collective. If it were, you'd all be on the hook for the fifteen-thousand-dollar nut I have to come up with each month. Do you know how much I put in my pocket, when you hand me $120 from a booking?'

The women all looked at me, dubious. 'About twenty bucks. The rest of it all goes to overhead. I'm not out here buying gold chains and shoes.'

'Hmf,' Tonya grunted, brushing the crumbs from her lap. 'So tell me, Madam Murphy. Would you do it?'

'What?' I asked.

'Sex work. And kissing. Would *you* let a client go down on you?'

I thought about that. 'Honestly? Yes. But I'm not young and gorgeous anymore.'

Tonya raised her eyebrows and didn't reply. She didn't believe me, I could tell. *Would* I do sex work? Maybe I would. But the truth was that I didn't have to. I had inherited money to start my own business. I had the discipline and skills to put this whole thing together, and Tonya had never finished school. It wasn't fair – I'd never say that it was. But I had options. And Tonya did not.

After our meeting, I put laminated signs in both of the Bach rooms, with a menu of services and prices. I posted the same thing on a sign in the dressing room, and Mysteek immediately defaced it. 'WHERE IS CONSENT??' she scrawled across the sign. 'HOW INSULTING!'

Mysteek and Tonya stopped showing up to work, though neither of them bothered to quit. 'I heard from Piper,' Wren reported to me. 'You know that girl's up on all the gossip. She says Mysteek and Tonya have been meeting with some rich guy up north, who wants to invest in their business. They want to start their own agency, something super-exclusive, with a helipad.'

I snorted. 'Oh, really? See if you can find out which businessman is investing in Miss Wingnut, will you? 'Cause I got a bridge I can sell him.'

I'm not proud of that comment. As much as those women infuriated me, I knew they were caught in a terrible trap. For decades, they'd relied on their sex appeal. They never got an education, or built up a mainstream career. All they had was escorting, and now they were both getting older. That's the real danger of sex work: believing that your youth will last you forever.

April was the worst month we'd had at The Bach. Some days I had to close altogether, because we just didn't have any ladies available. 'Don't worry so much, Antonia,' Wren told me. 'Remember, The Dick *Always* Provides.'

But it wasn't providing enough for us, and my kids' father was making things worse. Peter took the children for a week here and there, then announced he was flying his new girlfriend to Europe. *We'll be gone for four weeks*, he said in an email. *To the UK to visit her family, then Spain, maybe Portugal.* When he picked up the kids, he looked youthful and tanned, and that pissed me off even more. Plus Miranda thought his boat was just dandy. 'It's just like a *pirate ship,* Mama!' she gushed. 'It's like a house with my own little beddy, but then we move around and go *sailing!*'

'How come *he* gets to be a parent when he feels like it, and *we* have to do the work every day?' I raged at Patrice, but it wasn't just anger – it was the fear of being backed against the wall. One week in April, I couldn't pay myself a salary: there just wasn't enough cash in the bank. We put off some bills and we lived off our small savings, and I held my breath until the next week.

I wasn't sure if my stress was affecting the children. Silas and Matisse, of course, were oblivious. The teenagers, Nova and Maris, mostly just stayed in their rooms, on their phones. But there were signs, with Titou and Miranda, that they were nervous and needed attention. One day, they stole my cellphone and threw it in the bushes. And another time, when Miranda was teasing him, Titou put his fist through a window.

'Don't worry,' Patrice tried to soothe me. 'He didn't get hurt. And you'll find more women to work.' Then he called up a livestock agent, so we could sell the last two cows on our farm.

Desperate for cash, I started making bad calls. When a stunning eighteen-year-old backpacker reached out, I didn't bother to ask about her visa. Elke had long blonde hair and arresting green eyes, long legs and a chest like a porn star.

'I'd like to try this,' she told me, in her charming accent. 'It's an adventure! I would never do it back home in Germany. But here, no one knows who I am!'

Moneypenny took her pictures, and they came out exquisite: lying on the bed in a black leather dress, her hair loose, with six inches of cleavage. 'Eighteen's quite young,' Moneypenny said. 'I'd rather that she was in uni. But if she really wants to, I'm glad she found us. At least we give a shit about safety.'

'That girl could save us,' I said. 'She could turn this entire business around.'

'But she's a backpacker, right? So she's here on a tourist visa.' Moneypenny frowned. 'Doesn't that . . . mean she can't work?'

Of course she was right, and I knew it. The Prostitution Reform Act was clear on the subject: temporary visa holders couldn't do sex work, and they could be deported if they got caught.

I threw up my hands in despair. 'What else can I *do*? She's our only option! I can put her on the website as "European", and nobody's ever gonna check where she's from. Everybody does it, and no one gets caught. Especially if you're not doing *really* bad stuff, like human trafficking or selling drugs.'

'Just double-check all the rules before you take her on, will you please?' Moneypenny folded her laptop. 'I don't want to be involved in breaking the law.'

'Alicia!' I couldn't believe it when she answered her phone. 'D'you want to see Shaking Sammy Sikh at three?'

'Cool beans,' she said, ignoring the fact that she'd been ducking my phone calls for weeks. 'Wasn't he, like, my first booking? Gosh, I haven't seen him for *months.*'

'He's been in and seen some of the other ladies, though. I think you'll find he's a lot more confident.'

'Okie, no probs,' she chirped into the phone. 'I'll be down there in a couple of hours.'

That afternoon, there was a knock on the door. 'Come in!' I called out, and Debra, the motel manager, stepped inside. 'What's up, Debra?' I asked. 'You look worried.'

'Uh . . . the woman who's checked into Room 3.' Debra was drying her hands on her apron. 'Miss Wu? I think she calls herself? Asian woman, and . . . I've got an odd feeling about her. She said she needed a whole load of towels.'

'Towels? How many?'

'She asked for twenty, but I told her no – but I did give her five. But then . . . well, there's been loads of men rocking up at her door, and going in and out, and . . .'

'You think she's a sex worker?' Debra nodded. 'That's not gonna work. Leave it to me, I'll go take care of it.'

I went to Room 3 and I knocked on the door. A middle-aged Chinese woman answered. The room was dim, but I saw she had a massage table set up, and she was burning an odd, metallic incense. 'Hi,' I said. 'I'm the manager here. And I run an escort agency on site. And . . . I'm afraid I can't let you compete. You can stay for tonight, but tomorrow you need to leave.'

'Leave?' she asked, sounding confused. She had very few teeth in her mouth.

'Out,' I repeated. 'Go. Tomorrow. Don't worry, I'll give you a refund.'

'Okay, no problem. I go.' And she flashed me a pink, gummy grin.

'Shaking Sammy Sikh just earned a new name,' Alicia announced when she got back to the Dungeon. 'He's gotten so bossy! *Suck this, lick that, get down on all fours.* He asked me to spit in his *mouth!'*

She shuddered. 'You should start calling him Sammy Bossy Boots. And only put him with very experienced girls.'

'Good to know.' I tapped the phone and updated his contact, wishing I *had* more experienced girls.

'Anyway, someone's having a party, over there in Room 3!' Alicia shook her long hair out of its bun. 'Who's staying over there?'

'Some sex worker,' I said. 'I had to tell her to leave. And yeah – she's got some kind of incense burning.'

Alicia laughed, and skipped to the dressing room, tugging at the zip on her back. 'That's not incense, you egg!' she called out. 'It's *meth!* God, can't you even tell the difference?'

'I guess not,' I admitted, and I felt like an ass. But Alicia apparently could.

—

The next morning, I was in the waiting room for Silas's GP. Despite all our efforts with the purées and cream, he still wasn't gaining any weight. Now I thought he might be having seizures in his sleep – he'd woken that morning with a swollen black eye.

While Silas bounced on his chair, MP3 player to his ear, I tapped out a note to my stepbrother. Ned was a biotech founder in San Francisco, and though we'd never been super-close, he was one of the most brilliant people I knew.

I guess I'm reaching out because I have no one else to talk to about this stuff. I'm the only one I know who's running their own business, and who's responsible for supporting a whole family. I know day-to-day money issues aren't so much of a worry for you now, but were they in earlier days? Do you feel the overwhelming stress of being the one person in charge? How do you handle it?

I hit Send. Then my phone chimed with an email from Wren:

You know my residency is being reviewed for the next stage toward citizenship, and my criminal record has to be SPOTLESS. How could you even CONSIDER hiring that German girl? Do you know what could happen if we were caught, or if some angry escort (and there's two I can think of) decided to turn us all in? My residency could be REVOKED. My partner and I could be kicked out of NZ. I can't believe you would do this to me.
Take me off the roster for the next few weeks, please. I don't think I can work for you anymore.

Reading those words, I felt my throat constrict. But before I could reply, the nurse called us in.

The doctor shined a bright light on Silas's eye. 'I don't know what it is,' she finally admitted. 'Does he sleep with a hard toy? Could he be hitting himself?'

'*No*,' I insisted. 'There's a plastic lion he loves, but I take it away before bed. And look at his fingernails . . . see? How they're banded? And sunken, like he might have a fungus infection?'

'It's a bit of a mystery.' The doctor sat down. 'I can refer you to a nutritionist, for the weight and the nails. But otherwise, I can't see a problem.'

Silas was ten, and it was always the same answer – ever since we'd noticed he was different. The doctors could only describe what they saw: the broken chromosome, the intellectual delay, the seizures, the bruises, the frailty – but no one could cure him. No one could make it all stop.

I loaded Silas in the car and set off for school, dialing Wren on speaker phone as we drove.

'I'm *sorry*,' I said, when they answered the phone. 'Truly, I'm so, *so* sorry. You're not just a manager – you're a really good friend, and I would *never* intentionally hurt you.'

'Then why did you do it?' they asked. 'You know it's illegal for her to work.'

'Because I'm going broke!' I burst out. 'We have *practically* no ladies, and I'm kicking *meth addicts* out of the motel. This is serious, Wren.' I took a shuddering breath. 'I'm in survival mode here.'

Moneypenny knew how desperate things were, and she did her best to pitch in.

I've met a possible new woman today. Her name's Tina, and she just might be a go. The only problem is that she is missing many teeth, has no eyebrows and may have a learning disability or has sustained a mild brain injury. There is something about her but she'd need a makeover or some guidance at the very least.

Thanks, Moneypenny. I really appreciate you taking the time to meet her. But I don't think we can hire an escort with no eyebrows, many missing teeth, and a brain injury . . . do you?

No, perhaps not. But I tried.

—

'This chicken's *pink,'* Maris said when she cut it. 'Are you sure it's okay to eat?' It was a warm night for May, and we were dining outside. I'd made my mother's chicken breast with tomato and rosemary, served over buttered egg noodles.

I cut into my chicken. *Shit.* She was right. A trickle of warm, pink juice oozed out on the plate.

'Ew gross, it's RAW!' Miranda pushed her plate away. 'Can we just eat bread and Nutella?'

'No, you cannot.' Patrice picked up the platter. 'Antonia, you sit and relax. I'll put this back in the oven.'

'It's okay, I'm not hungry anyway.' Nova reached for the salad bowl. 'I'm fine with just salad and bread.'

'Aaaaaw, but we want *Nutella!'* Titou demanded. He picked up his fork and started pounding the table, and Miranda immediately joined him. 'Nutell-AH! Nutell-AH! Nutell-AH!' the two seven-year-olds chanted.

Matisse, who was sat in his high chair, started chortling and clapping his hands, spraying pureed beets in the air.

Silas tossed his sippy cup of milk on the ground. 'BUS-ah-bus-ah-bus,' he babbled. *'Whores.'*

I looked down at my plate, still smeared with bloody chicken juice. 'You know what?' I stood up. 'I *can't* with this.' I took my wine glass and moved away from the table.

'Mama?' Miranda looked startled. 'I'm sorry, we'll stop!'

'It's fine,' I held up my hand. 'I just – need a *break*.'

I went inside, passing Patrice in the kitchen, and he looked up, confused. 'Antonia?' he said. *'Ou vas-tu?'*

I knew if I opened my mouth I would cry, so I shook my head and headed downstairs. I sat on our bed, my knees to my chest, and

I rocked. Something inside me came apart just then. I put a pillow to my face and I screamed into the soft cotton fabric. I screamed that Peter could leave me with our disabled child, for months and with no end in sight. For the women at The Bach who had sex with strangers, because most of their partners had left them with kids, and it was the best way they had to make money. For the men who could just pay for sex if they felt like it, with a girl who was a third of their age. For the fear that I felt at who I had become: what was ethical about illegally pimping out an eighteen-year-old teenager, because she was hot and I was desperate for cash?

After a few minutes, I had nothing left. I put down the pillow, and I picked up my laptop. While we were at dinner, an email had come through from Ned. He'd written a few lines commiserating with me, telling me about the people who counted on him. And then he wrote this:

I think of it this way: it is an honor to bear the responsibility.
To be the only one strong enough to carry everyone else.
Much love,
N

'Antonia?' Patrice opened the door. 'Will you come and eat? I think Miranda is worried.'

'Yeah. Just a minute.' I folded my laptop, and Patrice sat down next to me on the bed. He reached out a hand and tucked back my hair, stroked his finger down the side of my face, down my neck. He leaned in, brushing his lips to my ear. 'I promise you, we will get through this.'

I flinched at his touch. 'You're tickling me!'

He picked up my hand and he kissed it, his blue eyes steady on mine. '*Non, mon amour. Je vous effleure.*' *I touch you so softly,* he whispered in French. *It's like touching with the petals of a flower.*

Chapter 20

'I've decided to practice radical honesty,' Moneypenny announced. 'Since we're right to the wire with bookings, we might as well stop faffing about with these clients. So far, it's working.'

'Oh yeah? What did you say?'

'Told Ben Smelly Dick the other day why Alicia wouldn't see him. I told him he had an odor problem, and sent him a link about hygiene. And d'you know, he actually thanked me!' Moneypenny laughed to herself. 'Guess his mummy never taught him to wash. So what about Wren?' she asked. 'Are they coming back?'

'I don't think so.' I shook my head. 'They want to go back on tour with a show again, and . . . they were pretty angry about Elke, to be honest.'

Moneypenny nodded. 'Sorry to hear that. But I won't lie, I could use the extra shifts. Oh, and there's good news!' She raised her eyebrows at me. 'We got a text through from a possible new lady.'

'She's not brain-damaged, is she?'

'No, not that. And she's not a German teenager, either. She's

Māori, a solo mum, and she's fifty. The selfie she sent me shows promise.'

'Thank Christ for that.' I let out a breath. 'I needed to hear some good news.'

'She's coming in later this evening,' Moneypenny said. 'If it's quiet like it's been lately, I'll try to take some nice pictures. Then as long as she's not totally bonkers . . .'

'I'll get her up on the website,' I said. '*Finally,* we're turning around.'

'I brought you a speaker!' Alicia sang out, setting it on my desk with a flourish.

'Oh . . . thank you.' It looked just like the one we used to have in Room 5, the one that mysteriously disappeared.

'What's this guy called?' Alicia asked, ducking into the dressing room.

'Eddie Titty Chomper.' I brought up his notes. 'He bit down on Sabra's nipples the last time, so make sure he knows you're not a chew toy.'

'Cool beans! Aaaw . . .' Alicia let out a disappointed moan. 'This used to be my favorite dress! Now it's baggy.' She came out in the black dress with spaghetti straps, which did seem to hang wrong on her slimmer figure.

'You *have* lost some weight,' I noted. 'Are you on a diet?'

'Pfff, no way.' She pulled the dress over her head and stepped back to pick out another. 'Just playing lots of netball, you know? Burns heaps of calories at practice.'

When she was ready, Alicia went to see Eddie, and I settled down with the Batphone:

4 cunts wanna ravage a box

Wow, who could resist such a seductive offer! We don't have any boxes here, but we do have some beautiful women if you'd like a date!

How much 1hr price for 2 short??

A one hour Girlfriend Experience is $240, which includes multishots, if the lady is willing.

Its too much
other girl she offer anal as well $150
and she is young girl only 22

Then you should definitely go visit her! Our women are sexy and skilled, and we do not barter.

I like to eat pussy n anal n thn fuck both the holes

I don't care and if you continue talking like that to me I will block you. Fuck off with this. Seriously.

I entered the last guy in our contacts as 'Gross Anal Creep', and then I flicked over to my email. There was a message from SunGoddessLibra@juicymail.com. It read:

Hello my working name is Zara and I've heard all about The Bach! Do you have any time for an interview? I've worked in parlours before, but I like how you do things. Here's a selfie if you want to see what I look like.

I clicked on the photo attached to the email. I won't say the sky opened up or the angels started singing, because that's silly and you wouldn't believe me. But I'll tell you this: the first time I saw Zara, I knew that The Bach would survive.

'I'm a palliative caregiver,' she said, when she came in to meet me. In her mid-twenties with shoulder-length blonde hair and strong features, Zara had a razor-sharp glint in her eyes. A bimbo, this woman was not.

She folded her hands on her lap. 'I work over at hospice,' she said, 'so I deal with disability, and when people need help with their toileting. There's actually more overlap with sex work than you'd think. I don't get grossed out by yellow toenails, or back hair. And both jobs are all about caring, and . . . nurture. That's what it is, I think. Nurture.'

I took in her slender black capri pants, her violet crop top and eye-popping curves. 'But if you've already got a good job, then why do you want to go back to this?'

For the first time since she'd entered the Dungeon, she faltered. 'My boyfriend . . . I love him, but he drinks a lot. Pretty bad alcoholic, actually. And I'd like to move out, but it's so expensive. Need to save up for a deposit and that. But also . . .' She tilted her head, considering her words. 'I *like* the work. I try to understand what they need, where they hurt. And then I try to make them feel loved. What's wrong with that, you know? It's caregiving work, basically. And sex has just always been easy for me.'

On her first day, Zara made a thousand dollars. And her bookings just went up from there. Unlike Mysteek, who never had a repeat, she quickly collected a core group of regulars, and some of them visited her twice a week.

'And she's *professional,'* I gushed to Moneypenny the next time I saw her. 'She's an adult woman, with no teenage drama. She shows up on time and she knows what she's doing.'

Moneypenny inspected her sign-up sheet. 'Doesn't hurt that she offers Greek, either. *And* golden showers. Good Lord, this girl is a star.'

'How did the photos come out, of that Māori lady?' I asked.

'Oh, Aroha! That's what she wants us to call her. It means "love", of course. Here, have a look.'

She opened her laptop and flicked through the shots: a beautiful woman in a black lace corset, seated on a plain office chair. 'These are *fantastic,'* I said, surprised. 'And . . . witty. Whose idea were the librarian spectacles?'

'Hers.' Moneypenny scrolled to her favorite one, of Aroha flicking the riding crop on the desk. 'She's fifty, but she looks great for her age. And she's *smart.* She works with people with disabilities. And of course they make nothing. But I think also . . . now her kids are grown up, she's wanting a bit of spice in her life.'

'Well, send me your best shots. I'll get them online today.'

'How much is Zara making?' Tonya demanded. 'That new girl, the blondie online. I heard she broke four figures on Friday.'

'She's doing great,' I told her. 'She's gorgeous, and she's also new.'

'*And* you advertised her every day this week. But you haven't put *me* up even once!'

'You haven't taken a booking in ten days.' I flipped through my log book to confirm. 'Tonya, last week we called you *six times* for jobs, and you turned them all down! How am I supposed to advertise you if you can't be reached? Or if you don't want to come in and work?'

'I'm not coming in at eight-thirty at night just to do a thirty-minute massage! *Especially* when Zara's getting two-hour bookings, *right* in the middle of the day!'

'Okay, but I can't advertise you if you don't pick up your phone, and I can't get you more bookings if you don't come in. So please, try to be more available.'

'I *will,* if you stop favoring the white girls.'

I tapped out of the call and leaned back in my chair. Aroha was finishing a three-hour session with Edward Older Canadian Gent, who was eighty-six years old. He'd been her first client, and this was her second booking with him. At this rate, he'd be her first regular.

She came in the side door, flushed, with a slight sheen of sweat. 'That Edward!' she said. 'Such a sweetheart! This time he brought in his photo albums from the war! After . . . you know, we just sat and had tea, and he told me the stories of his youth.'

'He's doing pretty well for his age,' I said. 'Can he get it up?'

'Yes! But I *do* think he takes a little pill just before. Oh! And he asked if I'd be interested in seeing him with another gentleman. A threesome! And he's eighty-six! He would have been *diabolical* in his twenties.'

'Is he still handsome?' I was updating the notes. 'Anything else we should know?'

'Well, he *is* old, but there's something about him. I just find him very sexy. He has a wonderful touch. Edward gives hope to us all!'

'See, here's the thing.' I pulled out the log books from the past several weeks. 'Tonya keeps saying I favor the white girls, and that's why she's not getting bookings.'

'She could answer the phone, for a start,' Moneypenny said. 'I had a three-hour for her with Dean Yachtee the other day, and she didn't bother to pick up.'

'And look at the two new girls: Zara and Aroha. Couldn't be more different, right? Zara's in her twenties and white. Aroha's fifty years old and Māori. But they're practically making the same money! Last week Zara cleared a thousand, and Aroha made eight hundred. If she hadn't caught a cold on Saturday, she might have earned the most cash!'

'It's because all the older gents love her,' said Moneypenny. 'Edward told me he doesn't want to see anyone under forty – it makes him feel like a paedo. Plus Aroha's educated; she can carry on a conversation.'

'So it's *not* just about the youngest and the whitest. Or the thinnest, either – Aroha has a tummy.'

'No.' Moneypenny shook her head. 'It's about making the clients feel loved.'

Alicia placed a big jar of honey on my desk. 'This is for you,' she said proudly. 'You said your son likes peanut butter and honey sandwiches, right?'

'Thank you,' I said, 'that's . . . really kind.' I was touched she'd remembered, but it was no longer true. Silas couldn't eat solid food anymore, just high-calorie Ensures and purées. 'How are things going these days?' I asked. 'You've been kind of hard to get ahold of.'

'Oh, you know . . . I'm just busy with netball!' She shrugged. 'Plus my boyfriend and I have been fighting. Actually, d'you think I could stay in Room 6 overnight? I kind of need some space – get my head straight, you know?'

'I guess so.' I wanted to be nice, since she'd brought in the honey. 'Usually you can only stay if you have an extra-late booking, but I'll make an exception. You'll have to wait till we close though, so you can't have it till ten.'

'Cool beans! Oh, and can my uncle rent out Room 7? Or whatever's available . . . it doesn't matter. He's in from out of town; it'll be nice to catch up.'

'I don't see why not.' I pulled up the motel booking app. 'Yep, Room 7's free. Are you going to pay, or is he?'

'Oh, he'll pay when he gets here.' And she gave me his name and his number. I reserved the room and forgot about it.

The next morning I was managing The Bach again, and Debra poked her head in the Dungeon. 'Ah, you might want to take a look at the security cameras from last night,' she suggested. 'I couldn't really sleep much, to be honest. There were people moving around all night long.'

Oh shit. Oh Alicia, what did you do?

Playing back the previous ten hours of footage was like watching a silent circus act on fast-forward. First, I saw Alicia buzz out of Room 6, her movements choppy on the accelerated film. She whizzed next door to her 'uncle' in Room 7, then another car zipped in, and Tonya scampered up the stairs to join them. At three in the morning, Mysteek joined the party, an accelerated stick figure in skin-tight pants, streaking back and forth between motel rooms, then pacing the parking lot to have a jittery cigarette. At one point, I thought I saw Alicia darting between the rooms stark naked, her pale bum plump in the moonlight. Throughout the night until dawn, the three of them popped in and out of motel units like a trio of methed-out clowns.

Suddenly, it clicked. The guy in Room 7 – that wasn't an uncle. Of course it wasn't. I opened the booking and noted the phone number. Then I cross-checked it on the Batphone with our client list.

Immediately, I got a match: 'Can I Pay With Drugs DO NOT TAKE BOOKING.' The man in Room 7 was a drug dealer – the kind that use bags of crack to get sex.

No one was surprised to find the rooms were trashed, with multiple items missing or broken. In Room 7 we even found a signature: someone had pulled out a drawer from the bedside table, and scrawled on its underside: *FUK U.*

Right away, I texted Alicia and called her, but of course she never picked up. Next, I tried Tonya.

'What were you doing at the motel at three in the morning?' I asked. 'I just watched the security footage. You, Alicia and Mysteek were all partying with the guy in Room 7.'

'What?' Tonya was instantly defensive. 'I was just visiting Alicia. Why, were you *spying?*'

'Were you smoking meth?'

'No, I didn't see anyone do drugs. How can you even *accuse* me like this? Are you asking me because I was there late at night? Or is it because my name's not *Zara?*'

I tried to keep my voice calm. 'I'm asking you because I'm looking at film that shows you up all night with a *known drug dealer.*'

Tonya just scoffed. 'Pfff. Whatever. Give *us* consequences, but not other people.'

'What are you talking about? I'm not playing favorites. Alicia's no longer welcome at The Bach.'

'Yeah? Well, maybe you should check out what *other* girls are doing, like when they're *alone* with a client.'

Later that day, Mysteek finally quit. She avoided my calls all morning, then at lunchtime she sent me a long text.

> I will no longer be working at your 'elite establishment' which is actually run like a cheap massage parlour. Your behaviour towards me has been unforgiveable. The lack of respect, the favouritism, your dismissal of all my ideas – and worst of all, your insistence on standard pricing for extras, which VIOLATES my right to run MY business.

'I have to hand it to her, she's got style,' I told Moneypenny over the phone. 'If I'd spent all night smoking meth with a drug dealer at the place where I worked, I don't think I'd have the balls to also tell my boss what an asshole she is.'

'But she has to,' Moneypenny reasoned. 'Otherwise, she'd have to account for her own actions.'

'Yeah, well, good riddance. She was toxic and unhinged. But Alicia . . . I know she fucked up. And she lied to me. But *goddamnit,* I still have a soft spot for that kid.'

Moneypenny said a few comforting words, but I only half heard. I was looking at that big jar of honey, still sitting there, right on my desk.

Chapter 21

Two days later, a new client reached out, asking if he could see Zara.

I'm sorry, she's not working today. Would you like to make a booking for tomorrow?

That is very unfortunate! A colleague of mine had sung her praises. I heard she goes the one extra mile with her special that uncovers the real feel . . . that's such a deal! Are there any other star ladies like Zara that I can see!!

I took a minute, letting the message sink in.

Are you speaking about natural services?

I am. My colleague has seen her a couple of times cause of her unique service she offers. So yes i am implying do your ladies offer this service separately from what is listed?

Thank you for informing me. I will speak to Zara and she may well lose her job. As to you and your little 'friend,' the two of you may think it's cute to put the health of vulnerable young women in danger, but I emphatically DO NOT. Are you aware there's a syphilis epidemic in New Zealand at the moment? Lose this number and don't contact me again.

I tapped out of the text and called up Diana, my contact at the Prostitute's Collective. 'It's tricky,' she said, when I asked her advice. 'As an operator, you'll never know exactly what happens with the girls in the rooms. And men will always offer to pay more for no condom. So I find the best thing to do is to share information about what you can catch . . . and of course you can't actually *see* most STIs. But I'll send you some flyers with horrible pictures on them; that should take care of the problem.'

The next day, I asked Zara outright. 'Did you give a blowjob with no condom?'

She stared at me, eyes wide with shock. 'How did you hear about that?'

I read her the text I'd received, and before I'd finished she was shaking her head. 'I did it *one time* with Dennis Langara! He's like a million years old and he couldn't get hard with the condom on. But that was *right* when I started, and it was only *one time!* I would *never* offer that as an extra.'

'Did you know there's a drug-resistant strain of gonorrhea in

New Zealand?' I handed her the printout from the NZPC. 'You can get open sores in your throat.'

She looked at the pictures of pus-filled cysts, and the tears spilled over her cheeks. 'I'm sorry,' she sobbed. 'It was only one time. I'm a trained caregiver! I *know* all the things you can catch!'

'It's okay.' I tried to back off. 'Everyone fucks up now and then. I don't know who sent me that text by the way, but I'm gonna figure it out. And in the meantime . . . I'm sorry, but you're going to have to take a break from The Bach.'

'Am I fired?' She dug in her bag for a tissue.

'No, but I want you to get a full STI screening. And I don't want the ladies gossiping that you got special treatment. There's already been some of that. So take a break for three weeks, okay? Make sure you're totally healthy. Then you can come back and we'll all put this behind us.'

—

Moneypenny drummed her fingers on her leg. 'Who do you think wrote the text?'

'Not sure. It *could* be an actual client. But I asked Dennis Langara, and he swore up and down it was only one time, and he hadn't told anyone. And Zara says it was just the one time.'

'Of course, they could both be lying.'

'Yeah, they could.'

Moneypenny thought for a minute. 'What about Tonya? She was so defensive about their night of absolute mayhem at the motel. She thinks you favor Zara; she never shuts up about it. And the call was from an unknown number – not one of our regulars.'

I shook my head. 'No, the English is too good. Tonya can't spell that well.'

'Then who?'

I considered. *This business is built on illusion and lies.* Luvely Lacey had been right: everyone lied, and they lied all the time. And one thing I'd learned about being a madam was that I had to trust in my instinct.

'Here's what we know.' I held out one palm. 'On the one side, we have a woman who's a trained caregiver. She's so scrupulous about her health that she makes clients use a dam when they go down on her. Yes, she screwed up. But I don't think she's doing it regularly. She values her health too much to do that.'

I held out my other palm. 'On the other side, we have an erratic, angry woman. She's furious at Zara because she's young and beautiful, and Zara makes more money than her. She just quit The Bach in a rage. *And* she's smart. Smart enough to get another phone and tap out a literate text.'

Moneypenny sucked in a breath. 'You think it was Mysteek.'

'I can't prove it,' I said. 'And no one will tell me the truth. But that's what my gut says.'

'Can I book a motel room?' Tonya asked the next week. She took a swig from a two-liter bottle of Coke.

'Sure!' I pulled up the booking app. 'Who's the client?'

'Dean Yachtee.' She took another gulp. 'He wants to see me for three or four hours.'

I glanced at the booking sheet. 'He does? That's not what it says here.'

'Oh, that's okay.' She swigged from the bottle. 'He wants to book me privately.'

I spun my chair away from my laptop. 'Let me get this straight. You're asking if you can see one of our clients here at the motel, but not pay the agency a cut? Are you asking me if you can *steal* Dean Yachtee?'

Tonya reared back. '*What?* No, I already knew him, before he even came to The Bach.'

'Since when?'

'I dunno.' She shrugged her shoulders. 'Like, February or something.'

I pulled out the log book and checked. 'But Tonya, your first booking with Dean was back in December. That's when he first made contact. You met him here – I remember the night.'

'Okay, so maybe I got the date wrong!' She tipped back the bottle. 'Why d'you *never* believe me?'

'I don't know, because there's a *record right here in my phone?* And on paper?' I held up the log book. 'Anyway, no, you can't see him privately while at The Bach. You can't poach our clients; you know that.'

'This is such bullshit.' She narrowed her eyes. 'It's one set of rules for me, and another set for everyone else, ay?'

'What are you talking about?'

'Zara, obviously. She's giving uncovered blowjobs and you don't even care. But I *asked* if I can see a client, who I knew from before, and you just accused me of stealing!'

'I very much care about Zara, who gave *one* uncovered blowjob. And she's been stood down for three weeks. But you can't see a client privately at The Bach. How does that even make sense? How could I run a *business* like that?' I turned back to my laptop and canceled the motel room.

'Fine. You know what? I quit.' She flounced back into the dressing room. 'You talk a lot of shit about being *ethical*, but in the end it's all about the *money* for you.'

'Well, that *is* a part of being in business,' I said.

She rummaged around in the dressing room, then came out with a big duffel bag over her shoulder. 'Whatever. I packed up my shit. *Bye.*' She pushed out the door before I could respond.

I got up and went back to the dressing room. Indeed, she had packed up her shit. And all of my BDSM equipment. The riding crop and paddle were gone, and the good leather restraints, even the gimp hood that Karli had left. Her big bottle of Coke was discarded in a small sticky puddle on the rug. I picked up the bottle, smelled it, and jerked back at the odor of rum.

—

'Good riddance,' Moneypenny sniffed, when I told her the news. 'That woman was poisonous. Here's to finding some women we can *trust,* around here.'

I leaned back on the couch. 'If building an agency's like starting a fire . . . I brought on Mysteek and Tonya when we were desperate for girls – but they always made me uneasy. Adding them was like tossing plastic bottles on the blaze. They melt, and the whole thing starts to stink.'

'Yeah, or a couple of bloody *grenades,* more like. Plus it's obvious they're all smoking meth.'

'Netball.' I shook my head. 'Alicia had me going with the netball.'

—

With Mysteek and Tonya finally gone, it felt like a curse had been lifted. Over the next several months, a steady stream of strong, healthy women reached out.

Chloe was a redhead in her mid-twenties, a single mother whose boyfriend had bailed out of town. To get her life back on track, she was training for the fitness test at the police academy. 'I think this job is gonna help me in law enforcement,' she said after her first couple of weeks. 'I can usually tell when they're lying. Plus I'm *really good* at telling if someone's on drugs. It's basically like a superpower.'

Jasmine was a free-spirited mother of two in an open marriage, and she came for the sex as much as the money. 'Would you please put "cock worship" as one of my services?' she asked when she read her description online.

'Okay, but what's that?' I opened the text box.

'It's sort of like . . . adoration through physical stimulation. I make them feel like their dick is the center of the world.'

'Get ready to get rich.' I typed in what she'd said. 'That's exactly what they all want to hear.'

'I just like making money,' Sadie said when I met her. Turned out in a well-tailored skirt suit, she worked in corporate law, and she could easily pay all her bills. But she liked to travel abroad and buy designer purses and shoes, and she was saving for a brand-new convertible. 'I *do* have a partner,' she said, 'but he loves that I'm doing this work. He's got what they call a Hot Wife Fetish. When I get home at night, he has dinner all ready, and then he draws me a nice, steaming bath. And he asks me to tell him about the men at The Bach, and exactly what I did with them that day.'

Phoenix was my age but incredibly fit, another mother with three kids and no dad. She'd taken loans out so she could be a pharmacist, thinking it would give them a more comfortable life. 'But I *still* can't make it work – everything's so expensive! We rent a one-bedroom house and the girls get the bedroom – I just make do with the couch. The other day, I was crossing the street in the rain, and the heel broke off from my boot. And I realized I didn't have the money for shoes! Working full time, and I can't buy *shoes.* And that's when I decided to ring you. Who knows? Maybe I'll even like it.'

After her first booking, she came down with a grin, and the same comment most ladies made. 'That was *dead easy!*' She collected her bag, tucking the cash into her wallet. '*And* more honest. When you go out with a man, he's paying for the dinner, and you think: what's he want in return? When does he expect sex? Is he even interested in what I'm saying right now? This way you know; it's all set in advance.' She sighed, sinking onto the couch. 'I quite like kicking ass, actually.'

And then there was Tasha, tall, blonde, and thin, who came in and got straight to the point. 'I've got a job,' she said, 'so I don't need the money. I just like really big dicks, you know? Also, I don't have a gag reflex. So I can offer deep throat. Is that something the men would pay extra for?'

'That is something the men will *line up* for,' I said. 'You can make as much money as you want.'

She thought about that. 'But could you just give me cute ones? And also just ones with big dicks.'

'I can't guarantee that.' I reached for the forms. 'Since they don't usually describe their penises when they call. But we put it in the notes, when they're a known client.' I thought back to Kostas, and his ginormous eel. 'Have you ever had lunch at the Olive Branch?'

All the new women were white, and most of them were young, and they all started doing great business. But the one who surprised us was Aroha – at fifty, the oldest woman at The Bach. Little by little, she built up her regulars – a group of elderly white men with money. There was Noisy Jerry Blueberry, a farmer who shouted at the top of his lungs when he came, and her favorite, Edward Older Canadian Gent. There was Donald Licky Sucky, but she didn't mind the slobber – passionate licking was an extra, so it earned her more money. Squawky Ted was also in love with her, and she never told him his nickname, or that his voice made him sound like a Muppet. Soon, she decided she would only work Fridays, and her regulars booked her from ten until five. She made over a thousand when you counted her extras, and we called it her 'day at the office'.

'Day at the gym, more like!' she said, coming in one evening from Room 6. 'Had a look at my Fitbit, after seven hours of bookings, and it said, "Do you want to get active?" Nah, mate, I've *been* active – you should see what I do lying down!'

In September 2018, Piper's case went to trial. We all followed the proceedings, excited for Ricky Titty to finally go to jail. With physical evidence and multiple witnesses, a conviction seemed like a no-brainer. The last day of the trial, the Batphone buzzed, and I saw I had a text from Piper.

Defendant found not guilty for sexual violation . . .

WHAAAAAA . . . Based on WHAT??

The fact that he paid for the service

But then you said NO!!! What do they say to that??

The detective was lost for words. I didn't take it so well . . . apparently the jury was majority males and that's why the detective is thinking there was doubt

'Son of a *bitch,'* I raged to Moneypenny. 'Even in New Zealand, where it's *literally decriminalized,* they think sex workers are asking to get hurt.'

'Course they do.' Moneypenny flicked at her phone. 'We've got no morals, our sex drive is out of control . . . don't you know? We're a perilous danger to society!'

'*Thinks her pussy's made of gold.*' I shook my head in disgust. 'That's what he said, the first time we talked. And you know what – it is! She's made a lot more with her body than he ever could! I don't care *how much* he goes to the gym.'

'Well, that'll get him properly livid.' She put down her phone. 'Too bad, Ricky Come On Titty. You can fuck right off back to America.'

—

By October, we were busy every day of the week, and Moneypenny and I were getting burned out. It wasn't the physical toll of the twelve-hour days, though we did get tired, running up and down stairs. It was the relentless male desire that gushed like a firehose out of the phone. It was **Can I have multishots** and **Can I fuck her in the ass** and **Can I fuck her as hard as I want.** It was **Can I come on her face** and **Can I get a discount** and **Can I get no condom** and **I can't see her pussy and ass.** It was **How many girls do you have** and **What's on offer today** and **What about you? Do you fuck for drugs?**

I didn't hate men, as Haley had predicted, but I was constantly wary of their needs and their lies. The ones who were rude and disgusting were easy to vet – we told them to behave, and if they didn't, we banned them. The trickier clients were the crafty ones like Rick, who knew how to hide their hatred for women. They'd start out polite, sometimes deferential – until we set a hard limit, or we told them 'no'. Then they'd let loose with what they *really* thought: we were 'uppity bitches', 'fat cows', 'filthy whores'. And that was emotionally exhausting.

So at the end of that month, I brought on Madam Foxx, and we split up the work week three ways. Foxx was stable, healthy and sexually adventurous, with an hourglass body to die for. She was easy to train, with great instincts about men, and she quickly settled into the job.

One day at the end of November, when the three of us were at breakfast together, Moneypenny and I started trading old stories. I can't remember exactly what we were talking about – the meth or the drunk clients, the domestic abuse or Robyn's ex torching her things on her lawn. But I remember Madam Foxx sipped her coffee and frowned. 'I don't know why you guys talk about drama so much. The Bach has been perfectly fine for me.'

My eyes met Moneypenny's then, and we both burst out laughing – a laugh that was empty of humor. 'I'm glad it's been good for you,' I said. 'And stable. It wasn't that way at the start.'

'*Fuck me,* it wasn't.' Moneypenny bit into her toast. 'Feels like I've been through the wars.'

Chapter 22

At the end of November 2018, at six in the morning, I woke up to a message on my phone from Piper: **I've just heard the news that Alicia has died.**

'What?!' I jerked myself upright in bed.

'Quoi?' Patrice asked, but I waved him away, and jabbed at Piper's contact.

'What *happened?'* I asked when she answered. 'Did she get in a crash? Was it drugs?' I hadn't seen Alicia since she trashed the motel back in March, but I knew she was just twenty-one. *Healthy young women don't drop dead out of nowhere.*

'They don't know.' Piper sounded distant, like she was in shock. 'Apparently she laid down to take a nap yesterday, and then she just died in her sleep.'

'Was she on drugs?' I asked, but that couldn't be it. *Who takes a nap when they're high?*

'I don't know. I don't think so . . . she was trying to be healthy.'

I finished the call and stared out into space, unable to believe what I'd heard. 'How does a young girl just *die* like that? I thought for *sure* it was drugs.'

Patrice stroked my leg. 'Maybe it was. She did a lot of bad shit. She wanted to be . . . this dangerous girl.'

'I know.' *And maybe that's why I loved her.* In Alicia, I saw my young self. I did plenty of stupid shit in my twenties – drove drunk, tried hard drugs, strolled alone down dark Mexican streets. I know what it feels like to hike all night in the desert, get high and hunt for psychedelic toads, take a pull of rum from the bottle at sunrise. It feels incredible. It feels *alive.*

I could imagine the rush that she felt smoking meth, the raw jolt of energy, the dream – no, the knowledge, the *absolute certainty,* that anything, anything was possible. How different that felt from the sober reality of life in a small town in Northland, with a high school diploma and no skills.

'MOM!' Miranda shrieked, from the living room upstairs. 'Silas is having a seizure!'

I leapt out of bed, grabbing my robe, and took the steps three at a time. Silas was draped half on the couch, his arms and legs twitching irregularly. Miranda was holding one arm so he wouldn't fall. His eyes were half-closed and unseeing, bubbles of foam in the corner of his mouth. 'Okay, babe.' I tried to sound calm. 'I can take it from here. How long has it been?'

'I don't know, a minute? Or less?' She looked white and scared. She'd seen Silas have seizures before, but there was always an adult in the room.

I pulled Silas up on the couch, and rolled him onto his side. The twitching slowed, and then stopped. He didn't wake up. I could see that he'd wet his pants.

'Is he gonna *die?'* Miranda sounded shaky.

'No, it's okay, he's just sleeping. Could you get me a towel?'

Patrice stood in the stairway, holding Matisse, who was trying to grab fistfuls of his hair. 'Should we keep him home from school today?'

Miranda gave me the towel, and I cleaned off the foam from his chin. He looked sweaty and pale, like he always did after a seizure. I tugged off his wet pajamas, draping the towel on his legs so he wouldn't get cold. 'I think he's all right, as long as he wakes up soon. He'll be tired, but he'll be okay. And they have their big outing to Snowplanet today – I don't want him to miss out on the snow.'

—

It was my day to manage The Bach, and once Silas woke up and got into the school van, I drove to the motel for work. The idea that Alicia was dead seemed unreal, especially since most of our new girls hadn't known her at all.

Chloe came in at ten, looking fit and toned, and at ten-thirty she had her first booking. 'I'm calling him Shane Shaky,' I told her, setting up a new contact. 'He sounds young, and incredibly nervous.'

One hour later, she was back in the office. 'Well, *that* was the easiest booking ever!' she declared, flicking on the jug for her tea.

'Why's that?' I was busy with planning our ads for the week, and I hardly looked up from my laptop.

'You said he was nervous, right? *I'll* say he was! He's never asked for what he wants his whole life!' She poured boiling water over her tea bag, and stirred in a spoonful of sugar.

'So what did he want? Is he kinky or what?'

She came over and sat on the couch. 'He wanted me to lie on the bed, right? On my tummy, with all of my clothes on. Didn't even want me to strip. Then he undressed and got on the bed, but he stayed on all fours.'

Now, this was getting interesting. I pushed away my laptop. 'And?'

'And he *sniffed my butt!*' She burst into helpless giggles. 'For an hour, he just sniffed my bum! I just lay there and tried *so hard* not to laugh, and he was just going *sniff sniff, sniff sniff.* It's like he was a bloody big dog!'

'No kissing?' I asked. 'No sex at all?'

'No! Easiest. Cash money. Ever.'

I updated his contact. Shane Shaky was now Shane Shaky Butt Sniffer.

That afternoon, Zara was straightening her hair for her booking with Frank Keen To Learn. 'What's he keen to learn, then?' she wanted to know. 'I can teach him to knit, if he likes.'

'Oral sex on a woman.' I read from the notes. 'He's Indian, and his wife won't let him. She's horrified if he even mentions it.'

She picked up a section of hair with her brush, then pressed it between the hot plates. 'Not *that* again. I was in a booking with DJ Diva Queen – you know that guy who always wants three heaters going? And he says, "In India, we do not go down on each other. It is tradition." And I'd *literally* just had his cock in my mouth. So I said, "But you like it when I do it to you, right?" And he says "Yes, but you are not married. And a man never does it to a woman."' She rolled her eyes. 'What kind of a numpty double standard is that?'

Jasmine came in the door, her face flushed with the sun. She had a small paisley bag which she set on the coffee table, then started unpacking her things. Out came a silk scarf, a small brazier for incense, a pair of rose-colored candles.

'What's all that then?' Zara asked.

'I wanted to show you the altar I'm making for my booking with Harry Sweaty And Nice. I've got some crystals here too . . .' She pulled a small, tissue-wrapped package from the bag. 'And I charged them under the full moon. Makes their orgasms incredibly potent!'

'Ah, yeah?' Zara stood up to go to her booking. 'I just put my legs right up over my head, grab their ass cheeks real hard and pull them right in.' She laughed. 'They go right away, no crystals required.'

'That's a good trick!' Jasmine packed up her things. 'If the crystals don't work, I'll try that one.'

'You're in 6,' I told Zara, 'and Jasmine's in 5. You better get over there, if you want time to set up your altar.'

Both girls went out, and I watched them on camera, making sure they were safely inside. It was nice how the ladies spent time in the Dungeon now, drinking tea and laughing about clients. It was starting to feel like a fun place to work, where women enjoyed hanging out. I wondered where Phryne was, and what she would think.

The Batphone buzzed.

Who's the hottest between Zara and Chloe?

And again.

How is Jasmine's assets like bust size and height?

I took a deep breath and got ready to answer, but then my personal phone rang. I looked at the number. It was a teacher from Silas's school.

'Is this Antonia?'

'Yes, what's going on?'

'Silas had a seizure on the van ride to Auckland. I'm sorry, but it was almost five minutes. We gave him Midazolam.'

I felt like I'd been punched in the stomach. 'Is he okay? Is he stable?'

The teacher hesitated. 'Yes . . . but we did call an ambulance. They're taking him back to Whangārei now. There's no rush – they won't get there for an hour at least. But obviously – well, I thought you'd want to know. We'll call you when they get closer, if you like?'

'Yes,' I said. 'I mean, thank you.' And I tapped the screen to finish the call.

Silas's first seizure had been when he was five, and I was flying back from America. Peter had taken him to the hospital then, and they'd kept him overnight for observation. 'Everyone is allowed to have *one* fit,' his jovial doctor had told us. 'After that, we start looking at epilepsy.'

The seizures kept coming. Silas had been medicated, and he had been studied. We'd slept overnight in the hospital once, with dozens of wires attached to his head, so the doctor could study his brain waves. But nothing they'd tried had ever made him better. When the medicines were strong enough to hold back the seizures, then he wandered around in a drug-addled haze, unable to form even one-syllable words. When we tapered the medicine, the seizures came back, often stronger than they'd been before.

The fits came without warning. The black eye wasn't the first time. Once, he'd smashed his head through the sliding glass door. Each fit was a horror, my child unconscious, flung about by an invisible hand. The piss and the shit and the foam in his mouth.

The guttural groan he could make, when the air was expelled from his lungs.

As I waited that day for the teacher to call back, all I felt was a dull sense of sick. I'd been punched in the guts for five years at that point. I didn't think anything else could surprise me.

One hour later, my phone rang. 'Antonia? Yes, it seems he's awake now. The medics think he can come home, no hospital needed. You can pick him up back at the school.'

I cashed out Zara and Jasmine, and closed up The Bach. At Silas's school, I found him in a playroom with a teacher, looking blankly down at a Spiderman doll. The school was unusually quiet, because the others were still off at Snowplanet. 'Such a pity he missed it!' the teacher said brightly, getting up and stretching her legs. 'The kids just *love* all the snow.'

Pity, I thought. *Yeah, it is.* 'Come on, Silas,' I said, and I held out my hand. He got up, still holding the Spiderman doll.

'Oh, he can keep that if he likes,' the teacher said. 'Poor lad, he's had a hard day.'

Silas looked pale, which was as I'd expected, and still dazed from the effects of the drug. He was quiet as I helped him into the car, and he fell asleep on the way home. The house was empty when we got there, with everyone still at school, and Patrice must have been out running errands. I opened the door and lifted out Silas, then carried him up to his bedroom. His legs were damp, with a sharp smell of urine, but it didn't seem safe to put him in the bath. I put a towel on his bed and laid him crosswise on top, then I pulled off all his clothes as he slept. I got a bowl of warm, soapy water and I gave him a sponge bath. He woke when the water rinsed his skin.

'Ah-bah,' he murmured, still half-asleep.

'Ah-bah is *right*,' I said. 'You gave us a scare, Silas – did you know that?' I dried him, and took out a nappy. They were sized for a six-year-old, and Silas was ten. He was small, and thin, and so small.

I eased him into his pajama bottoms and top, and lay down with him on his twin bed. He shut his eyes, and I kissed his head, and I sang one of his favorite songs, one I'd sung since he was a baby, when I'd had all the hopes in the world for him. *'Silas, row your boat ashore, halleluuujah, Silas row your boat ashore, halleluuujah . . .'*

He snuggled in against my body and slept. And finally, quietly, I found I could cry.

—

We rolled into our second Christmas season at The Bach with more confidence, and a whole lot less drama. The women on our team were emotionally healthy, and as far as I could tell, they didn't touch hard drugs. We also closed early, usually by ten – and that kept out most of the drunks.

After two years, I was good at this job – but I knew it had changed me. I saw through men's bullshit now, like I had Superman's X-ray vision for lies. One Saturday I got a call from a man named Richard, who said he was in town for business. 'I'd like two ladies for three hours each,' he announced. 'I've budgeted three grand for this.'

'That's great!' I said, 'but it won't cost that much.' I tapped at my calculator. 'Six hours incall will cost . . . just $1440. May I have a credit card number to lock in the booking?'

'I'll come see you in person,' he said. 'What's the address?'

Red flags were flying, but it *was* a big booking. And this time I had plenty of ladies. When he got there, I went out to reception.

He looked reasonable enough: mid-thirties, and well put-together. His shirt was tucked in, his hair neatly combed. I asked for his credit card.

'Oh, I'll pay by bank transfer,' he said, holding up his phone. 'And could I also get $200 cash out?'

'No, I'm sorry,' I told him. 'We're not a bank.' *And you're full of shit,* I thought to myself. 'If you want to do a bank transfer, I'll need to see some ID.'

He frowned. 'Why do you need that? I'll show you the bank transfer, and you'll see it's gone through.'

I smiled obligingly. 'I guess I'm just a suspicious American. Since it's Saturday, the money won't go through for two days. And if it doesn't, I'll need a record of your license when I call the cops.'

He flinched. 'Shall I go back to the hotel to get my ID then?'

I nodded, and he scurried away.

No surprise, he never returned. Back in the Dungeon, I did a little googling, and found all the apps you can get that will easily pull up a fake bank transfer page, and make it look as though money's been sent. *Can't play a player,* Queen Bee liked to say. *You can ride with me or collide with me. Bitch, please.*

It was a rush to see the booking sheet in the morning, a thousand dollars or more already locked in. Some days I closed off a motel room, or even two, so I could run four rooms all at once. The clients seemed to notice my confidence, too – Squawky Ted started calling me 'your Highness', and Dean Yachtee just went for 'O Great One'.

I was tough on the clients, but I tried to be fair, and I was never rude or abusive unless they crossed a line: begging for no condom, trying to pay with drugs, or repeatedly demanding a discount.

Then there was Patrick Parua Bay, who went *way* too far. So I put on my pimp hat. And I scared the living shit out of him.

'He didn't *pay,*' Sadie moaned, when she came down from her booking. 'He seemed so nice, and we had the best time. So I thought it was fine to hop in the shower, while he was still getting dressed. Then he left, while I was still washing! I got out, and he was just *gone!*'

'Don't panic,' I told her. 'You know I'll pay you. And maybe it was just a mistake.' I picked up the phone and texted Patrick.

> Hi Patrick, it seems you've forgotten to pay for your booking. Did you want to come back and settle up?

No answer. I cracked my knuckles.

'What else did he tell you?' I asked Sadie. 'Anything about his job or his family? All I have here is that he's from Parua Bay.'

'He's a landscaper,' she sniffled. 'I don't know if he's married. But he has his own business, I think?'

'That should work.' I turned back to my laptop. 'Patrick . . . Parua Bay . . . landscaping . . . *ha!*' I showed her the screen. 'Fantail Landscape Design. There's his phone number in bold, right there on the home page.'

I tapped out another text to Patrick, and this time I struck a new tone.

> Hi Patrick Simmons of Fantail Landscape Design in Parua Bay. You have one hour to transfer $240 to the following bank account. After one hour, I call up your office and all of your colleagues, and tell them you like to rip off sex workers for fun.
>
> Madam Murphy

I paid Sadie for her booking, and told her not to worry. When she left, I checked my bank account. The money was already there.

—

Men couldn't fool me, and they couldn't cheat me, but they did sometimes make me laugh. One thing was for sure: they all thought a lot about their dicks and their balls. Some of them were proud, and some were unsure, and some of them really did have unusual penises, which they felt safer revealing to a sex worker. There was One Ball Bob, with only one testicle. There was Colin Micropenis, who had, well, a micropenis. There were all kinds of dicks that were bent or else curved, and one man the ladies called Derrick Spiral Dick. And then we had clients with unusually large ones. A huge dick is something men are supposed to be proud of, and all women are supposed to be dying for it. But the truth was, a lot of those men told the ladies they had trouble with sex. They couldn't put it all the way in, or they were terrified of hurting her, or sometimes a girl took one look and refused.

'Do you want to see Larry Ogre?' I asked Phoenix one night. We'd spoken to him about the skid marks and blood, and since then he'd cleaned up his act.

'I think so!' She smiled. 'What do his notes say?'

'He looks like Shrek. But he's kind and respectful, and he's been a regular for more than a year. The only thing is . . .'

Phoenix waited.

'He's got a ginormous dick.'

'Hmm,' she wavered. 'How big?'

'Two cans of Coke, end to end. At least, that's what I've been told.'

'Okaaay . . .' Phoenix looked tentative. 'Can't be much worse than a baby head, I guess.'

I texted with Larry before his date with Phoenix.

Hi Larry, as you are unusually well-endowed, do you think you could take it slow with Phoenix? She's new to working with us and I don't want to scare her off! 💋

He replied:

I always drive with care. With what I have comes great responsibility and I take that seriously.

When I read that, I snorted. *Settle down, Spiderman. You're not saving the world with your two-Coke-can dick.*

The next day, I sent a text to Peter while I waited for Zara to finish a booking.

Silas's ambulance ride cost $90. Would you please pay half?

No. I'm not paying for an ambulance he should never have taken. That seizure was less than 5 minutes.

I looked at the text, and the old feelings came back. The numbness that comes with the fear. It was hard to believe that I'd married a guy who wouldn't pay $45 for his disabled son's ambulance after a seizure. Two years ago, that would have filled me with panic: the thought that I was on my own with three kids to raise, one of whom would never grow up.

But now things were different. I felt disdain for Peter, and sad about who he'd become. But I also felt strong, and proud of myself. I was supporting a family of eight people. I could easily pay for that ambulance. Men called me Your Highness; they called me O Great One. I had three thousand men in my Batphone, with notes on all their secrets in bed, who was married, and how often they'd cheated on their wives. They were the subjects of my little kingdom.

Peter didn't fill me with fear anymore. The French had a perfect expression for him: *Il peut chier dans sa caisse.* He could go shit in a box.

'Bossy Sammy Sikh has just gotten so *pushy!* I can't believe when he came here, he was timid!' Zara came in the side door and went right for the fridge, taking out a salad she'd brought for her dinner.

'We used to call him *Shaking* Sammy Sikh,' I told her, putting away my personal phone. 'He didn't try to get rough with you, did he?'

'Oh, no, I can handle him. He's mostly just so *scared* of women, you know? He wanted to do doggy, right? And he told me, 'Don't move. You no move.' Like I was his *dog* or something!' She crunched at a bite of her salad. 'So then I start queefing and he couldn't handle it, mate! He got *so* disgusted.'

'So what did you do?'

'I just lifted one leg and let out a long one, real long and slow, and I looked at him right in the eye, and I smiled and said, "You know that's my vagina, right?"'

I snorted.

'And he just about *died!* Didn't stop him going through with it though.' She put down her fork. 'It's all based in fear, I think. And ignorance. Like, you know Harish? He's so chauvinistic. Says the West is "ruining" Indian women. He goes, "I used to have a girlfriend in school. We would just look at each other across the school yard. Now women are laughing about how long their man lasts."'

'And how long *does* he last?'

'Not bloody long, mate! At least not with me.' She got up to toss out her salad container. 'Maybe that's why he's so threatened.'

I thought about Peter, and how he must see me. Running my own business, while he was still flailing around. And this wasn't just any business: it was my escort agency, where women had sex with whoever they wanted. And not only that, we charged for it.

The Bach flipped the male–female power dynamic, putting the women in charge. Men came to us on our terms, and played by our rules – or else they knew they wouldn't get laid. Most men loved it, or at least they put up with it, as long as they could have sex with beautiful women. But men like Sammy and Harish, and Peter – a woman in charge scared the shit out of them.

When men try to control women, when they put them down – Zara was right: it's based in ignorance and fear. Plus the worry, when they look down at their dicks, that they're weird looking – too big, too bent, or too small.

I tapped out a text to Sammy Bossy Boots.

> I'm sorry Sammy, but you can't order Zara around like a dog. I've heard from other ladies that you've also been rough with their nipples and breasts. I'm glad

you're feeling more confident in the bedroom, but please remember these ladies are *people*, and you need to ask for consent. I am placing a temporary ban on your contact, and we won't be able to service you for one month. See you in February back at The Bach! 💋

Yes mam I'm sorry. Please will you tell Zara I am sorry too.

I showed Zara the text, and she laughed out loud. 'If I said that to some guy on Tinder, he'd just swipe left and move on. But they *listen* to you!'

I shrugged. 'That's 'cause I'm not just one lady. They know I run a business with the twelve hottest escorts in town.'

'No shit.' She shook her head. 'It's like you're some kind of a *union organizer.*'

'I *am* a union organizer,' I said. 'For vaginas.'

Chapter 23

Please mam will you come out and talk to me please

Why would I do that? I texted to Sammy. It was February 2nd, and he'd just finished his ban. *Zara said you were perfectly lovely, and she'd be happy to see you again, any time!* 💋

Please mam I am at motel reception. This will only take just 1 minute

I glanced at the security camera. 'Oh, *Christ.*' There he was, Sammy Bossy Boots, formerly known as Shaking Sammy Sikh, hanging around at the motel reception. 'This is *all* I need.'

I walked to the entrance, prepared to kick him out. 'Sammy, we can't have you hanging around the motel. The Bach needs to stay discreet at all times, otherwise—'

'Please, mam,' he interjected, looking pained. 'I wanted to meet you, to say—'

'It's *fine,* Sammy. The one-month ban is finished. Zara is happy! There's no problem.'

'Thank you.'

That stopped me. 'For what?'

'You have given to me my confidence.' He clasped his hands on the front desk. 'You remember how nervous I was, when I first come here? In my culture, we know nothing, *I* know nothing, about . . . sex. You know about the rape that happened, in India, with many, many men? This is because no one *teaches* us.'

I knew what he was talking about. Last year, a little girl had been gang-raped and murdered in India. I didn't think a lack of sex education was any excuse, but Sammy was making an effort.

'So you don't get sex education in school?'

Sammy shook his head. *'No,* nothing. It is *very* taboo. Not about sex, or bodies, or . . . consent. They just say we should not be *having* the sex! So when I come to this country, I know *nothing!'*

'I'm sorry about that,' I said. 'That's not right. Thank you for coming and talking to me.'

Sammy pressed his palms together and bent his head, giving me a warm smile. He let himself out, and the Batphone buzzed in my pocket. I pulled it out and glanced at the screen. It was a photo of a semi-hard penis.

Wat cn u do with that

U r yummy I will eat u up

Out in the parking lot, Sammy got in his car. I wondered how he'd behave when he had his next girlfriend. Alicia had taught him about anatomy and STIs. Zara and I had taught him about consent. Maybe he'd be a better lover in the future.

My phone buzzed. It was the dick guy again:

what's your personal cell phone?
keen on sex?

HAHAHAHAHAHA
No. To everything. Have a nice night.

I waved goodbye to Sammy. Then I turned, and got back to work.

—

Two weeks later, I gave a Valentine's party at my house, and all of the Bach girls were invited. For the first time, I felt like I could trust all the ladies – nobody had gang ties, and no one was on drugs. They were just a big band of awesome, brave women, the kind you want to hang out with on a warm summer night.

We cleared out the kids to other parents and babysitters, and Patrice and I got ready for an all-night blow out. We filled a massive punch bowl with icy sangria, and Patrice heated the barbecue. In honor of Phryne, I set up a craft table with white plastic masks. I laid out trays of glitter and paint, sequins and feathers, so everyone could create their own disguise. That way, when people took pictures on their phones, the ladies could cover their faces.

Valentine's Day in New Zealand is hot, so the early night air brought a breath of relief. Piper and Moneypenny arrived before the others. They sat with me out on the deck, taking in the view of the wide, grassy paddocks. The neighbor's sheep bobbed in the distance, lowering their heads as they grazed.

Moneypenny rolled herself a cigarette, a habit she'd picked up back in Britain. She lit it and inhaled, tilting her head back as she breathed out the smoke. 'Did we ever find out what happened to Alicia?' she asked. 'Did the coroner come up with an answer?'

Piper was wearing tight, torn-up jeans, and a silver camisole with sparkly trim. 'It *wasn't* an overdose.' She shook her head vehemently. 'I'm *sure* she wasn't on drugs. She wanted to be healthy for her baby.'

'Her *baby?'* Moneypenny and I spoke simultaneously.

'She was *pregnant?'* I asked. 'But she *miscarried,* right?'

Piper shook her head. 'No. I mean yes, but this was a new one. She was only just six weeks along. And this time she wanted to do it right, and be healthy. Her boyfriend and her wanted to get married.'

The sun sank, glowing orange behind the pine trees. Alicia was so young, and she still seemed so vital. Dancing to Bollywood, prancing around in lingerie. Dodging the cops and then bringing me honey.

Patrice turned chunks of chicken on the barbecue, which sizzled as they released the scent of seared meat. 'I did a little research.' I sipped my sangria, which we'd made with boxed wine and brandy. It was harsh, but it did the job. 'There's something called cardiomyopathy. You can damage your heart, when you smoke a lot of P. And even when you stop using, you can die.'

'Makes sense,' Moneypenny said. 'And there's pressure on the heart when you're pregnant.'

I fished out an orange slice from my drink, flicking it into a guava bush. 'So I guess that was it. Her heart couldn't handle the strain.'

'Still, *fuck me,'* Moneypenny stubbed out her cigarette. 'Twenty-one years old. She had everything still left to go.'

Multiple cars came rumbling up the driveway, and soon half a dozen ladies were parading around the corner: Zara and Sabra, Jasmine and Phoenix, Sadie and Tasha, with Madam Foxx right behind them. They wore skimpy sundresses, jeans and camisoles in bright, splashy colors. 'Hiiiiii!' they called out, laboring under piles of camping equipment – blankets and tents, sleeping bags and rolled-up mats, along with more bottles of alcohol.

'We came all together!' Sabra dumped her gear in the grass. 'You're so far out in the country! Thought I'd get lost on the way.'

'What's this *old people* music then?' Tasha put a hand to her ear. We were playing a mix that Patrice and I liked, with a lot of Duran Duran and French rap. 'Where's your Spotify?' She moved to the sliding glass door. 'You oldsters need *help.'*

Phoenix took a deep breath, as MC Solaar gave way to Cardi B. 'It's lovely out here!' She threw her head back and inhaled. 'The air's so deliciously fresh!'

'Oooh, arts and crafts!' Jasmine moved straight to the mask table. 'Are the glue guns plugged in? I want to do one right now!'

'Get yourselves drinks!' I gestured at the sangria. 'There's plenty of time to make masks.'

Sadie sampled her cup and scrunched up her face. 'Too weak. Here, I'll fix it.' She took a bottle of rum from her bag, cracked it and poured the whole thing in the punch bowl.

Sabra came over and sat next to me, looking stunning in a black lace bustier, her face relaxed and refreshed after the long summer break. 'Third year of my program now!' She leaned back in her chair. 'We start again at the end of the month.'

'How's it been?' I asked. 'You were pretty stressed there, for a while.'

She stopped smiling and nodded. 'It *was* hard. And stressful. Don't know what I would have done without my mum, helping out with the childcare. But also – this place *saved my ass.*'

I looked around. 'This place? What place?'

'The *Bach*, silly!' Sabra knocked back her drink. 'I *never* could have done my program without it. I would have had to work a minimum wage job, with long hours, just to survive. I *never* could have got through a nursing degree.'

Phoenix was on her way to the drinks table, and she stopped. '*I* was paying my bills, but just barely. It's astonishing how little people earn. And dreams get narrowed.'

Patrice came over with two platters of food, barbecued chicken and veggie burgers and buns. 'Okay, *les* girls!' he called out. '*Venez manger! A table!*'

Jasmine grabbed at a veggie burger, loading hers up with ketchup, mayonnaise, and onions. 'Why *does* it threaten people so much?' She took an enormous bite, chewed, and swallowed. 'The whole sex work thing – honestly, people just lose their *minds.*'

I sampled my second glass of sangria, and I had to admit, Sadie's rum had made it much better – and stronger. At least you couldn't taste the box wine. 'It's every man's nightmare,' I said. 'Because think about it: what if *every* woman – every woman in the world – charged money for sex?'

'No more gender pay difference!' Sadie crowed. 'We could set our own prices!'

'Shit, I'd be rich,' Tasha joined in. 'They'd have to pay *us* what *they* earn if they want to get laid.'

'You're not doing half bad.' I raised my glass. 'You're who I would have liked to have been, at your age. Earning great money, confident and independent as hell.'

Tasha tilted her head with a quizzical look. 'But don't you know, Antonia? We all just want to be you.'

'You do?' That took me aback. I hadn't thought of myself as a role model, busy fighting each day to survive. Trying not to listen to the people who called me a pimp, an embarrassment, my business so dirty that it should be shut down.

The conversation paused for a minute. When she spoke, Zara's voice was unusually loud. 'We're all Lilith,' she said.

'Lilith?' I looked up. 'What's that?'

'You've not heard of her?' She smiled, and took a small bag from her purse. 'She was Adam's first wife. Before Eve.'

Piper put down her fork. 'She *was?* I didn't know.'

'Yeah, she was.' Zara took out papers and a small bag of weed, and set about rolling a joint. 'She refused to submit to him, or do what she was told, and finally she fucked right off out of the garden, and God started over with Eve.' She lit her joint and inhaled.

'So what happened to her?' Jasmine asked.

Zara blew out her smoke and passed Jasmine the joint. 'Some people say she's a demon, a monster who kills babies for fun. People are frightened of her, and I guess that's the point. She's a woman who won't do what she's told.'

And that's what we all were, why Peter divorced me, why I started The Bach in the first place. I wanted to have sex with more than one man, and when he told me to stop, I said no. The woman around me were just as defiant: they all refused to be poor. Single mothers and married women, employed or not, they knew what society expected of them. They should limit their options. Take what they got. Have sex for free, and with only one man. But these women know their sexuality has a monetary value – a bright, shiny coin they were born with. And since every man wants it, why *shouldn't* they sell it – isn't that supply and demand?

That party dissolved into the best kind of chaos; the kind you probably imagine when a bunch of hot escorts in bright, skimpy clothing let loose on a warm summer night. I won't tell you our secrets, but there was a hot tub, and bedrooms and tents, a bathtub of sangria, and a sky that was bursting with stars. And because we had masks on, with glitter and sequins, no one will ever know who we are.

But I know. I was the madam of The Bach. And I want *you* to know this: the women who worked there are smart, kind, and brave – and for a little while, I was lucky to know them.

Epilogue

This book covers the first two years of The Bach, because those were the years of chaos and adventure, when we were starting out and we all made mistakes – especially me. In the third year, everything settled down. Running The Bach became like running a neighborhood café: it was so routine, it was practically boring! By then we had a team of healthy, reliable women, who showed up on time and didn't do hard drugs. We had a core group of regular clients who knew our reputation: mind their manners, and they could keep visiting us. Step out of line, and they'd find themselves banned. For small infractions, like rudeness, the ban would be temporary – and they were always tame as kittens when we let them come back. For bigger violations, like pushing for no condom, or trying to pay for sexual services with drugs, they wound up permanently banned. And not many men wanted to test us.

I think it's clear from this book that I believe sex work should be decriminalized. When reporters hear that, they sometimes try to pounce. 'What about your *daughter*?' they ask me with relish. 'How would you feel if *she* sold her body for money?'

But that isn't the 'gotcha' they think it is. First of all, I always try to clarify the terms. 'Sex workers don't *sell their bodies*,' I explain. 'They consent to sell sexual services, and they sell their time.'

Once we get past that part, my answer is simple: 'If that's what Miranda wants to do when she's an adult, and she can consent, then she should have the right to do sex work. Everyone should. I just hope she can find a safe place to do it.' After all, I had demeaning jobs in my twenties. Didn't you? For chopping onions, folding T-shirts, and scrubbing other people's toilets, I rarely made more than $8 an hour. If sex work had been legal in New York when I was there, I probably would have given it a shot. I was *totally* a PSWG.

People do sex work for all the same reasons they do any kind of job: to make money, to survive, to feed an addiction, to have a flexible schedule, to buy bags and shoes, to pay rent or a mortgage, to afford opportunities for their kids. Every reason why capitalism compels people to work is also why people sell sex. It's also an industry where people who are marginalized, whether through sexual orientation, gender identity, or neurodiversity, can make a living. And sure – some people do it for fun, just like anyone might love their job. When consenting adults freely choose to do sex work, I think we should leave them alone.

But what about women who can't really choose? Women like Tonya and Mysteek, who had no other options? Or like Robyn and Mia, who were fleeing domestic abuse? Is sex work the best choice for them?

Let's put it this way: I think sex work was probably their best choice in the real world that we have today. The *ideal* option wouldn't be possible.

For those who need a leg up but who don't want to do sex work, or who want to leave it behind, the best path would be this: give them free childcare and decent, affordable housing. Make sure they have a car that's mechanically reliable. Provide a mentor to help them study or qualify for a trade, and assist them with study skills as required. Provide counseling and substance abuse support when they need it, and grant them enough money to cover the basics.

Is there a government, in any country in the world, that will provide all those services to people in need? No, there is not.

Does sex work lift women out of poverty? Or does it push them further into crime and degradation? In my experience, it's morally neutral. At The Bach, the major difference I saw between the women who got ahead and the women who spiraled wasn't how many bookings they took. *It was whether they had a supportive network of family and friends.* Women who were alone in the world, and who had no support, usually went back to bad habits: drinking and drugs, gambling and abusive partners. The women who had a network, meanwhile, did well. They put money aside; they fixed their cars; they went back to school. They kept their eyes on their goals. Importantly, they had loved ones to talk to when things got stressful, and people to help with their kids when they needed a break.

During the three years that I ran The Bach, one client refused to stop having rough sex when he was repeatedly told 'No.' That experience was horrible, and I won't try to deny it. But I would ask you not to use that as some kind of proof that sex work is inherently violent. Consider: during that same span of time, *three* of our women were raped *in their private lives.* One was a Tinder date; one was a flatmate; one was some asshole who slipped the girl drugs. None of those men knew their victims were sex workers – not one. Yet they were safer coming to work than they were in their own homes and their own private lives.

The fact is this: women are vulnerable to sexual abuse, whether single or married, sex workers or not. Women are also more vulnerable to poverty. We earn less than men and we often need more, since we're more likely to be raising our kids on our own. Sex work is the one job in which most women can reliably make more money than men, while choosing our own hours and working around our children's needs. To make that work criminal is to slam shut a door that could have provided an escape hatch from poverty.

After three years of running The Bach, my business lease came up for renewal. By that point, it was clear that while my escort agency was thriving, the budget motel was a dead weight on my neck. If I wanted to continue the business, I would need to lease or buy a building in downtown Whangārei – the only area in town where a brothel can operate without a resource consent. This would have meant selling my house, and putting the proceeds into the business, which in turn would have meant being the madam of Whangārei for the next couple of decades.

I'm a city girl, and I was bored up in Northland. I also saw a pattern among the single mothers at The Bach: they'd been smart young teenagers, growing up in a rural area without much to do. Often they fell pregnant, and dropped out of school. When their boyfriends left them with a baby and no skills, they were stuck in what Piper called a 'vicious circle': trapped on a benefit, caring for a child, with no time left over to go back to school or to better their options.

I want Miranda to have more choices than that. I won't be horrified if she goes into sex work, but if she does, I want her to *choose* that work – because it's an interesting, handsomely paid job – not because it's her last option.

So I decided to close The Bach, and put my house up for sale. For a nominal fee, I sold the business to Madam Foxx, who immediately started hunting for a new venue.

And then my world changed. In October of 2019, Silas had a massive epileptic seizure in his sleep. The next morning, when I went up to wake him, I discovered he had died in the night.

I don't remember the next two months very well. Everything was torn up at once. Patrice and I shut down The Bach and the motel while we packed up our home, all while I navigated a crippling grief. Losing a disabled child is the second of two deaths: first I'd grieved for the child I *thought* I would have, the strong, healthy boy with intact DNA, who would grow up to be an independent adult. And the second death, of course, was of the child I *did* have: condemned to be a baby forever. But Silas was full of joy, with a brilliant, bright smile. And he had a love for Broadway musicals that could light up a room.

Patrice, Miranda, Matisse and I moved to France for a year to recover. Maris and Nova decided to stay with their friends. Titou came with us for only three months, until Covid hit and his mother wanted him home.

In 2020, I swam in the Mediterranean; I leaned on the smooth, cool stones of old buildings. The perched hilltop villages along the French Riviera are intended as battlements, built to resist the onslaught of invaders and pirates. I walked in the shade of the parasol pines, thinking about my years at The Bach. The rush of male desire, that ancient beast, that we'd harnessed and tamed for a while.

When France shut down, we spent time with our kids, with no rushing or onerous schedules. I taught Miranda her times tables, long division, and fractions. She still says those mornings on the balcony, doing math with her mom under a sapphire sky, are among the best memories she has.

Madam Foxx worked valiantly to find another venue for The Bach, but she encountered the same prejudice and judgment that I had four years earlier. And sadly, the global pandemic made relaunching The Bach just about impossible.

In 2021, we moved back to New Zealand, this time settling in Auckland, where there are more educational opportunities for Miranda and Matisse.

Titou visits us every other weekend and on holidays, and though they're both teenagers now, he and Miranda still squabble over who sets the table.

Matisse has grown into a bright boy of seven, obsessed with *Calvin & Hobbes* and his Lego. I subject him to French lessons every morning, and he grumbles at the injustice.

Nova and Maris are both in college, working toward degrees in art and psychology.

Patrice and I married in 2023.

Now, there's a TV series called *Madam* about the story of The Bach – or at least, a fictionalized version of what happened in those years. I'm glad I could tell you this story, which is closer to the truth, at least as close as a madam's discretion (and the lawyers) will allow.

Will I open an agency again? No, but I hope more women will, and take on the values that I tried to hold: Be consent-based. Respect the rights and the dignity of workers and clients. Approach sexuality with more compassion and less shame.

And even though men are terrified of smart, independent women – never be afraid to go get that bag.

Antonia Murphy
Mount Albert, Auckland
August 2024

Acknowledgments

Because of the taboo against sex work, I cannot name the women to whom I am most thankful: in some cases, identifying them could ruin their lives. What an injustice it is that these gutsy, radical women should be forced into silence and shame. For this book, and for our eye-opening, three-year adventure, I am most grateful to the ladies and managers of The Bach. You know who you are.

Thank you to Alice Tasman, my agent at JVNLA, who believed in this book since its earliest incarnation in 2017.

Thank you to the talented and dedicated team at Simon & Schuster, including Rosie Outred, Michelle Swainson, Fleur Hamilton, Gabby Oberman, and Kelly Jenkins, their freelancers Celia Killen and Tricia Dearborn, as well as to my tireless editor, Anthea Bariamis. Special shoutout to cover designer Alissa Dinallo, and her psychic color-picking abilities.

Thank you to Annah Pickering, Catherine Healy, and everyone at the Aotearoa New Zealand Sex Workers' Collective / NZPC who taught me with patience, kindness, and grace.

Thank you to Bridie Sweetman, who provided sage legal counsel and never charged me a dime.

Thank you to my oldest friend, Ames Varos, who told me when I was at my lowest, 'Are you a writer or aren't you? Because if you're a writer, then go write something true, and make it funny.' Our best friends tell us truths we don't want to hear.

Thank you to the wise and witty community of anonymous sex workers online, who build each other up when the world tears them down.

Thank you to Dr Emma Batistich, who told me about cardiomyopathy and the lesser-known dangers of methamphetamine use.

Thank you to Tania Samarasinghe Kankanamge, who provided a thoughtful South Asian sensitivity read, and to our Māori sensitivity reader, who prefers to be unnamed.

Thank you to Patrice, who has stood solidly by my side through all these tumultuous years. *Tu es un amour.*

Resources

I could go on at length about my stance on the law, how criminalization and the Nordic Model fail, and how decriminalization is the best and least dangerous option. But others have made those arguments much more articulately. If you want to read further, try *Getting Screwed: Sex Workers and the Law* by Alison Bass, and *Revolting Prostitutes: The Fight for Sex Workers' Rights* by Juno Mac and Molly Smith.

If you feel you need domestic violence support services, please reach out.

- In New Zealand: Women's Refuge (womensrefuge.org.nz) 0800 REFUGE or 0800 733 843
- In Australia: 1800RESPECT (1800respect.org.au) 1800 737 732
- In the UK: Refuge (nationaldahelpline.org.uk) 0808 2000 247

Here are some excellent *peer-to-peer* resources for sex workers, whether you are currently working, thinking about working, or looking to exit the industry. These organisations are run for sex workers by sex workers, and they will not greet you with judgment or shame.

- In New Zealand: Aotearoa New Zealand Sex Workers' Collective / NZPC (nzpc.org.nz). They have offices in all the major cities; check their website for details.
- In Australia: Scarlet Alliance (scarletalliance.org.au) and Sex Workers Outreach Project / SWOP (swop.org.au).
- In the UK: National Ugly Mugs (nationaluglymugs.org). This group is not exclusively peer-to-peer, but they center sex workers in their effort to end all forms of violence.

About the Author

Antonia Murphy is an award-winning journalist and the author of *Dirty Chick* and *Madam*, which has been adapted into a television series. She is also the founder of The Bach, a legal, feminist escort agency. A San Francisco native, she lives in Auckland, New Zealand with her partner and two children.